The Great Powers, Imperialism and the German Problem 1865–1925

D1077288

University
...ation Services
...ROM STOCK

ONE WEEK
LOAN

1 9 MAY 1998

27th May

2 6 FEB 1999

25 SEP 1998

14 ... 2000

25 FEB 2000

3 DEC 1998

- 2 NOV 2000

7 DEC 1998

Th
un
po
in
th

Pu
ma
on
as
th
riv
bu
be

Th
sit
pr
an
W

Jo
Or
Eu
In

The dramatic events of the early 1990s in central and eastern Europe underline the importance of political change, as well as power politics on the grand scale. John Lowe introduces the critical issues in international affairs from the period of German unification to the aftermath of the First World War.

Pursuing a lucid thematic approach to problems in European diplomacy, John Lowe examines the impact of imperialist expansion on international relations. He highlights the global rivalries and tensions of an increasingly powerful united Germany. He shows that the intertwining of the German Problem with Austro-Russian rivalries in the Near East, aggravated by Balkan nationalism, contributed greatly to the escalation of international tension in the decade before 1914.

This book sets out a clear framework for understanding the complex tensions and major issues in international affairs of this period. It provides an ideal text for students of European and German history, and for courses on Imperialism, and the Origins of the First World War.

John Lowe was formerly Principal Lecturer in European History at Oxford Brookes University. His publications include *The Concert of Europe: International Relations, 1814–70* (1990) and *Rivalry and Accord: International Relations, 1870–1914* (1988)

The Great Powers, Imperialism and the German Problem, 1865–1925

John Lowe

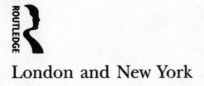

London and New York

First published 1994
by Routledge
11 New Fetter Lane, London EC4P 4EE

Simultaneously published in the USA and Canada
by Routledge
29 West 35th Street, New York, NY 10001

© 1994 John Lowe

Typeset in Baskerville by Intype, London

Printed and bound in Great Britain by
Clays Ltd, St Ives plc

All rights reserved. No part of this book may be reprinted or
reproduced or utilized in any form or by any electronic,
mechanical, or other means, now known or hereafter
invented, including photocopying and recording, or in any
information storage or retrieval system, without permission in
writing from the publishers.

British Library Cataloguing in Publication Data
A catalogue record for this book is available from the British Library

Library of Congress Cataloging in Publication Data
Applied for

ISBN 0–415–10443–2 (hbk)
ISBN 0–415–10444–0 (pbk)

SHEFFIELD HALLAM UNIVERSITY LIBRARY
WL
940.28
LO
COLLEGIATE CRESCENT

Contents

Illustrations

All illustrations are contemporary cartoons from *Punch*

Maps

Introduction
The European powers in the late nineteenth century

Between 1865 and 1871 the political map of Europe changed more dramatically than it had done in the previous fifty years. Admittedly, the Vienna settlement of 1815 had been modified in a number of ways before 1865, in particular by the creation of an independent Belgium in the 1830s and by the formation of the Kingdom of Italy in 1859–61. For the most part, however, the European states system set up after the Napoleonic Wars had withstood outbreaks of revolt in the 1820s and 1830s, as well as the great revolutionary ferment of 1848–9. The leading states of Europe in 1865 were the same great powers (Britain, Russia, Austria, Prussia and France) which had presided over the destinies of Europe in 1815, albeit with some changes in their rank order, especially as regards Russia and France.

The momentous change during the brief spell between 1865 and 1871 was the emergence of a united Germany. The new German empire, proclaimed in 1871, transformed the political power situation in central Europe. In place of a weak German Confederation of thirty-nine states, flanked by the two German powers, Prussia and Austria, there now existed a Prussian-dominated Germany, from which Austrian influence was excluded.

After 1870 Germany was the most powerful state on the continent, following the defeat of both Austria and France. The fact that this was the result of Bismarck's skilful diplomacy and the efficiency of the Prussian military machine inevitably gave rise to uncertainty as to Bismarck's future intentions. Such fears seemed well founded in April 1875 when Germany seemed to be preparing a pre-emptive strike to check France's recovery. After warnings from Russia and Britain, however, Bismarck was quick to reassure the powers that Germany was committed to the cause of peace. Consequently, the 'German Problem', although latent, was not raised in an acute form for another two or three decades.

THE BALANCE OF POWER AND THE CONCERT OF EUROPE

The balance of power, a concept to which most statesmen in the nineteenth century subscribed, implied that no one state should be permitted to dominate the continent. The experience of Napoleon I's attempt to create a French hegemony in Europe provided ample evidence that Europe was more likely to enjoy peace and stability if a 'just equilibrium' could be created among the great powers.

A complementary device for avoiding conflict among the leading states was the Concert of Europe. Although it lacked institutional form (in contrast to the League of Nations or the United Nations later) it provided a means of resolving problems as they arose on an *ad hoc* basis – usually in the form of a conference of ambassadors of the great powers. For the Concert to be effective, a measure of self-restraint was needed if the good of 'Europe' as an entity was to prevail over the conflicting national interests of the individual powers. Despite the emergence of an ideological divide, between the reactionary 'holy alliance' of Russia, Austria and Prussia on the one hand and the 'liberal alliance' of Britain and France on the other, the Concert of Europe operated quite successfully for about forty years – until the outbreak of the Crimean war in 1854.

The Crimean war, the first conflict among any of the great powers since 1815, had an important impact on international relations for a decade and a half. Not only was Russia's influence in European affairs greatly reduced after its defeat by France and Britain, but the tsar was also much less committed to preserving the *status quo*. Resentment at the neutralization of the Black Sea, as part of the terms of the Treaty of Paris of 1856, converted Russia into a 'revisionist' power in marked contrast to its previous role as a champion of conservatism and stability. In addition, Russia's anger was directed against Austria, whose association with the western powers in 1855 was regarded as base ingratitude, in view of Russian aid to Austria in 1849 during the suppression of the Hungarian revolt.

Russia's volte-face provided the opportunity for the French emperor, Napoleon III, with his prestige enhanced as the victor of the war, to champion the cause of 'nationality' in Italy at Austria's expense in 1859. It also meant that Bismarck, the minister-president of Prussia from 1862, had a freer hand to resolve the situation in the German states to Prussia's advantage between 1865 and 1870.

The Crimean war also had an important influence on British policy. Despite being one of the victors, Britain felt that the results of the war were not commensurate with the sacrifices of lives and money made to win it. This led to a sense of disillusionment with the policy of active intervention in continental affairs and an abandonment of concern for the balance of power – that 'foul idol', as some British leaders now termed it.

The international scene after 1856 was therefore significantly different from that prevailing earlier in the century. The temporary eclipse of Russia tilted the balance of power initially in favour of France, but subsequently to Prussia's advantage. Furthermore, the spirit of cooperation in the interests of 'Europe' seemed to be on the wane in the 1860s, as shown in the failure of the Concert to act effectively over either the Polish revolt of 1863 or the Schleswig-Holstein affair of 1864. Even the more restricted 'liberal alliance' was gravely impaired when Britain rejected a French proposal for a conference of the great powers, on the grounds that Britain 'would feel more apprehension than confidence at a congress ranging over the map of Europe'.

THE GREAT POWERS

The basic test for a great power, suggests A. J. P. Taylor, was its ability to wage war. Success on the battlefield raised Prussia, the weakest of the five great powers in the 1850s, to continental predominance by 1871, while Austria and France, vanquished by the Prussian army, suffered a decline in status. Similarly, tsarist Russia experienced a deep sense of humiliation following defeat by Britain and France in the 1850s and again half a century later by Japan. By the same token, Italy's military weakness excluded it from the front rank of the great powers.

Modern opinion naturally stresses economic resources, especially iron and steel capacity, combined with financial strength, as necessary components of a great power's war potential – not that potential was necessarily the same thing as military power. Historians such as Paul Kennedy tend to utilize other indices of comparative war potential as well, such as energy consumption, shares of world manufacturing output and total industrial potential. They also stress the significance of less obvious factors, for example literacy, orderly state administration and national cohesion. All the same, contemporaries tended to regard population size – translated into 'rifle strength' – as the key factor in a state's ability to wage war. This traditional attitude was reinforced by the successes of the Prussian army, which relied on universal short-term military service to provide large numbers of well-trained reserves.

Although all the continental powers adopted conscription as the basis of their military organization after 1871, none of them succeeded in creating an efficient command structure to match the Prussian general staff. Furthermore, before 1900 few of them gave enough priority to the construction of strategic railways that would permit the rapid deployment of troops in wartime. Austria's defeat in 1866 owed something to the slowness of its mobilization in Bohemia, so that, in Trebilcock's view, 'victory went as much to the Prussian train-drivers as to the Prussian generals'.

In terms of land forces, Britain fell way behind its continental neighbours after 1871. Its regular army, most of which was on active service in the empire, was numerically dwarfed by the new conscript armies of the continental powers. The British army sent to France in 1914, for example, was only one twentieth of the size of the French army. Britain's position as one of the leading great powers in the nineteenth century was based on the country's sea power, industrial strength and overseas possessions – factors which came to be regarded as increasingly important to the status of a great power in the late nineteenth century.

All the great powers had some diplomatic objectives in common. If the most obvious was security from invasion, the maintenance of prestige was almost as important as the defence of their national interests, political and economic. After 1871, territorial gain was less obviously an important diplomatic objective than the desire to assert political influence over weaker states. In an age of so-called 'international anarchy', the fact that none of the great powers fought against each other between 1871 and 1914 suggests that great power diplomacy was conducted with a fair amount of success in this period.

THE 'FLANKING' POWERS: BRITAIN AND RUSSIA

The basic aims of British foreign policy were twofold: the protection of the country's overseas trade and possessions and resistance to domination of the continent by any one state. Britain also regarded the independence of Belgium as important to its security, in view of the proximity of the Belgian ports to its own shores. In the absence of any such threats, involvement in the affairs of the continent was, to some extent, a matter of choice – thanks to Britain's position as an island state whose security, before the age of the aeroplane, depended on the strength of its navy. In this respect Britain was, of course, unique among the great powers.

Naval supremacy was in fact vital to the country's prosperity, if not to its survival, since Britain, as has been observed, 'could not feed herself and her industry could not function without regular shipments of raw materials from abroad'. In the late 1850s Britain's dependence on overseas trade was such that over 90 per cent of its imports were raw materials and foodstuffs, while 85 per cent of its exports were finished goods. By 1880 Britain's seaborne trade was valued at over £700 million a year – three times that of France and ten times that of Russia. A prime concern of British policy was therefore to maintain an uninterrupted flow of trade by ensuring the safety of the sea-lanes throughout the world.

Although the defence and extension of British commercial and political influence overseas were major concerns for most British governments, this did not necessarily imply indifference to continental affairs. In fact, between 1815 and 1856 Britain played an active role in the Concert of Europe. But the distinction between overseas and European affairs is somewhat artificial, since developments in areas such as the eastern Mediterranean and the Near East (in particular the fate of the Ottoman empire) were a constant preoccupation of British foreign policy throughout the nineteenth century.

What began as a determination to keep the Russians out of Constantinople, an important centre of the overland trade routes to the east, broadened into a more general fear of the spread of Russian power in the eastern Mediterranean after the opening of the Suez Canal in 1869. In the 1890s, however, the British government quietly abandoned the defence of Constantinople – a decision which gave added importance to Egypt (occupied 'temporarily' in 1882) as a centre of British power in the eastern Mediterranean.

The strategic significance attached to both the Suez Canal and the Cape for the sea route to India shows just how crucial the Indian empire was judged to be in maintaining Britain's imperial position. This was not just a matter of trade and investment, substantial though they were. India provided Britain with a power base on which much of British influence east of Suez rested.

In 1865 Britain was at the peak of its industrial and commercial supremacy in the world, while its overseas investments probably exceeded those of all other countries combined. The country was the world's banker as well as the world's greatest trading nation whose merchant fleet dominated the oceans throughout the globe. By 1900 Britain had added even more territory to its existing empire, which made it the greatest imperial power in the world. Well before 1900, however, Britain's ascendancy was being challenged by its European rivals, especially Germany and France, as well as by the United States, so that British trade and industry suffered a relative decline. Britain's share of world trade dropped from about 23 per cent in 1880 to 14 per cent in 1912, while its share of world industrial production fell from 23.2 per cent in 1880 to 13.6 per cent by 1913 – by which time Germany's share had risen to 15 per cent and that of the USA to a startling 32 per cent. In terms of the annual increase in industrial production from 1885 to 1913, Britain's rate of growth was a mere 2.1 per cent – less than half that of Germany, let alone the USA (5.2 per cent) and Russia (5.7 per cent).

The sense of being overtaken in the industrial race, aggravated by clinging to the principle of free trade in an increasingly protectionist world, explains some of the stridency that coloured Britain's overseas policy in the late nineteenth century. It also accounts for the mood of pessimism among British statesmen, exemplified by Lord Salisbury's comment that 'whatever happens in the world will be for the worse and therefore it is in our interest that as little should happen as possible.' Defending commercial interests scattered across the globe and the largest empire in the world placed a heavy strain on Britain's limited resources, necessitating what Kennedy calls a 'diplomatic and strategical juggling act'.

Although ministers worried whether '*demos* would foot the bill' for rising government expenditure on colonial administration, the army and the navy, the fact was that Britain – unlike some of the other great powers – was a wealthy country with a sound financial system. Despite alarmist fears about its decline, Britain was probably still the 'number one' world power in 1913, whose heavy expenditure on defence absorbed a smaller percentage of its national income than any other power's. If a consensus existed that an important national interest was at stake, British policy would not be constrained by financial considerations. The problem was to achieve a consensus. The foreign (or colonial) secretary had first to convince his cabinet colleagues, including the Treasury ministers, that the end justified the means. The government had then to carry Parliament with it, especially if funds had to be voted. Unanimity was not necessarily to be found within a government party, let alone between government and opposition.

The real distinction, however, was not so much between a Liberal and Conservative view of foreign policy as between two tendencies

– abstentionist and interventionist – which cut across party lines. Thus Gladstone's and Lord Granville's abstentionist approach was shared by the Conservative Lord Stanley (later Lord Derby), while the views of the Liberal Imperialist Lord Rosebery were not very dissimilar from those of Lord Salisbury, Derby's successor as Conservative foreign secretary in 1878. There were even times when it almost seemed to be a case of 'Gladstone versus the Rest', – so addicted was the Liberal leader to a highly moralistic view of international affairs, which few of his colleagues shared.

British foreign policy was usually formulated by a relatively small, select group of people – the foreign secretary, prime minister and senior cabinet ministers, in consultation with the queen and with the advice, if needed, of Foreign Office staff and the service chiefs. Once a policy had been decided upon, however, it had to be made acceptable to a much wider circle, including the press and public opinion. The growth of the popular press caused Lord Salisbury to lament in 1901 that 'the diplomacy of nations is now conducted quite as much in the letters of special correspondents as in the despatches of the Foreign Office.' All the same, British ministers did not have to contend with the sort of difficulties that plagued their continental counterparts, such as incompetent monarchs, nationality conflicts and extremist groups. Although there was much diversity of opinion in Britain, and pressure groups and lobbies in abundance, overall it was a unified nation (Ireland excepted) with a sense of common purpose.

In contrast, Russia's defeat in the Crimean war dealt a serious blow both to its status as a great power and to the prestige of the tsarist regime. The new tsar, Alexander II, recognized the need for a programme of modernization, including the abolition of serfdom, to overcome the backwardness of Russia revealed by its military shortcomings. This attempt at reconstruction (*perestroika*) and openness (*glasnost*) in the 'reform area' of the 1860s, following a long period of repression, created tensions and uncertainties not unlike those found in the Russia of the 1980s under Mikhail Gorbachev. The sense of instability and unrest, combined with serious financial problems, placed a premium on cautious, unadventurous policies in Europe.

Russia was not just a passive spectator of the momentous changes taking place between 1865 and 1871, but its diplomatic protests and interventions could not be backed by the threat of force. The country also had interests of its own to pursue in Poland and the

Near East, which meant that its natural ally was no longer Austria, but Prussia.

The main objective of Russian policy in the 1860s was to secure the abrogation of the clauses of the Treaty of Paris of 1856 which prohibited the keeping of warships and arsenals in the Black Sea. The opportunity to repudiate this humiliating restriction of Russian sovereignty came in 1870, after the outbreak of the Franco-Prussian war. In the late 1860s Russia's policy of supporting discontented Balkan states against Turkey had foundered on French indifference and Austrian hostility. A safer outlet for Russia's expansionist drive was found in the resumption of its advance across central Asia, begun in the 1840s by military conquests and conducted at a faster tempo during the 1860s through Turkestan and eventually to the Far East. The founding of Vladivostok on the Pacific Ocean after treaties with China in 1858 and 1860 symbolized Russia's position as an Asiatic as well as a European power. As such, it gave the country added scope to indulge in the 'Great Game', a sort of cold war confrontation with the British empire in regions adjacent to India, especially Afghanistan, at a safe distance from Britain's dreaded ironclads.

Expansion across Asia was, however, something of a side-show, enacted by the War Ministry with the tsar's assent. Russian public opinion was not very excited by it, while the Treasury and the Foreign Ministry disliked it because of its financial and diplomatic repercussions. Until the 1890s, the real drama was, as ever, the fate of the Ottoman empire.

The tsarist government accepted that the so-called 'Eastern Question' was a matter which concerned all the great powers and that changes in the Near East required the sanction of the Concert. No such caution restrained pan-Slav enthusiasts, a motley collection of influential journalists such as Katkov and Aksakov, academics and army officers, such as General Fadeev. In their view it was Holy Russia's mission to liberate fellow Slavs and Orthodox Christians from the yoke of the Muslim Turks. Official Russian policy in Balkan affairs was therefore liable in certain circumstances to be swept aside by a wave of pan-Slav enthusiasm. It has to be admitted, however, that the tsarist government itself was periodically prone to spasms of romantic dreams of recovering Constantinople, the ancient Byzantine capital, from the Turks.

Russia's interest in the Straits, linking the Black Sea and the Mediterranean, was, by contrast, perfectly rational. Uninterrupted passage of merchant shipping through the Straits was vital to the Russian economy for the export of grain and import of machinery. Control of the Straits could therefore not be permitted to pass from the Turks to any other power, except Russia. Economic interest, as well as considerations of prestige, made it desirable that Russian influence at Constantinople should be greater than that of any other power.

In the 1890s, however, tsarist foreign policy was directed once more towards the Far East, with the aim of establishing Russian influence, both political and economic, over northern China, especially Manchuria. This involved the ambitious project of the Trans-Siberian railway.

Russia's effectiveness as a great power was considerably impaired by serious financial and economic weaknesses and by the sheer inadequacy and incompetence of the tsarist political system. Significant progress was undoubtedly made on the economic front as the programme of industrialization got under way in the 1880s and 1890s, especially that associated with Count Witte, the finance minister from 1892 to 1903. Expansion of the railway system, begun in the 1860s, was accelerated in the 1890s along with the growth of heavy industry. Russia's rapid industrialization was heavily dependent on massive foreign loans, with France replacing Germany as the main source of credit. An important political pay-off (the Franco-Russian alliance of 1892/4) resulted from this financial switch, reinforced by a brief but fierce tariff war with Germany. The heavy borrowing of foreign capital, the interest on which placed a strain on a Treasury already burdened with military and naval expenditure, inevitably increased the size of the state debt. The problem was the need to raise state revenues.

Although large grain exports from southern Russia were an essential complement to the import of machinery for its farms and factories, Russian agriculture in general was not productive enough to yield the amount of revenue the state needed. The harshness of Witte's fiscal policies, which laid much of the financial burden of industrialization on the backs of the peasantry, led to mounting rural discontent. Given the grievances of a ruthlessly exploited industrial proletariat in the big cities, a revolutionary upheaval was never far from the surface in the 1900s. Defeat by Japan, quickly followed by the 1905 revolution, led to Russia's partial eclipse as a great power for several years, with important repercussions on international relations.

By 1914 the country had made a good recovery and, although its army reforms needed another two years for completion, in terms of population size Russia seemed a formidable adversary. 'By the yardstick with which armies were measured in 1914', Russia was undoubtedly powerful. With a population almost three times as large as Germany's, it could put an army of 1.3 million into the field, backed (supposedly) by reserves four times that number. Russia's heavy military expenditure and rapid railway construction between 1900 and 1914 (averaging 1,000 miles a year) not surprisingly caused alarm in Berlin.

Rapid industrialization succeeded in reducing Russia's economic backwardness to such an extent that by 1914 it ranked as the fourth industrial nation in the world. The statistical evidence for increases in output of steel, coal and oil, as well as for the expansion of foreign trade from 1890 to 1914, looks impressive enough. Nevertheless, in Kennedy's view, 'Russia was not, in reality, a strong state.' Its fourth ranking still left Russia way behind the leading industrial nations and its productive strength was actually decreasing in relation to Germany's. The progress of modernization concealed serious flaws. For example, an enviable rate of growth of 5 per cent per annum in industrial output only resulted in a 1 per cent rise in real national product and little improvement in living standards for the rural and urban masses.

Similarly, the enormous size of Russia's army was offset by a shortage of good officers and well-trained NCOs. Its fifty cavalry divisions looked impressive, but transporting fodder for 1 million horses was probably beyond the capacity of a railway system built 'on the cheap'. Just as the semi-literate military transport personnel could not cope with deploying masses of infantry, so the incompetent civil servants could not run the state effectively.

No equivalent modernization of the governmental system had taken place. The granting of a parliament, the Duma, in 1905 did not result in a perceptible increase in governmental efficiency. Effective power still resided in the tsar and his ministers, but since he lacked the ability to provide the vital element of coordination, ministers frequently worked at cross-purposes. This weakness was also evident in foreign policy when the tsar allowed himself to be persuaded by individuals or groups to pursue a policy at variance with the more cautious aims of his foreign minister.

THE CENTRAL POWERS: AUSTRIA(-HUNGARY) AND (PRUSSIA-)GERMANY

The Austrian empire, territorially the second largest state in Europe in 1815, was something of a lame duck for much of the nineteenth

century, as a result of Hungarian unrest and severe financial problems. Nevertheless, it preserved the illusion of being a great power
between 1815 and 1848 by a diplomatic conjuring trick, using the
spectre of revolution to frighten successive tsars into upholding
the *status quo*.

Austria's decision to align itself with the western powers against
Russia in 1855–6 was a major foreign policy error, since the tsar
regarded this ingratitude for Russian aid against the rebellious Magyars in 1849 as little short of treachery. With Russia no longer acting
as the underwriter of the 1815 settlement in Europe, Austria had
to face alone the challenges to its influence in Italy and Germany.

By 1865 the Austrian empire was in grave danger from three
different directions. Negotiations to appease the Magyars had not
been brought to a successful conclusion. The emperor refused to
buy off Italian hostility by ceding to them the province of Venetia.
But the greatest danger of all lay in the rejection of Prussia's claim
to hegemony over north Germany. Following the country's shattering defeat by Prussia at Sadowa in July 1866, all three issues were
settled to Austria's disadvantage.

Austrian foreign policy after 1871 was based on the determination
to preserve intact what remained of the multinational empire and to
extend its political and economic influence in the Balkans. Austrian
policy towards the Ottoman empire was not altogether consistent.
While for the most part anxious to prevent that empire's disintegration, Austria also sought to create or protect 'client states'. The
emergence of independent national states in the Balkans with irredentist claims to co-nationals within the borders of Austria-Hungary
(as the country was called after 1867) constituted a major threat
to its integrity and survival. Its prosperity was also linked to the
development of Balkan markets, since most of its exports could not
compete against German or other manufactures in central Europe.

Cooperation with Russia on the basis of agreed spheres of influence in the Balkans was not usually official policy, although it was
favoured by some circles within the Dual Monarchy. For the most
part, therefore, Vienna turned to Berlin or London for support
against signs of Russian threats, since it was too weak to risk war
alone against Russia.

Austria-Hungary's weakness stemmed from a series of problems,
some of which were almost insoluble. As a multinational state
(containing about a dozen nationalities) in an age of growing
nationalism, the country was in a sense living on borrowed time.
Appeasement of the Magyars, the most dangerous internal threat,

through the *Ausgleich* of 1867, which was been called 'probably the least unworkable of the available alternatives', meant that the emperor could do little to conciliate the Serbs, Croats and other nationalities within the Kingdom of Hungary. Their oppression by the Magyars, the dominant ruling group, exacerbated their grievances and led to the growth of the south Slav problem, which became increasingly troublesome in the early 1900s. In a similar way, though to a lesser extent, the Germanic dominance in Austria created crises with Czechs and Slovenes. Attempts to satisfy some of their demands usually led to violent protests by the Germans. In such circumstances it was not easy to foster national or cultural cohesion.

The actual constitution of Austria-Hungary was an added source of friction and led to serious delays in decision-making in both domestic and foreign affairs. The emperor, Franz Joseph, had insisted on the need for common ministers for foreign affairs, war and finance for the sake of the Dual Monarchy's status as a great power, but fiscal and commercial issues had to be approved by representatives (delegations) from the two parliaments. The result was that decisions on matters such as tariffs, commercial treaties and strategic railways were subject to prolonged hard bargaining. Furthermore, the Hungarian prime minister had the right to be consulted on important issues in foreign affairs, as did, of course, the emperor himself, who regarded diplomacy as his special prerogative ('meine politik'). These obstacles to decision-making, exacerbated by periods of domestic crisis in the 1890s and in 1903–6, contributed to a rather negative stance in foreign affairs until 1908.

Public opinion exercised little influence over foreign policy, partly because no consensus existed, apart from Magyar hostility to Slavs in general and to the Russians in particular, and support for war against Italy. This was the only war that would be universally popular with public opinion throughout the Dual Monarchy – which was unfortunate, since Italy was an ally from 1882. The press was not under tight government control since, according to the constitution, the Dual Monarchy was a liberal parliamentary state.

Another problem was Austria-Hungary's financial and economic weakness relative to most of the other great powers. The fact that the population spent over three times as much on beer, wine and tobacco in 1903 as the government spent on the armed forces indicates a dubious set of priorities for a country that claimed to be a great power. Between 1904 and 1910 the Dual Monarchy only devoted about 12 per cent of its revenue to armaments – less than half the figure for Russia (and even Italy) and under one third of the British total. After meeting the salary bill for 3 million civil servants, there was not much money left for the army, which was deficient in weapons and could only afford to conscript 30 per cent of the available manpower. Avoidance of war was therefore almost a financial necessity.

Inadequate state revenues were partly the product of an under-developed economy, in which agriculture was still predominant, especially in Hungary, whose interests clashed with those of Austrian manufacturers. Nevertheless, regions such as Bohemia had developed modern textile and metal industries, while Austria itself produced the Porsche car. But if the Skoda and Steyr armaments works were among the best in Europe, regional disparities in levels of output and per capita income remained quite marked. Although by 1914 Austria-Hungary's level of economic attainment was, in some respects, superior to that of Russia, it was, in Stone's view, 'trying to act the part of a great power with the resources of a second rank one'.

As for Austria's neighbour, Prussia, the transformation of its position from the weakest of the five great powers in 1850 to one of the strongest was accomplished in two stages. The defeat of Austria in 1866 established Prussia as the dominant force in central Europe and the defeat of France in 1870–1 made it the foremost military power on the continent. The creation of the German empire in 1871 represented the realization of the *Kleindeutsch* (lesser German) programme for German unity, dating from 1848, which excluded the Austrian Germans.

For the next two decades Bismarck gave priority to the consolidation and the security of the Reich. Since Germany had nothing to gain and possibly much to lose from war, its interests were best served by preserving peace in Europe. As chancellor, Bismarck took responsibility for both domestic and foreign affairs and he was not averse to exploiting foreign policy issues for short-term political advantage. His main objectives in diplomacy were to isolate France and to maintain a semblance of harmony in Austro-Russian relations, on which his 'system' depended. Apart from a brief flir-tation with colonial expansion in the mid–1880s, Bismarck clung to his belief that Germany was essentially a 'land rat', whose destiny lay on the continent.

It was the abandonment of this limited continental outlook, and the non-renewal of the alliance with Russia, that characterized post-Bismarckian diplomacy, certainly from the late 1890s onwards. The mood of unrestrained overseas expansion found expression in the concept of world policy (*Weltpolitik*) and the popularity of the idea of a powerful fleet which might challenge Britain's naval supremacy. More obviously related to Germany's economic interests and to the spread of its influence was the greater attention paid after 1890 to the Ottoman empire and the Near East, symbolized by the Berlin-Baghdad railway project. By about 1907 the links formed by Britain, France and Russia gave rise to a feeling of 'encirclement' in Germany, which gradually led to greater emphasis on the alliance with Austria-Hungary as Germany's only reliable ally, even though this necessitated greater involvement in the tangle of Balkan politics. The objectives of German foreign policy after 1890 are therefore not altogether clear.

Germany's dominant position in European diplomacy in the Bismarck era was a fair reflection of the country's military might and growing economic strength. Rapid industrialization and population growth enabled it to overshadow France between 1870 and 1890, by which time it was also beginning to challenge Britain. During the next twenty years Germany forged ahead of both France and Russia in terms of national power, partly because its economy was not encumbered with an inefficient agricultural sector. By 1913, in Kennedy's view, it had probably overtaken Britain, which made it economically supreme in Europe. Germany's phenomenal growth in manufacturing output, in chemicals and electrics, in overseas trade and in maritime and naval strength enabled it (or, in the German view, entitled it) to challenge the existing order in the European states system.

From the evidence of the press and the activities of pressure groups such as the Kolonialverein, it is clear that a substantial body of German opinion expected Germany's influence in the world to be commensurate with the country's economic strength and, perhaps, its cultural vitality. A minority, such as the Pan-German League, also stressed the racial superiority of the Germanic people – an exaggerated form of the social-Darwinist attitudes prevalent at this time. The adoption of a world policy was therefore popular with public opinion, but whether the German Foreign Ministry viewed it as 'for real', as opposed to a public relations exercise, is a matter of controversy. Certainly *Weltpolitik* was part of a strategy to make the Kaiser's regime, and the Kaiser himself, more popular. Before the late 1890s, foreign and overseas policy had not been used in a systematic way as a diversionary tactic. It could be argued that the need for it arose during Wilhelm II's reign because the anachronistic nature of both the political system and the social structure had become that much more evident.

Political power in imperial Germany was largely concentrated in the executive, particularly the chancellor and the Kaiser, as the rest of the ministers were subordinate to these two. Although the Reichstag was elected by universal suffrage it was not much more than a façade of parliamentary government, since the deputies exercised little control over the ministers, except on budgetary issues. Furthermore, the vital role of coordinating government policy was inadequately fulfilled by most of Bismarck's successors as chancellor, while the Kaiser's unpredictable personality made him something of a political liability rather than an effective leader. The pluralism in decision-making which became apparent after 1890 contributed to the confusion in German policy after Bismarck. By the turn of the century Germany had become a powerful nation that was inadequately, if not irresponsibly, led.

The effect on German policy of the survival, despite industrialization, of the influence of the traditional 'feudal' elite, the *Junker* landowners, together with the deference paid to the agrarian interest, has been the subject of much comment by German historians such as Fischer, Wehler and Berghahn. They see the growth of the socialist party and its success in the 1912 elections as signs of a fundamental crisis in domestic affairs that induced Germany's leaders to favour war in 1914 as an escape from the socio-political impasse that supposedly existed.

FRANCE

In 1865 France, still regarded as the foremost military power on the continent, seemed to hold the balance between the two contending German powers. Ten years later, by contrast, only Bismarck and a few German generals could regard France as a serious threat, and their fear of a war of revenge was an illusion.

If the idea of *revanche* for the humiliation of 1871 and the loss of Alsace-Lorraine lived on in France into the 1880s and 1890s, it was increasingly confined to the nationalistic right or was exploited by politically ambitious officers, such as General Boulanger in the late 1880s. The majority of Republican leaders, in line with public opinion, were primarily concerned with the consolidation and defence of the Republican regime against threats, real or imagined, from Catholics and monarchists.

Nevertheless, the defeat of 1871 did have at least three significant effects on French policy for the next thirty years or so. First, although *détente* with the victors of 1871 became a possibility in time, an alliance or even simply an entente was virtually impossible as long as the 'lost provinces' remained in German hands. Second, the desire to strengthen France's security made Republicans willing allies of autocratic Russia when the opportunity presented itself in the 1890s. Third, the blow to French prestige led some Republican leaders to seek to restore French greatness through overseas expansion which, by adding over 3 million square miles to the French empire between 1871 and 1890, made France the second greatest colonial power in the world by 1914.

Ironcially, colonial expansion made Britain, not Germany, France's main antagonist in overseas affairs, at least until 1904–5, partly because of rivalry over Egypt. Furthermore, the Franco-Russian alliance of 1892/4 was, for a decade, directed more against Britain than Germany. Although public opinion in France was sensitive to challenges to French pride, arising from colonial clashes with Britain in the 1890s and with Germany in the 1900s, it tended to be preoccupied with domestic issues. The French press, on the other hand, was a force to be reckoned with, but its thunder was mitigated by its venality. Foreign affairs were not often discussed in the French cabinet, and even less frequently in the Chamber of Deputies. The formulation of French foreign policy usually only involved a discrete group – the foreign minister, officials at the Quai d'Orsay, the prime minister and the president of the Republic. A determined foreign minister, such as Delcassé, who held office from 1898 to 1905, or premier/president, for instance Poincaré (1912–14), consequently could usually get his own way, regardless of the vagaries of Republican politics.

Both economic and political factors had a considerable bearing on France's attempts to sustain its position as a great power between 1871 and 1914. The country's most obvious weakness was demographic. French population growth after 1870 was one of the lowest in Europe – a mere increase of 3 million to give a total of about 39 million by 1910. These figures contrasted unfavourably with Britain's total of 45 million, Austria's 50 million, Germany's 65 million and Russia's staggering total of 160 million. The only consolation for France was that in 1914 it had, proportionately to its total population, more men of military age than Germany had. Even so, France had to conscript 80 per cent of its eligible youth to enable it to mobilize eighty divisions in 1914 to face Germany's 100 divisions. The latter also had twice the manpower reserves to call on in the event of a long war and twice as many experienced NCOs to provide the training cadres for fresh recruits.

France's economic growth was also much less impressive than Germany's, despite a phase of vigorous expansion after about 1900 which, in per capita terms, produced some impressive statistics. In coal, iron and steel production France lagged way behind Britain and Germany and was slipping behind Russia by 1914. There is meaning to Trebilcock's jest that the French could see little point in manufacturing, given France's limited mineral resources, and turned instead to drink. French industry was a mixture of traditional small-scale producers, usually inefficient, surviving alongside modern, large-scale innovative manufacturers such as Citroën, Peugeot, Michelin and Schneider. The survival of the former against foreign competition seems to have depended on protective tariffs, which reached their peak with the Méline tariffs of 1892–4.

High tariffs also enabled small farmers to survive, so that as late as 1910 40 per cent of the active population were still employed in agriculture. The crucial statistics, however, are those that show the disparity in France's economic strength relative to Germany's. By 1913 France's share of world manufacturing production and total industrial potential were both only about 40 per cent of Germany's, while it enjoyed only about half of Germany's GNP and national income.

Nevertheless, in spite of its commercial and industrial short-comings, France was a wealthy nation investing large amounts of capital abroad, which paid useful diplomatic dividends in its relations with Italy, the Balkan states and, above all, Russia. But successive governments failed to face up to the politically unpopular challenge of modernizing the tax system to yield additional revenue for the expenditures of a great power. However, the fact that the French navy resembled a 'fleet of samples' by 1900 was not due to financial constraints but to constant changes of personnel and strategy at the Ministry of Marine.

A characteristic of the Third Republic was frequent changes of government, giving the appearance of political instability, aggravated by occasional crises and periodic scandals, which tarnished the image of the Republic abroad. The political system was also particularly prone to manipulation by commercial pressure groups and colonial enthusiasts. Weak governments in Paris were liable to find themselves presented with a *fait accompli* by ambitious officers in the colonial army.

At the turn of the century, France's ability to play a full part as a great power was seemingly impaired by several developments in domestic politics. The revival of confrontational politics in the Dreyfus affair was followed by syndicalist strikes and the growth of pacifism and anti-militarism on the French left. The latter, aggravated by politicking by radical Republicans, certainly had a disastrous effect on the morale and effectiveness of the French army. Further uncertainty about the direction of French policy arose from the activities of prominent radicals from the business world who were advocates of a Franco-German entente, to be based on financial and commercial cooperation. Other Republican leaders, however, remained fiercely 'patriotic' and loyal to the Anglo-French entente of 1904, especially Clemenceau and Poincaré – the latter associated with the so-called 'nationalist revival' after 1911. Such uncertainties were dispelled, however, in August 1914 when even the extreme left participated in the *union sacrée* to defend the *patrie*.

THE LESSER POWERS: ITALY AND TURKEY

In 1865 the process of Italian unification, which had begun in 1859 with French military aid and was accelerated by Garibaldi's daring exploits, was still incomplete. Italy was a beneficiary of 'Bismarck's wars', securing Venetia from Austria in 1866 despite defeat on the battlefield, and occupying Rome in 1870 when the French garrison was withdrawn.

Italy, 'the least of the great powers', was only granted admission to the great power club as a matter of courtesy, since it failed to qualify for membership according to the normal tests applied. In terms of population and economic resources the country ranked sixth in Europe, while its industrial production as late as 1901 was only the equivalent of that of Belgium and Luxembourg. Even in 1913 its industrial muscle was only a fraction of that of the leading powers. Italy remained basically an agrarian state, without much wealth and hampered by budget deficits at least until the turn of the century. The army was kept short of funds for modern weapons and its low esteem was reflected in the poor quality of its officer corps. If ability to wage war was the acid test of great power status, Italy clearly failed to pass it.

The Italian right, fully aware of the country's weaknesses, concluded that Italy needed peace and good relations with both France and Austria-Hungary. This 'low-profile' approach to international affairs, however, was rejected by Crispi, an influential politician of the left from 1887 to 1896 who conceived a dynamic role for the nation, in emulation of ancient Rome. Italy's destiny, in Crispi's view, was to become a Mediterranean power, with ambitions directed towards north and east Africa and the Balkans, especially Albania.

Italy's role in the alignments of the great powers was a modest one. It was a junior member of the Triple Alliance of 1882 with Germany and Austria-Hungary, and an associate of the latter and Britain in the Mediterranean Agreements of 1887. Cooperation with France, perhaps a more obvious direction for Italian foreign policy to take, was precluded by the French occupation of Tunis in 1882 (largely to forestall the Italians) and the escalation of a tariff war in the 1880s. Italy's imperial ambitions subsequently found an outlet of sorts along the Red Sea, in the Horn of Africa and in Tripoli.

By 1914 Italy had become a more considerable power, the leading industrial power, at least, of the Mediterranean region. Lavish expenditure created a modern navy, which provided a boost to general technological advance – reflected in the now-famous names of Fiat, Lancia, Olivetti and Pirelli. The handicap of having no coal was partly offset by the use of electric power, in which Italy led Europe.

Despite this economic progress, the Italian army was quite unprepared for war in 1914, lacking not only mortars but even overcoats. In the view of the foreign minister, it was 'wise and patriotic' to doubt the army's capacity to fight – even against the Austrians!

As for the Ottoman empire, it was no longer a great power in its own right during the late nineteenth century, although it remained a seemingly indispensable element in international affairs. A vast empire in decline, stretching from the borders of Austria-Hungary and Russia to Persia, Arabia and north Africa, it confounded its critics throughout the nineteenth century by failing to disintegrate. Even so, by 1914 its European territorial base had been reduced to a mere fraction of its former size, while the sultan's authority had long been little more than nominal in north Africa and elsewhere. Not surprisingly, therefore, the main objective of successive Turkish regimes was to preserve the integrity of what remained of this once great empire.

The Turkish government contributed to its own decline by failing to create a reasonably efficient system of administration, as well as by heavy borrowing. Bankruptcy in 1879 led to the creation of the Ottoman Public Debt Commission, which included representatives of the great powers. Increasing European penetration of the Turkish economy, which had been encouraged by 'Westernizing' grand viziers earlier in the century, resulted in the grant of substantial privileges to European nationals. The popular reaction against this

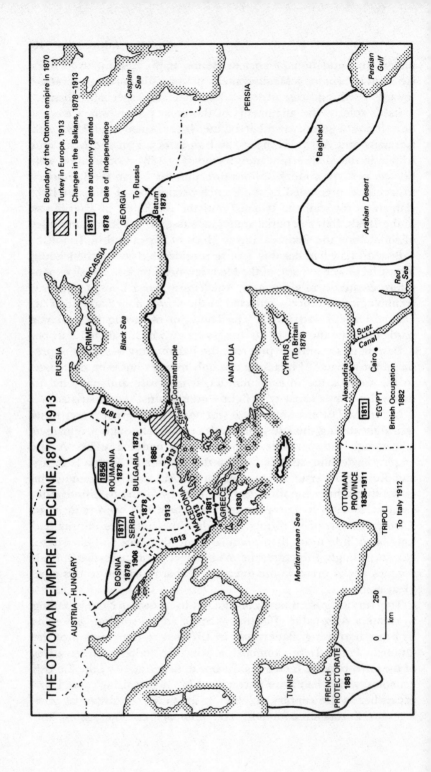

THE OTTOMAN EMPIRE IN DECLINE, 1870 – 1913

	Boundary of the Ottoman empire in 1870
	Turkey in Europe, 1913
	Changes in the Balkans, 1878–1913
1817	Date autonomy granted
1878	Date of independence

AUSTRIA–HUNGARY

RUSSIA

CRIMEA

CIRCASSIA

GEORGIA

To Russia

Batum
1878

Caspian
Sea

PERSIA

Black Sea

• Baghdad

Arabian Desert

Persian
Gulf

BOSNIA
1878/
1908

SERBIA
1817

1878

1913

MACEDONIA
1913

1913

GREECE
1830

1881

ROUMANIA
1878
1856

BULGARIA 1878

1885

1913

1878

Straits Constantinople

ANATOLIA

CYPRUS
(To Britain
1878)

Suez
Canal

Alexandria

Cairo •

EGYPT
1811

British Occupation
1882

Red
Sea

Mediterranean Sea

OTTOMAN
PROVINCE
1835–1911

TRIPOLI

To Italy 1912

TUNIS

FRENCH
PROTECTORATE
1881

0   250
km

enabled Abdul Hamid II to restore the sultan's authority between 1876 and 1908, by posing as the champion of the traditional Islamic order. After his removal by the 'Young Turks' in 1908 the new regime attempted to rejuvenate the empire through political and economic modernization, but this met with only limited success, partly through lack of support from the great powers.

The 'Eastern Question', at its simplest, was the problem of what the great powers should do about the declining Turkish empire. Apart from a consensus, usually respected, that it was a European question to be decided by the Concert and not by unilateral action, the attitudes of the powers diverged. Russia and Austria-Hungary could not agree on an east-west partition of influence in the Balkans. As long as Britain regarded Constantinople as 'the key to India', Russia would be denied possession of the Turkish capital or control of the Straits and so would be checked in Asia Minor. Whereas in Bismarck's time Germany disclaimed any interest in Turkey, his successors sought to extend German political and economic influence throughout the Ottoman empire.

Three factors in particular made the Eastern Question an inflammatory issue in international affairs in the late nineteenth century. One was the reluctance or inability of the sultan's regime to satisfy the grievances of the Christian population without antagonizing Muslim opinion. The second was the growth of nationalist feeling among the Balkan Christians and Slavs. Finally, there was the failure of the great powers, especially Russia, to restrain the expansionist tendencies of their client states in the Balkans. The eclipse of Turkey-in-Europe in 1912–13, by removing the great 'shock absorber' of great power rivalries, left the other empire-in-decline, Austria-Hungary, dangerously exposed to the force of Serbian nationalism.

THE RISING POWERS: JAPAN AND THE UNITED STATES

The Meiji restoration in 1868 paved the way for Japan's emergence from obscurity to become a major power in the Far East, defeating China in 1894 and Russia a decade later. The morale and discipline of the Japanese infantry greatly impressed western observers, but they drew erroneous conclusions from this with regard to future warfare in Europe.

The transformation of Japan from an inward-looking, agrarian, decentralized, feudal society into a modern, industrial and military state was achieved with the aid of western experts against the handicap of few natural resources and limited land fit for cultivation. Modernization was imposed from above to prevent Japan from being dominated by the west. By 1913 its level of industrialization in per capita terms equalled Russia's, but its industrial base, especially iron and steel output, remained weak in comparison with that of the lending powers. Nevertheless, Japan ranked fifth in warship tonnage by 1914, ahead of Russia, Austria-Hungary and Italy, while its naval and military forces were nearly twice as large as those of the United States.

In 1914 the United States was an economic giant but a military pygmy, whose war potential greatly exceeded its actual military power. Although it had undoubtedly become a great power, America did not form part of the great power system until its entry into the war against Germany in 1917. The USA's geographical isolation from Europe was not the key factor in explaining the delay. It was probably more significant that the focal point of international affairs reverted away from the Far East, an area of concern to the United States, and back to Europe in about 1905. But the decisive factor seems to have been that Roosevelt's successors as president were content to return to isolationism after his participation in negotiations to end the Russo-Japanese war in 1905 and the crisis over Morocco in 1906.

In economic and demographic terms, the USA's credentials as a great power were unquestionable by the turn of the century. The pace and scale of the expansion of the American economy after the ending of the civil war in 1865 were quite staggering. In 1901 one American steel firm produced more steel than the combined output of all the steelworks in England, while Americans produced more motor vehicles than the rest of the world put together. The country's national income in 1913 exceeded that of the four richest European powers. Between 1860 and 1914 America's exports increased seven-fold but its imports, thanks to high tariffs, only fivefold; yet the role of foreign trade in its economic growth was much smaller than in the case of Britain.

By 1914 the USA was well on the way to overtaking Europe as the region of greatest economic output in the world. On the other hand, its military might was ludicrously small in relation to that of the European Great Powers. Admittedly, the USA's navy ranked third in the world after those of Britain and Germany; yet its army was not only one tenth the size of Russia's but scarcely bore comparison with Serbia's.

SOURCES AND FURTHER READING

Grenville, J. A. S., *Europe Reshaped 1848–78*, London, Fontana, 1976.

Kennedy, P., *The Realities behind Diplomacy*, London, Fontana, 1981. (Ch. 1 very useful for Britain.)

——, *The Rise and Fall of the Great Powers*, London, Fontana, 1989, (Ch. 5, sections 1 and 2, pp. 249–320.)

Kent, M. (ed.), *The Great Powers and the End of the Ottoman Empire*, London, Allen & Unwin, 1984.

Stone, N., *Europe Transformed 1878–1919*, London, Fontana, 1983.

Taylor, A. J. P., *The Struggle for Mastery in Europe 1848–1918*, Oxford, Clarendon Press, 1954. (Useful introduction, but tables dated.)

Trebilcock, C., *The Industrialization of the Continental Powers 1780–1914*, Harlow, Longman, 1981.

1 International relations: Biarritz to the Berlin *Post*, 1865–1875

International affairs between 1865 and 1871 were dominated by three issues, two of which were closely interwoven. The unification of Germany under Prussian leadership was a triumph for Bismarckian diplomacy, but its success depended on the nature of the French response to the aggrandizement of Prussia. Prussia's unexpectedly rapid victory over Austria in 1866 altered the balance of power in central Europe without any corresponding advantages for France. The French attempt to correct the imbalance led to a crisis in Franco-Prussian relations by 1867, sometimes called the 'Western Question'. Although this interacted with Austro-Russian disputes over developments in the Ottoman empire – the Eastern Question – France was unable to capitalize on the situation by securing an alliance with Russia.

In 1865 Napoleon III seemed to possess the diplomatic advantage, since Bismarck was anxious to secure a guarantee of French neutrality in the event of an Austro-Prussian war. After preliminary discussions in Berlin and Paris it was agreed that Bismarck would meet Napoleon III at Biarritz in October 1865. For Bismarck, the purpose of the meeting was to discover what price the French would ask for their neutrality.

By October 1865 Bismarck had abandoned any earlier thoughts he may have entertained of reaching a negotiated agreement with Austria which would concede to Prussia a predominant position in north Germany. Since Austria would not recognize that the time had come to shift its centre of gravity to the east and abandon its historic influence over the German states, war was unavoidable, in Bismarck's view, if Prussia was to obtain 'the air so vitally necessary to our political existence', as he put it in 1862.

Whether Bismarck had an overall strategy from the outset for resolving the situation in Germany in Prussia's favour has naturally been the subject of an extended historical debate. Broadly speaking, three main schools of historical opinion can be identified.

One, exemplified by Eyck, presents Bismarck as the 'master-mind' who planned to unite all the German states under Prussia (the *Kleindeutsch* solution of 1848) through 'blood and iron'. It is argued that the three wars between 1864 and 1870, against Denmark, Austria and France, were minutely prepared by Bismarck so as to isolate his victims diplomatically, who obligingly fell into the traps set for them.

This traditional view of Bismarck the diplomatic genius, which leaves no room for twists of fate, has been countered by A. J. P. Taylor, a great believer in historical accidents, with the assertion that Bismarck had no overall plan. Rather he was the master opportunist, skilfully exploiting situations created by others to his own advantage – an unusually lucky 'innocent bystander', perhaps? A rather different form of the 'de-bunking' of Bismarck's genius has been made by Mosse, who argues that the unification of Germany owed far more to the favourable diplomatic situation than to skill on his part.

A position between these two main schools of opinion has been taken up by many historians, including Medlicott and Pflanze. They believe Bismarck did have a specific aim – to unite Germany under Prussia – but credit him with devising alternative strategies for realizing it. This flexibility of approach not only enabled him to confuse his opponents as to what his objectives were but also permitted him to delay his final decision as to the policy he would pursue until the situation had developed more clearly. This sort of interpretation has been powerfully reinforced in a recent study of Bismarck by Lothar Gall. Gall believes Bismarck had to devise a maximum and minimum programme, especially with regard to Austria, because of the manifold difficulties he faced on both the domestic and foreign policy fronts between 1862 and 1870. In Gall's view, ingenuity rather than genius characterized Bismarckian policy, since he frequently made blunders, especially in domestic affairs, which alienated the liberal nationalists, whose backing was useful to his policy.

A successful outcome to war with Austria depended on two factors: the skill of the Prussian army and Bismarck's ability to localize the conflict by isolating the enemy. Although the military were ready to consider war against Austria in May 1865, Bismarck was in no hurry to provoke its outbreak. The international situation seemed to him to be full of uncertainties and he needed time to persuade opinion in Germany and in Europe that this war was a necessary stage in the unification of Germany and not just a matter of the aggrandizement of Prussia.

With hindsight, it looks as though Bismarck was being unduly cautious in his appraisal of the international scene in 1865–6. Admittedly, Italy was the only state with a direct interest in siding with Prussia against Austria – for the sake of securing Venetia. But British intervention could safely be ruled out, as Bismarck predicted, since its policy of bluff and bluster over support for the Danes in 1864 in their dispute with Prussia over Schleswig-Holstein had been an ignominious failure. In any case, from the perspective of London there seemed no reason to fear that British interests would be adversely affected by the creation of a more powerful state in central Europe that might act as a counterweight to the unpredictable French. As regards Russia, on the other hand, Bismarck was much less confident, despite some goodwill over Prussia's overt hostility to the Poles in 1863 and the tsar's coolness towards Austria. In fact, however, the memorandum prepared by Gorchakov, the foreign minister, in September 1865 advocated a policy of total abstention by Russia in any conflict between the two German powers. In addition to St Petersburg's continuing need for peace, Gorchakov stressed the valuable role played by Germany as a barrier to French threats to aid the Polish cause in 1863; thus a strengthening of Prussia as 'the road to Poland' was in Russia's interests.

Mosse's case that Bismarck was able to benefit from a diplomatic situation which was unusually favourable to Prussia is echoed by Kolb's view that 'Germany waged war in 1870 under optimum conditions.' Britain was abandoning concern for the balance of power, Russia was prepared to give up its support for 'dualism' in the affairs of Germany, while the Franco-Russian entente was destroyed by the Polish revolt. This left France as the only great power which could play a decisive role in a conflict between Prussia and Austria.

Bismarck was under pressure to reach an agreement with Italy and France from March 1866 onwards, following the decision of the Prussian crown council in late February to prepare for war against Austria. The Prussian military attached particular importance to securing an offensive alliance with Italy, which would oblige the Austrians to fight on two fronts. After protracted negotiations the alliance was concluded in April 1866, but with a limited duration of only three months – a sign that the Italians were wary of being used as a pawn in a game between the two German powers.

Bismarck's attempts to reach a firm understanding with France, however, were unsuccessful despite the meeting at Biarritz in October 1865 and further negotiations in March and late May 1866. In the absence of wholly reliable evidence about Bismarck's and Napoleon's intentions, historians have had to speculate about the reasons for their failure to reach an agreement.

Traditionally, Bismarck has been credited with a major diplomatic achievement in pursuing a 'stalling policy' towards France which kept the French out of the war with no rewards for their neutrality. In a more recent interpretation, on the other hand, it has been suggested that Bismarck was forced to gamble on the outcome of the war because French diplomacy left him very little room for manoeuvre. This view seems to be based on the supposition that French policy pursued a clear and consistent course from October 1865 to June 1866, which is hard to see. Gall also charges Napoleon with adopting a policy of 'temporizing neutrality' with the overriding aim of achieving a lasting French hegemony on the continent.

A more sympathetic interpretation of Napoleon's policy is provided by Pottinger's detailed study of French diplomacy in the prelude to the Austro-Prussian war. In her view, the key to the riddle of the twists and turns of French policy is that Napoleon encountered so many obstacles to his aims from public opinion and the political opposition in the legislative body, not to mention his own foreign minister, that he was obliged to explore a range of alternative possibilities. Napoleon's own sympathies lay with Prussia, consistent with his reputation as the champion of the principle of 'nationality'. Thus, providing Bismarck's aim was limited to creating a north German state under Prussian leadership, 'compensation' for France was not necessary. If, however, French intervention was necessary, then France would expect some territorial reward.

Bismarck seemed willing enough to pay a price for French neutrality, but at Biarritz and in subsequent negotiations his offers were limited to 'anywhere where French is spoken'; that is, Belgium and Luxembourg. Napoleon knew well enough that a French occupation of Belgium would excite violent opposition in Britain, possibly leading to war. With French opinion so averse to adventures, this was an unduly high-risk course to pursue. The dilemma was that a pro-Prussian policy was unpopular in France, as the public reaction to speeches by Napoleon himself and by leading opposition spokesmen in early May 1866 clearly demonstrated. If Napoleon were to persist with his pro-Prussian line he would need a 'sweetener' for French opinion, which would have to be a return to the frontiers of 1814 or the acquisition of some Rhenish territory. Bismarck's generosity, however, did not extend to sacrificing German territory. It was easy enough to pay off the Italians with the Austrian province of Venetia but the offer of independent Belgium to France, however tempting for Napoleon, was not an acceptable solution. Since Bismarck rejected Napoleon's March 1866 offer of benevolent neutrality with 'consultations' if Prussia's action upset the balance of power, no agreement seemed possible between France and Prussia.

In an attempt to break the deadlock, Napoleon revived in late May an earlier idea of a European Congress to consider reform of the German Confederation, Venetia and the Danish duchies of Schleswig-Holstein. Austria's refusal to allow territorial changes to be discussed killed the project, leaving Napoleon with a diminishing range of options. After yet another abortive exchange with Prussia, the 'Kiss Mission', Napoleon swung back to the idea of an agreement with Austria. The treaty, signed only days before the outbreak of war in June 1866, promised the cession of Venetia to Italy and also offered France some rich pickings if Austria were victorious. The concession to Italy resolved a problem that had been worrying Napoleon since the conclusion of the Italo-Prussian alliance in April – the fear that Italy would lose all if Prussia were defeated. Napoleon's concern for Italy was certainly rather quixotic, giving priority to its claims to Venetia (which French intervention had failed to secure for Italy in the War of Liberation of 1859) over territorial gains for France itself. Italy therefore enjoyed the privileged position of being a beneficiary regardless of which side was victorious.

France's prospects, by contrast, were wholly dependent on the outcome of the war, since the only agreement Paris had made was the last-minute alliance with Austria. Napoleon, in common with most contemporary opinion, expected the Austrians to win by virtue of their superiority in artillery and cavalry, their larger population and the advantage of support from at least the south German states. Historians with the benefit of hindsight have to remember that the reputation of the Prussian army was made on the battlefield of Sadowa in July 1866. Before then it was not all that highly rated as a military force and even Moltke, the chief of staff, was uncertain whether the Prussian infantry had been trained sufficiently to exploit the advantage of the new needle rifle, which demanded precision aiming to be effective. In the event the new weapon was devastating in its accuracy of fire, with the Austrians suffering heavy losses in every encounter with the Prussians. But this was not what most contemporary opinion expected. It made sense for Napoleon to console himself with the thought that his failure to secure an understanding with Bismarck might not be all that significant. With the two sides supposedly evenly matched, the war would be a long and exhausting struggle, providing Napoleon with the opportunity to step in at the right moment to impose an armistice and extract payment for his services.

An element of 'temporizing neutrality' was therefore evident in French policy from Biarritz to the outbreak of war, as Gall claims. But Gall's assertion that Bismarck avoided specific offers to France because he sensed that its benevolent neutrality was unobtainable does not seem justified. Even stranger is his argument that the Franco-Austrian treaty of June 1866 vindicates Bismarck's doubts, when its conclusion came after the failure of a series of negotiations with Prussia, which failed because Bismarck had nothing to offer apart from the 'poisoned chalice' of Belgium, which French public opinion would not allow Napoleon to accept.

THE WAR OF 1866, SADOWA AND THE POLICY OF *POURBOIRES*

Provoking Austria into war in June 1866 caused Bismarck little difficulty. He had prepared the ground with such consummate skill by persuading the Austrians to take joint action with Prussia in the dispute with Denmark over the status of the duchies of Schleswig-Holstein that there was no difficulty in creating a confrontation. Once the Austrians attempted to break out of the trap in which they had been ensnared, they could not avoid violating their latest agreement with Prussia, the Convention of Gastein, signed in August 1865. This was enough to overcome the scruples of the Prussian king, whose resistance to war against the Habsburg emperor had been an obstacle to Bismarck's plans for some time.

Even so, Bismarck preferred to widen the apparent cause of the war from a rather narrow quarrel over the duchies, in which Prussian policy had aroused much hostility in Germany, to the broader issue of a reform of the German Confederation. The Prussian proposal made on 10 June, involving the exclusion of Austria, taken together with an earlier one for the creation of an elected parliament, was intended to signify Prussia's role as the standard-bearer of the German national cause, rather than that of a protagonist in a power struggle between the two German powers. Its impact, however, was virtually nil, since the vast majority of the states of the German Confederation sided with Austria. Prussia's disregard for their views in the Schleswig-Holstein dispute had been too blatant for

Bismarck's new pose as the leader of the nationalist cause to carry credibility.

Within three weeks of the opening of hostilities the Austrian army was routed at the battle of Sadowa (Königgrätz) on 3 July 1866, a testimony to Prussia's superior planning and military organization. Following a truce, definitive peace terms were agreed in the Treaty of Prague in August. In this treaty Prussia made substantial territorial gains by annexing some of the smaller German states and the Danish duchies. The states north of the River Main were to form a confederation under Prussian leadership, but the southern states, notably Bavaria, Württemberg, Hesse and Baden, were to enjoy an independent international existence. The Austrians had to pay an indemnity to Prussia and to cede Venetia to Italy, despite the victories of their army on the southern front.

Overall, the terms of the Peace of Prague were regarded as reasonably lenient. Napoleon's intervention may well have contributed to limiting Prussian demands but it is quite possible that Bismarck was reasonably content with this peace, for the time being at least. Not so the king of Prussia, aided and abetted by the Prussian military, who complained bitterly at being denied the chance of inflicting a humiliating peace on the vanquished. Bismarck later joked that his two main problems in the Austro-Prussian war were to persuade King William to go into Bohemia and then to get him out of it. More serious was Bismarck's reminder to the king that: 'We are not the only inhabitants of Europe, but live in it with three other powers that detest and envy us.'

Prussia's crushing defeat of Austria in early July 1866 produced consternation in France, summed up in the phrase 'it was France that was beaten at Sadowa'. On 5 July the council of ministers decided, with Napoleon's full backing, to send a French army of observation to the Rhine frontier as a warning of possible 'armed mediation'. This decision was reversed the next day in favour of purely diplomatic pressure. The rapid abandonment of the threat to intervene was probably not, as has sometimes been argued, a reaction to hostile public opinion but a result of determined opposition by some of Napoleon's senior ministers. The emperor himself, indecisive by nature and possibly ailing at the time, was also influenced by mistaken reports that all the combatants were willing to allow him to play a mediating role. As a result, he was able to exercise some influence over the broad outline of the peace terms, especially as regards the independent status of the south German states. This slight boost to Napoleon's prestige, however, could not conceal that France had made no tangible gains to console it for the fact that Prussia's spectacular victory had transformed the situation in central Europe. Under pressure from some of his ministers, who thought Prussia's gains were excessive, Napoleon embarked on the disastrous 'policy of *pourboires*', seeking compensation for France to redress the imbalance.

Whatever may be thought of the logic behind France's demands for territorial gains after – rather than before – a decisive battle, for sheer bad timing the French ambassador's approach to Bismarck, as he was preparing to sign the truce of Nikolsburg in late July, was hard to beat. Worse was to come. The elaboration of France's demands to include the Bavarian Palatinate and the Mainz district of Hesse enabled Bismarck to reveal the hollowness of France's claim to be the defender of the south German states and thereby to conclude military treaties with them in 1866. In a subsequent proposal early in 1867, France agreed to allow the incorporation of the southern states into a united Germany in return for Prussian support for the acquisition by France of Belgium and Luxembourg. The reply was ominously non-committal.

A proposal that made sense as a face-saving policy for Napoleon was the plan to purchase the French-speaking Duchy of Luxembourg from the king of Holland in the spring of 1867. Even so, the plan misfired, partly through maladroit tactics by the French in Luxembourg, partly through Bismarck's double-dealing. The fact that Luxembourg had been a rather anomalous member of the German Confederation since 1815, garrisoned by Prussian troops, prompted a somewhat spurious campaign in the North German parliament to preserve its 'Germanic' identity. The evidence suggests that if Bismarck did not promote the campaign, he certainly exploited it for domestic political reasons. What threatened to become a dangerous crisis was defused by British pressure for a conference, which ended in a face-saving formula providing for the Prussian garrison to be withdrawn and the duchy to become a neutral state. The comment made by the British foreign secretary in April 1867 seems very apposite: 'Luxembourg would have been a small price to pay for a reconciliation between France and Prussia.' Perhaps the most alarming aspect of the crisis was Prussia's prolonged reluctance to compromise on an issue of minor importance to it but of major significance to Napoleon III in his desperate search for a boost to his prestige.

KÖNIGSSTRASSE

PEACE—AND NO PIECES!

BISMARCK. "PARDON, MON AMI; BUT WE REALLY CAN'T ALLOW YOU TO PICK UP ANYTHING HERE."
NAP (the *Chiffonnier*). "PRAY, DON'T MENTION IT, M'SIEU! IT'S NOT OF THE SLIGHTEST CONSEQUENCE."

FRANCO-PRUSSIAN RELATIONS, 1867–1870

After the fiasco of the Luxembourg affair, Franco-Prussian relations were set on a collision course which culminated in the war of 1870. A parallel development in Austro-Russian relations also began to emerge, though it took until 1914 to come to its full fruition. Its origin lay in Austria's greater interest in Balkan affairs after its influence in central Europe had been diminished by the creation of the North German Confederation under Prussia and the loss of its last remaining Italian province. Hence the suggestion that 1866 marks the beginning of the modern form of the Eastern Question, characterized by Austro-Russian rivalry and a shift of emphasis away from Roumania to Bosnia. Between 1867 and 1870 the Eastern Question in its new form interacted with what Mosse calls the 'Western Question', producing new alignments of the powers in the form of a Russo-Prussian agreement in March 1868 and a Franco-Austrian entente. Mosse makes the interesting suggestion on the basis of these developments that the key issues in European affairs for the next fifty years stemmed from the crises of 1866–7, so that 'the events of 1914 were the direct consequence of the war of 1866.'

In 1867 Napoleon, believing (perhaps rightly) that he had been duped by Bismarck in the Luxembourg affair, came to the conclusion that a partnership with Prussia-Germany was not, after all, a serious possibility. French policy now changed to determined opposition to any Prussian moves to incorporate the south German states into the new, and supposedly hostile, North German Confederation.

Bismarck's attitude towards France between 1866 and 1870 is still open to doubt, despite Kolb's denial that he deliberately sought to provoke France into war in 1870. On balance, the evidence suggests that by 1867 Bismarck was sceptical of the genuineness of French proposals for Franco-German cooperation, his doubts reinforced by the negotiations between France and Austria, and he regarded a military clash as inevitable. Linked to this was Bismarck's recognition that the North German Confederation of 1867 was not a lasting solution to the question of German unity and that it was necessary to create a momentum for unification, especially in the southern states. Schemes to draw the south closer to the north, through their military systems and through economic ties, could kill two birds with one stone. They would advance the *Kleindeutsch* cause of unification – an end desirable in itself – while possibly provoking France into action to preserve the independence of the southern states, which Prussia could exploit to its advantage. Hence Gall's suggestion that, although clumsy diplomatic moves by the French tended to obscure the fact, 'German policy after 1866 was clearly on the offensive while that of other powers, principally France, was on the defensive.'

One of the main objectives of French diplomacy between 1867 and 1870 was to secure allies in case of conflict with Prussia. Superficially, the prospects seemed promising. Austria might want to reverse the verdict of 1866 and Italy might be willing to assist France out of gratitude for French military and diplomatic aid for the cause of Italian unification.

The reality was less encouraging. The stumbling block to an Italian alliance was the continued presence of French troops in Rome to protect the Papacy from Italian desires to regain their ancient capital. Withdrawal of French protection from the pope would outrage Catholic opinion in France, not to mention the empress. Napoleon also failed to appreciate that Germans in Austria and Magyars in Hungary would strenuously oppose an attempt to reopen the Austro-Prussian conflict. So, despite the desire to increase Austrian influence in the southern states, the Habsburg emperor and his new foreign minister, Count Beust (the displaced Saxon prime minister who hated Bismarck), favoured alternatives to direct confrontation with Prussia. Hence their rejection in 1867 of an anti-Prussian alliance which would secure the Rhine frontier for France and bring gains in south Germany for the Austrians.

Beust's alternative strategy was to provoke a war with Russia over issues in the Near East, in which Prussia was expected to join, thus opening up the possibility of gains for France. Not surprisingly, Napoleon found this rather blatant pursuit of Austrian interests unappealing, but his persistence with alliance proposals in the period 1868–70 produced little more than verbal assurances of support. Even then Austrian intervention in a Franco-Prussian war would not commence until six weeks after the opening of hostilities; thus, in effect, France had first to demonstrate its ability to beat Prussia.

Napoleon encountered similar obstacles to an alliance with Russia. Although the tsar was uneasy at the aggrandizement of Prussia, which bordered on Russia, his advisers had no sympathy for French ambitions towards the Rhineland. Equally, no French interest could be served by supporting Russia in the Near East, where Austria was the main antagonist to Russia. The tsar's visit to Paris in July 1867 was not a success. The French would not back Russia's proposal to solve the revolt in Crete by transferring the island from Turkey

to Greece. Nor did they share Russia's concern at the prospect of a
Balkan rising against the Turks in the spring of 1868, or of an
Austrian occupation of Bosnia. Russia therefore turned to Prussia
for support, concluding an agreement in March 1868 whereby each
undertook to move 100,000 men to the Austrian frontier if either
side were threatened by joint Franco-Austrian military action. Russia
thereby tacitly accepted the eventual unification of Germany in
return for a renewal of Prussian sympathy over the Black Sea issue.

By 1870, therefore, when a dispute over a Prussian prince's candidacy for the vacant Spanish throne created a major crisis in Franco-
Prussian relations, France had made no real progress in its search
for allies. To make matters worse, 'the international mood was quite
favourable to Bismarck and rather hostile to France', Kolb suggests,
because the French neglected to give as much attention to the
political aspects of the diplomatic situation as Bismarck did. Furthermore, French diplomacy failed to take note of the fact that between
1868 and 1870 the military alliances of the south German states
with Prussia came under severe scrutiny, or even attack, in Bavaria
and Württemberg. A possible conclusion from this is that France
was presented with an opportunity to strengthen the independence
of the south German states by pursuing a policy of peace, but that
it failed to take advantage of this in 1870.

BISMARCK AND THE HOHENZOLLERN CANDIDATURE

Bismarck was aware that, for the sake of international opinion, it
was important to present the process of unification as an expression
of German national feeling rather than as a further stage in the
aggrandizement of Prussia. The south German states had previously
agreed to place their armies alongside Prussia in the event of a
French attack. The next stage was to create an economic union
between north and south through the agency of the existing *Zollver-
ein* (customs union). His initial strategy was to enlist the support of
nationalist opinion by setting up a permanent Customs Diet with
an elected parliament. This plan misfired almost completely.

Elections for the *Zollparlament* in 1868 in the southern states
demonstrated strong anti-Prussian feelings, while the Bavarian parliamentary elections in the following year revealed the strength of
particularism in parts of the south. These expressions of anti-Prussian sentiment showed that Bismarck's evolutionary approach to
union with the south was, for some time at least, quite unrealistic.
Unless he was prepared to let the southern question drift on

indefinitely, therefore, he had to look to the international scene for a solution. His best bet would be an issue which would arouse national sentiment throughout Germany, so that the south German states would make common cause with the north. The most likely issue for such a purpose was, of course, a confrontation of some sort with France. The fact that such an issue presented itself in the candidacy of a Prussian prince for the Spanish throne and that it led to war in 1870 has naturally led some historians to see this as a deliberate trap which Bismarck laid for France.

The new Spanish government that came to power after a successful army coup against Queen Isabella in September 1868 was in the market for a European prince who was prepared to face the hazards of Spanish political life in becoming king of Spain. The junior branch of the Prussian royal house had a prince with suitable credentials in the person of Leopold of Hohenzollern-Sigmaringen, whose brother had become king of Roumania in 1866. By the spring of 1870, however, both Leopold and the Prussian king, whose approval was necessary in such matters, had become less than enthusiastic about the candidature which was then withdrawn. Bismarck, however, continued to press for an acceptance, which was eventually given in June 1870. What turned a drama into a crisis was a muddle at Madrid which frustrated plans for Leopold's rapid confirmation as king by the Spanish Cortes, or parliament. Instead of France being presented with a *fait accompli*, the secret was out in early July that a Hohenzollern aspired to the throne of Charles V, the Habsburg emperor whose dominions had encircled France in the sixteenth century.

Bismarck's close involvement in the Hohenzollern candidacy from at least the winter of 1869–70 cannot be denied. Equally certain is that but for the enormous pressure exerted by Bismarck, the candidacy, strongly disapproved of by the Prussian king, would have been dropped. Bismarck's apologists nevertheless insist that his objective was neither war with nor even provocation of France. Bismarck's critics, who accuse him of laying a trap for France with the intention of provoking a war, tend to neglect the fact that there were too many uncertainties in the situation for even a diplomat as skilful as Bismarck to be able to make precise plans and be confident of their outcome. The candidacy certainly contained numerous possibilities, but it was not without its dangers. For a scheming statesman like Bismarck there was no doubt a potential in the situation to be exploited, but precisely how and when could hardly be determined at the outset and would have to be decided as the situation developed.

Some of Bismarck's apologists attest his innocence of 'war guilt' on the grounds that the complicity of the Prussian government in the affair was highly secret and could not be proven. Bismarck's plan was to insist that it was purely a family affair, involving the Hohenzollerns, not the Prussian government. As such, there would be little that France could do about it and any complaints it had would have to be addressed to Madrid rather than to Berlin. Other apologists (such as Kolb, writing in 1970) argue that Bismarck could not foresee how the French government would react, so that his intention cannot have been to provoke France. This viewpoint, however, ignores considerable evidence of Bismarck's awareness of how Paris might respond to such a challenge. Naïvety, after all, was hardly one of his traits. Halperin's charge that Kolb is indulging in special pleading, by placing the entire blame for the war on Paris so as to exonerate Bismarck, seems fair comment.

Nevertheless, some of the blame for the escalation of the crisis does rest with the French government. It seems quite clear that the Napoleonic right wing, which included the Duc de Gramont, appointed foreign minister in May 1870, hoped to inflict a diplomatic defeat on Prussia over the Hohenzollern candidacy. Gramont's appointment is significant in another way, in that it may well have influenced Bismarck's decision to go all out for a confrontation with France which would probably result in war. Crucial to this argument is the view that it did not greatly matter which side suffered a diplomatic defeat since, Gall believes, 'escalation of the conflict to the point of war was the probable outcome.'

Gramont's reckless and inflammatory speech on 6 July raised the tension until the Prussian king, William I, responded in a conciliatory manner to the appeals of the French ambassador, Benedetti. The announcement of the withdrawal of Leopold's candidature represented a major diplomatic triumpth for France – but it was short-lived. Gramont instructed Benedetti to obtain reassurances, or guarantees, from King William that the candidature would never be renewed. The king's report of his latest encounter with the French ambassador, at which Benedetti attempted to implement his somewhat impertinent instructions, provided Bismarck with the opportunity for some skilful editing of what became known as the Ems Telegram. Published in the press, this so-called 'red rag to the Gallic bull' helped to provoke a French declaration of war on 19 July 1870.

THE FRANCO-PRUSSIAN WAR

The Franco-Prussian war was a disaster for France and for the Napoleonic regime. Within months, the two main French armies had been defeated at Sedan and Metz by the Prussians and their south German allies. The French army was not so much outnumbered or outgunned as outmanoeuvred. True, inefficient mobilization meant that only two-thirds of France's 300,000 men were ready for action at the start of what turned out to be the decisive campaign of the war, lasting only five weeks. By contrast, over 300,000 German troops were mobilized and transported to the forward zone within three weeks of war being declared. The French therefore missed the chance to disrupt the deployment of the German forces. The German army also exploited the tactical advantage of its superior breech-loading artillery, but the French *chassepot* rifle demonstrated its withering fire-power against advancing infantry. Furthermore, France's 'secret weapon', the *mitrailleuse*, capable of firing 125 shots per minute, had a devastating potential, if only the French army had known how to use it effectively. The crucial factor in 1870, however, seems to have been the lethargy and incompetence displayed by the French high command in the face of the momentum and mobility of the German advance, directed by Moltke and the Prussian general staff.

When the emperor himself was taken prisoner, the Second Empire was replaced by a Provisional Republic which continued the war until an armistice was signed in late January 1871. By this time the king of Prussia had been acclaimed German emperor (a title he disliked) in the Hall of Mirrors at the palace of Versailles. The victorious war against France had provided the national issue which induced the southern states to accept unity with the north, even if it required disbursements from the secret funds to bribe the king of Bavaria, a Wittlesbach, to defer to the parvenu Hohenzollern dynasty. The terms of the peace treaty signed at Frankfurt in May were severe. France had to pay an indemnity of 5 milliard francs and accept a German occupation of the eastern region of France until it was paid. Worst of all was the cession of Alsace and one third of Lorraine to Germany.

The Prussian demand for Alsace-Lorraine provoked some fleeting thought of British diplomatic intervention. Before the Prussian victory at Sedan in September 1870, Russia had actively promoted the idea of intervention by the neutral powers 'to redress the European balance' and preserve the integrity of France. The response from

Austria was negative having declared its neutrality at the outbreak of the war, refusing to become involved when French bellicosity had inflamed national feeling throughout Germany. In September, Russia, rebuffed by Austria, took advantage of the preoccupation of the powers with the war to denounce the restrictions placed on it in the Black Sea by the 1856 treaty. Fear that Britain and Russia might reach a compromise on this issue and launch a peace intiative in early 1871 induced Bismarck to conclude an armistice with France.

Once the armistice was safely in his pocket, Bismarck was willing to participate in the London Conference of February 1871, in which Russia assented to the proposition that international agreements should not be renounced unilaterally. In return, St Petersburg secured the substance – the recovery of sovereignty over the ports and littoral of the Black Sea. The decline of France marked the resurgence of Russia as a great power. But the greatest power in European affairs was now the new German Empire.

GERMANY AND THE GREAT POWERS, 1871–1875

After 1871 Europe had to contend with the 'German Problem', as A. J. P. Taylor calls it: the existence in central Europe of a modern, bureaucratically organized state whose potential for economic growth could now, after unification, be fully realized to provide the resources, if and when needed, for the most efficiently organized military system in Europe. On the other hand Calleo denies that Germany was 'uniquely aggressive', suggesting that tension arose because 'modern Germany was born encircled'. He sees the 'German Problem' as an essentially geopolitical issue since, for reasons of geography, 'Germany's vitality was an immediate threat to the rest of Europe.' That Bismarck himself was slow to appreciate the power of the new Germany and the anxiety this caused other states is shown by the 'War in Sight' crisis of 1875.

The rise of Prussia-Germany on the ruins of the military reputation of the Austrian empire and the French Second Empire destroyed the old multiple balance of power, in which several permutations of alignments had been possible to preserve a 'just equilibrium' in Europe. After 1871 the other powers had to come to terms with the novel situation in which Germanic central Europe was no longer the weakest point of the great power constellation, but a formidable force to be contained and somehow integrated or absorbed into a new balance of power. Hence, despite Bismarck's assurances that Germany was now a 'satiated' state, whose main interest lay in upholding the new *status quo*, the European chancelleries were understandably anxious. As Disraeli, the Conservative leader warned in 1871: 'There is not a diplomatic tradition which has not been swept away. . . . The balance of power has been entirely destroyed.'

From the perspective of Berlin, however, the fluid diplomatic situation in 1871 contained uncertainties and dangers for Germany, whose geopolitical position burdened it with two exposed flanks – to the east and to the west. The hostility of France needed to be neutralized lest it provide a focus for an anti-German coalition, which might include Russia.

In 1871 the wisdom of Bismarck's refusal in 1866 to allow Austria to be humiliated paid dividends, facilitating a reconciliation between the German powers. Bismarck's reassurances to Vienna that Germany harboured no expansionist designs towards the 10 million Austrian Germans coincided with Austria-Hungary's desire for a *rapprochement* with Berlin. The abandonment of the anti-German policy of the Beust era was personified in two ways. The first was the meeting of the two emperors in August 1871; the second the appointment in November of the Hungarian Count Andrassy as Austrian foreign minister. Andrassy's idea, however, of utilizing a display of Austro-German solidarity as a warning to Russia became converted by the tsar into an odd demonstration of monarchical solidarity. The tsar's visit to Berlin in September 1872 was followed by a rather meaningless Russo-German military convention the following May. More significant was the Convention of Schönbrunn in June, a statement of Austro-Russian solidarity against unspecified 'subversive forces', to which the German emperor acceded in October. This *Dreikaiserbund*, or Three Emperors' Agreement, of 1873 was a strange beast, asserting the common interest of the monarchs in consulting together to settle their differences, in defence of peace and of those 'principles which they consider themselves alone capable of defending'.

To an outsider, such as Britain, the *Dreikaiserbund* of 1873 looked suspiciously like a revival of the union of the 'Three Eastern Courts' of the 1840s, or even the 'holy alliance' of 1815. Its initiation by the Habsburg and Romanov emperors, however, suggests that it might be seen as a sign of Austrian and Russian anxiety not to be too dependent on Germany. A contemporary German verdict, on the other hand, implied that Bismarck's objective had been 'so to emphasise our relationship with Vienna that both France and Russia would have to accommodate themselves to it', but this had misfired. Even so, the *Dreikaiserbund* served the purpose of emphasizing the isolation of France at a time when the replacement of the pacific Thiers as president by a more bellicose monarchist, Marshal MacMahon, caused Bismarck some concern.

In 1875 Bismarck's worries over France's unexpectedly rapid recovery from defeat and the concern of the Prussian high command at French army reorganization sparked off a brief crisis. It began with the publication in the *Berliner Post* on 9 April of an article entitled 'Is War in Sight?' The article, believed to have been inspired by Bismarck, together with some very indiscreet remarks by the German ambassador in Paris, was cleverly exploited by the French foreign minister as a sign of Germany's intent to launch a preventive war against France. The evidence suggests that the Prussian general staff, who misinterpreted the purpose of the French army reforms and exaggerated their effects on the size of the French army, may have considered military action as a riposte. On the other hand, there is little doubt that Bismarck's plans did not extend beyond warning France not to increase its military strength too fast.

The outcome of the crisis was something of a diplomatic humiliation for Bismarck – a rare event. Britain and Russia made plain to Berlin their objections to any unprovoked attack on France and Bismarck had to tolerate the self-congratulatory stance of the conceited Russian foreign minister, Gorchakov, to the effect that he had saved Europe from war.

The 'War-in-Sight' crisis of 1875 taught Bismarck an important lesson – that other nations regarded the enormous growth in German power as a potential threat to European peace and stability. This threat had been recognized by Disraeli as early as February 1871, when he warned: 'This war represents the German Revolution, a greater political event than the French Revolution', which meant 'a new world . . . new and unknown objects and dangers with which to cope'. Henceforth Bismarck had to conduct German diplomacy with more finesse and avoid arousing fears of the use Germany intended to make of its dominant position on the continent. Consequently, for the next twenty-odd years the 'German Problem' was in abeyance.

SOURCES AND FURTHER READING

Bridge, F. R. and Bullen, R., *The Great Powers and the European States System 1815–1914*, Harlow, Longman, 1980.

Calleo, D., *The German Problem Reconsidered: Germany and the World Order, 1870 to the Present*, Cambridge, Cambridge University Press, 1978.

Echard, W. E., *Napoleon III and the Concert of Europe*, Louisiana State University Press, 1983.

Eyck, E., *Bismarck and the German Empire*, London, Allen & Unwin, 1950.

Gall, L., *Bismarck. The White Revolutionary*, vol. I: *1815–1871* (transl. J. A. Underwood), London, Allen & Unwin, 1986.

Geyer, D., *Russian Imperialism 1860–1914* (transl. B. Little), Leamington Spa, Berg, 1987.

Grenville, J. A. S., *Europe Reshaped 1848–1878*, London, Fontana, 1976. (Chs XV and XVII.)

Halperin, S. W., 'The Origins of the Franco-Prussian War Re-visited: Bismarck and the Hohenzollern Candidature', *Journal of Modern History*, 1973, vol. XLV(1): 83–91.

Kolb – see 'Halperin's' article.

Medlicott, W. N., *Bismarck and Modern Germany*, London, English Universities Press, 1965.

Medlicott, W. N. and Coveney, D. K. (eds), *Bismarck and Europe*, London, Arnold, 1971.

Mosse, W. E., *The European Powers and the German Question 1848–1871*, Cambridge, Cambridge University Press, 1958.

Pflanze, O., *Bismarck and the Development of Germany, vol. 1: 1815–1871*, Princeton, NJ, Princeton University Press, 1963.

Pottinger, A., *Napoleon III and the German Crisis 1865–6*, Cambridge, Mass., Harvard University Press, 1966.

Steefel, L. D., *Bismarck, the Hohenzollern Candidacy and the Origins of the Franco-German war of 1870*, Cambridge, Mass., Harvard University Press, 1962.

Taylor, A. J. P., *The Struggle for Mastery in Europe 1848–1918*, Oxford, Clarendon Press, 1954.

Bismarck's aims and policies are effectively analysed and discussed by Lothar Gall. A work of comparable scholarship is Otto Pflanze's first volume. Medlicott offers a good brief introduction to Bismarck's policies in general, while Medlicott and Coveney focuses on diplomacy and has useful documentary extracts. The views of Erich Eyck are now, perhaps, mainly of historiographical interest. A. J. P. Taylor's views are best pursued, perhaps, in Chapters VIII–X of his magisterial work on Europe.

French policy is not well covered (Taylor has a blind spot on most of French history) except for Anne Pottinger's study, which could be supplemented by W. E. Echard's more recent work.

On the war of 1870, L. D. Steefel's study is quite detailed. A much shorter treatment of some aspects of the debate (including Kolb's controversial views, published in German in 1970) can be found in S. W. Halperin's article.

The favourable diplomatic situation for Bismarck's achievements is well presented by W. E. Mosse. Russia's role is perceptively described by D.

Geyer. Good general accounts of the period are Bridge and Bullen and also Grenville.

Finally, David Calleo's views on the 'German Problem' are presented in the form of an extended speculative essay.

2 The dilemma of Bismarckian foreign policy, 1875–1887

The basic dilemma of Bismarckian foreign policy in this period was how to maintain good relations between Russia and Austria while ensuring that both of them were well disposed towards, and dependent on, Germany. Failure to satisfy either of these two powers could result in the formation of a coalition, which would inevitably include France, directed against Germany. For the sake of Germany's security, Bismarck was impelled to perform a delicate balancing act in order to placate Russia while offering some reassurance to Austria. The issue most likely to generate tension between the two powers was, of course, a revival of the Eastern Question. If a serious crisis arose in the Balkans, Germany, which had no direct interests of its own in this part of the decaying Ottoman empire, had to avoid being pressured into siding with either the Russians or the Austrians. But both powers regarded Berlin's support on Balkan issues as the acid test of German goodwill. This was a dilemma from which there was no real escape. The problem consequently remained a persistent, if latent, threat to the security of the German empire.

This problem was compounded by the need to assume French hostility towards Germany after the loss of Alsace-Lorraine in 1871. While France alone posed no real threat to Germany, the combination of France with one or more of the other powers certainly did. A Franco-Russian alliance, obliging Germany to face the prospect of a war on two fronts, was Bismarck's greatest nightmare. A disaffected Austria was marginally less serious but its participation in a revived 'Crimean coalition', alongside France and Britain, would leave Germany isolated or dangerously dependent on Russian goodwill.

Bismarck's main objection to seeking security for Germany through an alliance with Russia seems to have been his fear of dependence on Russia. Another reason was that such an alliance might involve Germany in Russia's wide-ranging disputes with Britain, with whom Germany had no serious quarrels, at least until the colonial era. Perhaps an alliance with Britain was the best solution to Bismarck's dilemma? But this would have the obvious drawback of alienating Russia.

An exploration of Germany's foreign policy options between 1871 and 1890 does seem to suggest that Berlin's freedom of manoeuvre was limited after 1871 (and partly because of 1871). This was recognized by a key official in the Wilhelmstrasse, Holstein, when he complained in 1886: 'we are literally immobilized by France.' Security without commitment, the pursuit of the free hand in diplomacy, was seemingly an illusion. Germany's geopolitical situation in the centre of Europe denied it the luxury of a policy of isolation that was, to some extent, an option for an island power such as Britain. The most drastic solution to Bismarck's dilemma – to abandon Austria-Hungary to its fate – might have resulted in the disintegration of this ramshackle multinational empire. For Bismarck, the prospect of 10 million Austrian Catholics seeking to incorporate their homeland into his creation, the Prussian-dominated and mainly Protestant *Kleindeutsch* German empire, was unthinkable. Partition of the Ottoman empire seemed to Bismarck a less traumatic solution to the dilemma posed by Austro-Russian tension over the Balkans. His oft-repeated suggestions for a solution to the Eastern Question on these lines, however, were not received with any enthusiasm by the other great powers, who doubted that their political or economic interests would be well served by a 'carve-up' of the Ottoman empire. The Austrians, in particular, insisted that Russia could not be trusted to honour an arrangement that confined the growth of its influence to the eastern side of the Balkans.

THE NEAR EAST CRISIS OF 1875–1878

In July 1875 a revolt broke out in Herzegovina which rapidly spread to neighbouring Bosnia, the north-western extremity of the Ottoman empire. The revolt began as a protest by mainly Christian and Slav peasants against the heavy burdens imposed on them by their Muslim landowners. Unrest in Bosnia was nothing new and this was not primarily a nationalist revolt, since most of the Muslim landowners were Islamic converts of Slavic descent who spoke Serbo-Croat, not Turkish. Serbian and Montenegrin support for the revolt however, revived earlier hopes of liberation from Turkish rule.

A subsequent rising in Bulgaria in May 1876, initiated by a revolutionary committee, had a more pronounced nationalist flavour to it. It also complicated the crisis by shifting the focus of the revolt from the western to the eastern Balkans. As a result it was Russian rather than Austrian interests that were affected. This in turn had implications for Britain if the security of Constantinople and the Straits was to be put in jeopardy. Furthermore, the massacre of Bulgarian peasants by Turkish irregular forces – a reprisal for the slaughter of Muslims by the Bulgars, which passed largely unnoticed – aroused widespread indignation against the Turks in both Russia and Britain. When the semi-independent states of Serbia and Montenegro declared war on Turkey in July 1876 it looked as though a Slav crusade was developing, which might put an end to Turkish rule in the Balkans. In reality the outcome was quite different.

After a series of palace revolutions in Constantinople in the summer of 1876 a new vigour was imparted to Turkish policy, exemplified by the crushing defeat of Serbia in September despite unofficial Russian aid. By April 1877, the tsarist government faced such strong pressure to intervene on behalf of the Slav cause that it reluctantly declared war on Turkey.

Russia's unilateral military action against the Turks without a mandate from the other powers was not the expected outcome of the Balkan unrest of the previous two years. Rather it was a sign that the inability of the great powers, acting in concert, to resolve the crisis left St Petersburg in a quandary. Indeed, one of the most remarkable aspects of the crisis from 1875 to 1877 was Russia's desire to cooperate with Austria in the search for an agreed policy to bring the upheavals in the Balkans to an end. The Andrassy Note of December 1875, proposing a series of modest reforms in Bosnia, was accepted by all the powers and by Turkey only to be rejected as inadequate by the insurgents. A second Austrian initiative, the Berlin Memorandum of May 1876, containing a more extensive reform programme, was accepted by Russia but failed to secure British approval, partly because it was held to infringe the sultan's authority. The worsening of the crisis in the summer of 1876, after the Bulgarian rising and the Serbian revolt, put a strain on Austro-Russian relations until a new compromise was reached. In the Reichstadt Agreement of July 1876, the two powers agreed on a united front regardless of the outcome of the Serb-Montenegrin revolt.

This agreement marked a shift in Andrassy's stance in that he now accepted the idea of a partition of some Ottoman territory, laying claim to most of Bosnia, while Russia was to recover southern Bessarabia, lost in 1856. However, the Reichstadt Agreement, like the previous ones, was soon overtaken by events – in this case the

'Bulgarian atrocities'. The subsequent attempt by the powers to impose a solution on the Balkans, by requiring the sultan to grant a form of autonomy to both Bosnia and Bulgaria, was frustrated by a typically devious Turkish strategem. An Assembly of Notables, Christian as well as Muslim, rejected these proposals made at the Constantinople Conference (December 1876 to January 1877) and the sultan announced his intention of promulgating a new constitution for the whole Ottoman empire, thereby rendering the powers' proposals superfluous. Short of coercing Turkey by force, which Britain opposed, there was now little scope for collective action by the powers to solve the crisis.

The failure of the Constantinople Conference left the Russian government with little alternative but to prepare for war against Turkey. Consequently it once again sought an accommodation with Austria. In the Budapest Conventions (January and March 1877) the Austrians agreed to stay neutral in the forthcoming war on condition that Russia kept out of the western Balkans. Moreover, in return for Austria's acceptance of the creation of an autonomous Bulgarian state, the Russians recognized Austria's right to occupy Bosnia. Additional articles (agreed in March 1877) made provision for the collapse of the Ottoman empire. Even so, Russia did not declare war on Turkey until after the failure of yet another reform scheme (the London Protocol of 31 March) and the refusal of the other powers to participate in concerted action against the Turks.

The tsarist government acknowledged that Russia's prestige as the protector of the Slavs obliged it to intervene on their behalf. Preparations were accordingly begun in October 1876 for an offensive in the following spring, but the tsar's ministers, determined not to repeat the mistakes that had led to the disaster of the Crimean war in 1854, wanted at all costs to avoid provoking intervention by Britain and Austria. A further consideration was that the Russian Treasury could scarcely stand the strain of a long war. But the failure of the government to relieve the sufferings of the Slavs and Orthodox Christians, despite the Bulgarian massacres and the near-defeat of the Serbs in the autumn of 1876, produced mounting discontent inside Russia, directed against the tsarist regime, whose apparent inactivity was denounced by the clergy, Slavic committees and nationalist press.

Austria's readiness to negotiate with Russia over the crisis in the Balkans was partly prompted by the Dual Monarchy's financial and military weaknesses and also by the need to avoid appearing hostile to the Slav cause. Andrassy was nevertheless very suspicious of Russia and found its proposal of autonomy for Bosnia and Herzegovina very embarrassing. The creation of a semi-independent Slav state situated between the Dalmation and Croation provinces of the Dual Monarch would only add to Austria-Hungary's existing difficulties with its Slav populations. Another factor influencing its response to Russian policy in the Balkans was the marked lack of support from Germany.

The Near East crisis of 1875–8 was the first of several occasions that pointed up the basic dilemma which Bismarck faced – how to keep both Russia and Austria well disposed towards Germany and prevent a war over Balkan issues. Bismarck naturally tried to capitalize on Germany's disinterestedness in the Eastern Question, but even this had its dangers. For example, his assurances of Germany's neutrality in Balkan matters were misinterpreted initially by the tsar as giving Russia a free hand to make war against Austria. Furthermore, a display of total indifference to the outcome of the crisis might leave Germany isolated if the other powers succeeded in reaching an agreement. Bismarck's reaction to the crisis was twofold. First, he proposed partition of the Ottoman empire. Second, he sought to restrain the Austrians while encouraging Britain 'to entirely take the lead in the Eastern Question'. When pressed to clarify Germany's attitude to the issues that arose, however, his enthusiasm for some sort of alliance with Britain fluctuated markedly according to the vicissitudes of the crisis.

Not that consistency was a hallmark of British policy, despite Britain's former commitment to preserving the integrity of the Ottoman empire. Disraeli, the Conservative premier from 1874 to 1880, was a novice in foreign affairs whose initial aim was mainly to split the *Dreikaiserbund*. It was not until the autumn of 1876 (ironically, after the 'Bulgarian atrocities' had swung public opinion violently against the Turks) that his mistrust of Russia's aims led him to insist that Constantinople was the 'key to India' and must be defended. In contrast, Lord Derby, the foreign secretary until March 1878, was totally committed to peace and non-intervention, whereas the queen became more belligerent and anti-Russian than Disraeli. The equivocations in British policy, combined with the influence of the turcophile ambassador at Constantinople, seem to have played a part in encouraging Turkish resistance to the reform schemes proposed in 1876 and thereby contributed to the failure of concerted action by the great powers, especially at the Constantinople Conference.

The diplomatic situation at the outbreak of the Russo-Turkish war in April 1877 was consequently unusually favourable to Russia.

Austria's neutrality had been secured in advance, Germany and France were indifferent, while in Britain the anti-Turkish mood of public opinion precluded war with Russia. The military situation, however, was much less promising, particularly the lack of strategic railways to the Danube. Although the war began well enough, by the summer of 1877 the Russian advance into the Balkans was halted by fierce Turkish resistance centred on the fortress of Plevna, which held out until the end of the year. Thereafter the Russians advanced rapidly to Adrianople and by late January 1878 were within striking distance of Constantinople, forcing the sultan to sue for an armistice.

The Treaty of San Stephano in March 1878 signalled the magnitude of Russia's victory. The Turks assented to the creation, under Russian influence, of a Greater Bulgaria stretching from the Black Sea to the Aegean. Full independence was conceded to Serbia, Montenegro and Roumania, while territory in Asiatic Turkey was surrendered to Russia. The terms of the treaty fulfilled the exaggerated hopes of Russian opinion, including the pan-Slavs, that the 'War of Liberation' would result in great gains for Russia and the Slav cause, even though Constantinople itself had not been occupied. Many diplomats and ministers, on the other hand, regarded San Stephano as an 'act of stupidity', since they were well aware that the other powers would have to be consulted about such sweeping changes to the 1856 Treaty of Paris. They also recognized that the Russian army, exhausted by the long campaign, was in no condition to fight on if Britain and Austria challenged the Treaty of San Stephano. The siege of Plevna had in fact swung British opinion behind the 'heroic little Turks', which made it possible for the Disraeli government to adopt a warlike posture towards Russia in the early months of 1878.

The Russian threat to Constantinople and the peace terms served to confirm the worst fears of both Disraeli and Andrassy that Russia was out to destroy the Ottoman empire. The early months of 1878 were the most critical phase of the Near East crisis. The danger of an Anglo-Russian conflict seemed very great; war fever ran high in London, exemplified by the popularity of 'jingoism' in the music halls' repertoire, with the defiant climax: 'The Russians shall not have CON-STAN-TI-NO-PLE!' To counter Russian designs against Turkey the government asked Parliament for a war credit of £6 million and ordered the fleet to Constantinople. After publication of the peace terms, the government called up the reserves and summoned troops from India.

This threat of resolute action, facilitated by the resignation of the pacific Lord Derby, was not lost on the Russians, or on Britain's potential ally, Austria. In Vienna, Andrassy complained that 'Russia has played us false' when his earlier fears were confirmed by the Treaty of San Stephano. The grant of autonomy to Bosnia and the creation of Greater Bulgaria contravened the spirit, if not the letter, of the Austro-Russian agreements. Despite this, for military and financial reasons Andrassy shrank from anything more than diplomatic protests. Even diplomatic cooperation with Britain was hindered by the divergence of interests between the two states, since Austria's main concern was the spread of Russian influence towards the western Balkans, not Constantinople and the Straits. Suggestions for Anglo-Austrian cooperation, dating back to May 1877, did not therefore bear fruit until almost a year later, when the full extent of Russia's demands on Turkey was revealed.

Andrassy's proposal in March 1878 for a European conference to review the Treaty of San Stephano was seconded by Salisbury, Lord Derby's successor as foreign secretary, in the form of a diplomatic circular objecting to frontier changes in the Balkans which threatened Constantinople. Under pressure from Britain and Austria, the Russians agreed to a conference to be held in Berlin. The choice of Berlin may have attested to Germany's new importance in European affairs but it was not at Bismarck's prompting, since he had no desire to be pushed into the limelight on Balkan issues.

Throughout the crisis from 1875 to 1878 he had maintained a low profile, insisting that the Eastern Question was not of direct concern to Germany or, as he put it in December 1876, 'not worth the healthy bones of a single Pomeranian musketeer'. He had, at various times, encouraged Austria and Russia to cooperate, recommended partition of the Ottoman empire and assured Russia of Germany's neutrality, all in the hope of preserving harmony within the *Dreikaiserbund*. These manoeuvres were not without a measure of success. It can be argued that A. J. P. Taylor has dismissed the *Dreikaiserbund* too readily as just a 'fair weather system', even if Bismarck had to fend off Austrian and Russian requests for Germany's support in the event of a conflict over the Balkans. In his negotiations with Britain, Bismarck's attitude varied from expressions of studied vagueness to pressing hard for an alliance. During his ten months' absence from Berlin after mid-April 1877, he did little more than advise the Austrians to let Britain take the lead in opposing Russia. By February 1878, however, the tension created by Russia's military advance towards Constantinople led

Bismarck to offer his services as an 'honest broker', whose role would be to facilitate a compromise settlement but not to act as an arbitrator. However, as he was to discover during the Congress of Berlin, even the role of mediator carried the risk of offending one or both of the parties in dispute.

The Congress of Berlin, which assembled in June 1878, was attended by representatives of the five great powers as well as Italy and Turkey, and by some of the Balkan states. As such, it was the largest international gathering since the Congress of Vienna in 1815. Bismarck, who presided over the congress, was at the height of his influence as a European statesman. The fact that his support was sought by all sides enabled him to expedite the work of the congress within one month, through a mixture of cajolery and bullying, the latter being used quite ruthlessly with regard to the Turks and the lesser states.

Another reason for the successful outcome of the congress was that important preparatory work had been done in advance. Britain and Russia, for example, reached agreement on several key issues, such as the division of Bulgaria and Russia's gains in Bessarabia and Asiatic Turkey. The Anglo-Russian Convention, signed in May, was followed by British agreements with Turkey and Austria. The sultan reluctantly agreed to cede Cyprus to Britain in return for a guarantee of Turkey-in-Asia, where reforms were to be introduced. Britain also promised support for Austria's claim to occupy Bosnia and Herzegovina. The preliminary conventions, however, did not mean that the congress itself was all plain sailing.

The most contentious issue was naturally the division of Greater Bulgaria. When the Russians tried to renege on the terms agreed prior to the congress, Britain, backed by Austria, insisted on the creation of a separate state (to be called Eastern Rumelia) with defensible frontiers and remaining under Turkish sovereignty. In return, it was Britain which put to the congress Andrassy's 'solution' to the problem of Bosnia and Herzegovina. Their 'occupation', strongly opposed by Turkey, was designed to block Serbian and Montenegrin designs on the two provinces, while Austria-Hungary's 'administration' of Bosnia–Herzegovina was a compromise between the emperor's desire to annex the provinces outright and the aversion of both German and Magyar opinion to the inclusion of any more Slavs within the multinational Habsburg empire. Andrassy also virtually dictated the extent of the territorial gains made by Serbia and Montenegro, which, together with Roumania, secured their complete independence from Turkey in 1878.

THE BALKANS AND THE CONGRESS OF BERLIN, 1878

Vienna

Budapest

A U S T R I A — H U N G A R Y

RUSSIA

BOSNIA
(Occupied
1878–1908)

HERZEGOVINA

Belgrade

SERBIA

ROUMANIA

River Danube

DOBRUJA

Novibazar

BULGARIA

Plevna

Black Sea

MONTENEGRO

Sofia

1885

EASTERN RUMELIA

'MACEDONIA'

Adrianople

Constantinople

T U R K E Y   I N   E U R O P E

Straits

GREECE

Mediterranean Sea

Territory ceded by
Turkey, 1878–1881

Limits of Greater Bulgaria
in Treaty of San Stephano

Boundary of Turkey in Europe
before 1878

0   200
km

Russia's gains from the war which it had fought and won single-handed, at considerable human and financial cost, were relatively modest, at least when compared to the San Stephano treaty. It recovered southern Bessarabia but its rights of occupation over Bulgaria, which was expected to become a Russian satellite, were reduced to a period of a mere nine months. In Asia, Russia secured Kars and Batum, partly because Disraeli, who reportedly 'had never seen a map of Asia Minor' in his life, failed to notice Gorchakov's deft switching of maps at the crucial moment in the negotiations. France fared badly in 1878. Its only consolation for seeing the British acquire Cyprus was the suggestion that it might like to occupy Tunis.

Some of the issues seemingly resolved by the Congress of Berlin continued to cause friction for several years. The Russians, for example, sought to evade implementation of the Bulgarian settlement, with the result that by the time Eastern Rumelia was eventually restored to Turkish rule the sultan's authority over the province was virtually non-existent. For his part, the sultan created serious difficulties for the Austrians by employing delaying tactics over relinquishing his authority over Bosnia, where fierce opposition to the Austrian occupation necessitated extensive military operations. The Turks also tried to evade implementing reforms in the administration of Asia Minor, despite British threats. Ironically, Britain and Austria, the two powers who had most actively resisted Russian encroachment on the Ottoman empire, ended by being more unpopular than Russia in Constantinople. But then, their professions of concern for the integrity of the sultan's empire seemed somewhat at variance with their acquisition of Turkish territory in 1878.

Some historians are dubious about the value of the Berlin settlement. Lord Salisbury himself once remarked that Britain had 'backed the wrong horse' in propping up the Turkish empire. Certainly, in 1878 Disraeli seemed blind to a possible alternative policy of recognizing the full potential of the Balkan states for self-government. The artificial creation of Eastern Rumelia lasted less than a decade. More serious was the return to Turkish misrule of part of Greater Bulgaria, thus paving the way for the 'Macedonian Problem' in the early 1900s. The failure of the reform programme in Asia Minor led to the subsequent Armenian massacres, while Austrian rule over Bosnia was scarcely trouble-free. The eventual annexation of Bosnia in 1908 created yet another major crisis in Austro-Russian relations. These flaws in the work of the Berlin Congress have consequently led some historians to suggest (perhaps simplistically?) that allowing Russia to keep its gains under the Treaty of San Stephano might have been the lesser of two evils.

Although Salisbury abandoned hope of a regeneration of the Turkish empire as early as 1880, the British government was, in general, well pleased with the Berlin settlement. Disraeli rejoiced that 'our great object . . . to break up the *Dreikaiserbund*' had succeeded and at Austria's obvious dependence on Britain in Balkan matters. More important was that by resisting the apparent Russian threat to Constantinople, Britain had safeguarded the route to the east as well as its position in the Mediterranean. As A. J. P. Taylor remarked in a gem of a comment: 'Great Britain won a bloodless victory with a music-hall song and a navy of museum pieces.'

Whereas the congress safeguarded Austrian interests in the Balkans, in Russia the Berlin settlement (and especially the truncation of Greater Bulgaria) was naturally regarded as a great humiliation which damaged the prestige of the tsarist regime. For Bismarck, the Congress of Berlin was only a partial triumph. Although the *Dreikaiserbund* still existed on paper, the estrangement between Russia and Austria persisted for some years even though the German chancellor had attempted to direct Russian animosity away from Austria and towards Britain. Furthermore, despite giving Germany's support to Russia on many issues he had failed to convince the Russians of his good faith as a reliable friend and ally.

THE CREATION OF THE 'BISMARCKIAN SYSTEM' 1879–1882

Between 1879 and 1882 Bismarck created an alliance system in which Germany and Austria-Hungary, as allies, became linked first with Russia and then with Italy. This network of alliances was extended by treaties made by Austria with Serbia and Roumania. Some historians have regarded this alliance system as being of major significance for Germany and for Europe as a whole. For example, Gordon Craig has drawn attention to the fact that the Austro-German alliance of 1879 was not only a peacetime commitment that became permanent, it was also the first of a series of secret treaties which eventually divided the European powers into two hostile camps. As such, the alliance system came to be regarded as one of the long-term causes of the First World War.

Historians have naturally questioned the impulse behind Bismarck's decision to seek alliances. Was it perhaps a sign of a deterioration in Bismarck's nerves rather than a rational response

A BLAZE OF TRIUMPH!

to an actual worsening of the international situation? Was Russia really so formidable a power that alliances were essential to Germany's security? Lothar Gall argues that the alliance system represented a decisive change in Bismarck's strategy after 1878, related directly to his experience of the Near East crisis. This crisis revealed the shortcomings of his negative, low-profile approach to issues which caused serious tension between Austria and Russia. Instead, Gall suggests, Bismarck now believed it was necessary for Germany to seize the initiative and seek to influence events, rather than merely respond to them.

In 1879 the most pressing problem was what to do about Russia's overt hostility to Germany after the Congress of Berlin. The Russians talked of a 'European coalition under the leadership of Prince Bismarck' and in August 1879 the tsar complained of Bismarck's animosity towards Russia in a personal letter to his uncle, the Kaiser, emphasizing the 'disastrous consequences' that might result from a Russo-German estrangement. Bismarck, unlike the Kaiser, had no intention of yielding to Russian pressure. An alliance with Russia would mean, in his view, that German policy would be subordinated to Russian policy and result in the loss of any freedom of manoeuvre. Furthermore, Austria's likely reaction to a Russo-German alliance would be to try to revive the Crimean coalition. In Bismarck's view, therefore, the best response to pressure from Russia was to secure an alliance with Austria in which Germany would be the dominant element. This would oblige Russia to seek a partnership with the German powers in a revived *Dreikaiserbund* which, he assured the Kaiser, would be 'an ideal political objective'.

Although this line of reasoning has a clear logic to it, it leaves two factors unexplained and makes no allowance for Bismarck's habitual deviousness. One factor is that the German chancellor was not simply the innocent victim of Russian pique. The deterioration in Russo-German relations was partly the result of Bismarck's own actions and policies in 1879, such as tariffs, complaints about Russian troop movements and a press war. Some historians have consequently wondered whether Bismarck was not deliberately trying to increase Russo-German tension in order to justify his preference for an alliance with Austria, which the Kaiser did not share. The second factor which is hard to explain is the curious nature of the alliance that Bismarck proposed to the Austrians. Presented as a return to 'the good old days' of the German Confederation, the revived 'German bloc', consistent with the imperial tradition, was to be a permanent insurance pact, ratified by both parliaments. The Austrian response to this was discouraging. Although Andrassy had been seeking closer ties with Germany since 1871, he found these proposals totally unacceptable because what Vienna wanted was firm German backing against Russia, not a general commitment that could involve Austria in a Franco-German quarrel. Furthermore, Andrassy, a Magyar aristocrat and foreign minister of a multinational empire, disliked the emphasis on the German interests of two states. As a result of his objections, the eventual form of the Austro-German alliance was quite conventional.

In the Dual Alliance of October 1879 the two powers promised mutual support in the event of an attack by Russia, but only benevolent neutrality if attacked by another power. The treaty was to remain secret unless both parties agreed to its communication to a third power and it was to run for five years. That Bismarck was dissatisfied with the form of this alliance, whose terms were largely dictated by Andrassy, seems quite clear. The elimination of the 'German bloc' element, which he had hoped would win support for the government from the Catholic Centre Party and south German opinion, destroyed its potential usefulness to Bismarck in domestic politics.

Even before the treaty was signed Bismarck had agreed to hold talks with Saburov, soon to be the Russian ambassador to Berlin, on the possibility of reviving the *Dreikaiserbund*. From the point of view of both Russia and Germany a new tripartite agreement had much to commend it. By drawing Russia back into the fold, Bismarck hoped to weaken the influence over Russian policy of anti-German elements, especially the pan-Slavs. This would help to reduce the risks of an Austro-Russian conflict in the Balkans and of a Franco-Russian entente. The Russian approach to Germany stemmed from a number of anxieties. Foremost among these was, of course, the rumours of an impending alliance between Germany and Austria. But the Russian government was also concerned at the general implications of Anglo-Austrian cooperation in the Near East. More specifically, it feared a reassertion of British influence at the Porte affecting the Straits and the situation in Eastern Rumelia. Although the Russians were over-optimistic about Bismarck's willingness to support their interests there, it was the Austrians who reluctantly made most of the concessions, which shows the importance Bismarck attached to restoring good relations with Russia.

Berlin's view of the Austro-German alliance as a first step towards a new *Dreikaiserbund* was not shared by Vienna. The emperor may not have been averse to a new agreement with the tsar but Andrassy objected strongly that the Russians were 'full of perfidy'. He regarded the alliance with Germany as the 'tombstone' of the old *Dreikaiserbund*, not a stepping stone to a new one. The only extension of the 1879 alliance that Andrassy favoured was the inclusion of Britain and possibly France. But to Austria's dismay Gladstone returned to power in April 1880, signifying a change in British policy. Instead of cooperation with Austria to enforce the provisions of the Berlin treaty, the British government would work with Russia against Turkey. The Austrians were therefore left with little alternative but to seek a *modus vivendi* with Russia in Balkan affairs. Under heavy pressure from Bismarck, they eventually agreed to the terms of a new *Dreikaiserbund* in June 1881.

This secret treaty, which was renewable after three years, naturally provided for the benevolent neutrality of the other signatories if one of them should be at war with a fourth power. This proviso even extended to a war against Turkey, providing a prior agreement had been reached on the outcome of the conflict. The main substance of the Three Emperors' Alliance was an attempt to identify Austro-Russian interests in the Balkans. The 'mutually obligatory character of the principle of the closing of the Straits' was reaffirmed to satisfy Russia's anxiety at the apparent desire of Britain to withdraw from the Straits Convention of 1841. Austrian fears about Russia's intentions were met by the stipulation that changes could not be made to the territorial *status quo* in European Turkey without prior agreement. In a separate protocol, Austria reserved the right to annex Bosnia and Herzegovina in the future. Russian interests were covered by a declaration against a Turkish reoccupation of Eastern Rumelia, whose eventual reunion with Bulgaria 'by force of circumstances' was conceded. To avoid collisions of interest the local agents of the three powers were to be instructed to cease working against each other in the Balkans.

The terms of this *Dreikaiserbund* were not particularly advantageous to the Austrians. Of more direct benefit to them was a secret political agreement with Serbia in 1881, buttressed by a commercial treaty. Two years later, they succeeded in drawing Roumania into a similar alliance which was reinforced by Germany's adherence to it. In both cases, however, the link was largely a dynastic one, with no popular support for it in either state.

Not that Austrian or Italian public opinion was taken into account in the formation of the Triple Alliance of May 1882. On paper this alliance seemed to increase Germany's security, but in reality the main beneficiary was the Austrians, who were relieved of the threat of an Italian stab in the back if they became involved in a conflict in the east. In the event of a war in the west, the two German powers were only obliged to assist Italy if it were the victim of an unprovoked attack by France.

Bismarck seems to have played a less active role in the making of the Triple Alliance than Kalnoky, the new foreign minister of Austria-Hungary in November 1881. It took a renewal of Bismarck's fears of pan-Slavist influences over the new tsar, Alexander III, to persuade the German chancellor of the merits of an alliance with Italy. Italian feelers for an alliance with Austria were renewed after the French occupation of Tunis in May 1881, which blighted Italian hopes of an empire in north Africa. But having a quarrel with France hardly added to Italy's already dubious attractions as an alliance partner. Two factors eased Italy's path in 1882: Austrian fears for the stability of the monarchy in Italy, and Bismarck's anxiety at the welcome given in Paris to the pan-Slav General Skobelev, which revived old fears of a Franco-Russian alignment. Hence the stipulation that Italy would assist its allies if either were attacked by two powers, whereas in the event of an attack by only one power Italy's neutrality would suffice. It was therefore 'the dreadful confusion prevailing in Russia', as Kalnoky put it, rather than the French occupation of Tunis, that explains the conclusion of the Triple Alliance.

The treaty of May 1882 did not, as is sometimes suggested, convert the Dual Alliance of 1879 into a Triple Alliance. The two treaties remained quite separate entities, though the latter, with its basically anti-Russian thrust, was a useful adjunct to the Austro-German treaty. The new alliance also had some value to the Austrians in obliging the Italian government to restrain the irredentist groups inside Italy which laid claim to Austrian territory, notably the Tyrol. Perhaps the main disadvantage of the Triple Alliance from Austria-Hungary's point of view was psychological, in that it deprived the Dual Monarchy of the freedom to attack Italy, the one and only war that would have been universally popular throughout the Habsburg lands. Even so, the existence of the alliance did not prevent a future chief of staff from constantly advocating a preventive war against Italy. Apart from this, the only outlet for Austrian frustration and aggression as a non-colonial power lay in the east, the Balkans, where Russia's historic interests lay.

In 1884, when the *Dreikaiserbund* was renewed for a further three years without difficulty, Bismarck's alliance system seemed stable and secure. Yet only a few years later its fragility was made plain. Germany's security seemed to be put at risk by a renewal of Austro-Russian tension, following a crisis in Bulgaria, and by a revival of pan-Slavism, coinciding in part with an apparent resurgence of revanchism in France.

PAN-SLAVISM AND REVANCHISM

Bismarck confessed to suffering from a 'nightmare of coalitions'. In December 1872 he noted that 'our chief danger for the future will be the moment France is once again regarded by the royal courts of Europe as a potential ally.' His description of the French as 'incorrigible disturbers of the European peace', however, hardly fitted the majority of Republican leaders in the late 1870s and 1880s. Their main preoccupation was to consolidate the newly established Republican regime against the machinations, real or imagined, of their monarchist and clericalist opponents inside France. In so far as Republicans had ambitions for restoring French greatness, these were directed primarily towards Africa and Asia and resulted in clashes with Britain, not Germany. By the early 1880s the desire to recover Alsace-Lorraine was such a dying sentiment in France that the Ligue des Patriotes was founded in order to remind the French of their patriotic duty towards the 'lost provinces'. Apart from the Boulangist episode in the late 1880s, therefore, revanchism was either a spectre that Bismarck chose to frighten himself with or, more probably, exploited in order to frighten others with it.

Pan-Slavism, on the other hand, exerted a significant influence on Russian foreign policy on two occasions in this period. Although it was at its peak in 1876–8, its resurgence during the Bulgarian crisis of 1885–7 coincided with the emergence of Boulangism in France, thereby reviving Bismarck's nightmare of a Franco-Russian coalition against Germany.

During the 1860s the multifaceted concept of the brotherhood of Slav peoples (Poles excepted) was being defined more narrowly in terms of Russia's leadership of the Slav cause. Russian pan-Slavs called for the liberation of fellow Slavs from Austrian as well as Turkish rule, arguing that the road to Constantinople and the Straits lay through Vienna. Although no official government support was forthcoming for pan-Slavist committees and congresses, the pan-Slav movement had the backing of influential figures at court and in the army, the bureaucracy and the clergy as well as the support of journalists and writers of note. Despite restrictions on the press, pan-Slavist editors such as Aksakov and Katkov, as well as writers such as Dostoevsky, were able to mount campaigns in support of the cause and to publicize their views. The point of convergence between the pan-Slavs and the tsarist government lay in the belief that Russia needed some dramatic successes in foreign affairs to make up for its defeat in 1856 and to compensate for its relative decline as a great power following the aggrandizement of Prussia-Germany between 1866 and 1871. Where they differed was in their estimate of the feasibility of pursuing an expansionist policy, given the government's acute financial weakness in the 1870s and 1880s.

During the Near East crisis of 1875–8 pan-Slavist agitation in favour of Russian intervention to aid the Serbs and Bulgars reached its height. The campaign launched in the nationalist press aroused the urban population and the clergy and even touched some of the peasant masses, creating a wave of 'Slavomania' across Russia. Some 5,000 Russian volunteers went to fight alongside the Serbs, while funds were raised by Slavic committees. When diplomatic efforts to resolve the crisis came to nothing the tsar was forced to recognize Russia's 'holy mission' to aid the cause of the Slavs and Orthodox Christians against their Muslim 'oppressors'. Hence despite the parlous condition of the state finances, the war minister was led to proclaim in February 1877: 'Russia's honour forbids us to stand about any longer with lowered guns just for the sake of peace.' After the military successes in early 1878, both public opinion and the army high command demanded that Constantinople be occupied by Russian troops.

The Treaty of San Stephano in March 1878 was literally a pan-Slav peace, negotiated by General Ignatiev, the pan-Slavist ambassador to Constantinople. Russia's subsequent climbdown at the Congress of Berlin created widespread disillusionment in Russia which led to the government being accused by Aksakov of 'a conspiracy against the Russian people'. Pan-Slavist enthusiasm therefore not only pushed a reluctant government into military action against Turkey, but it also brought Russia to the brink of war with Britain by threatening Constantinople and by its unrealistic peace terms.

Pan-Slavist agitation in the mid–1880s mainly took the form of denouncing the new *Dreikaiserbund* with the German powers and advocating an alliance with France. Katkov's press attacks on official foreign policy were tolerated to a remarkable degree by the government, while General Skobelev preached a militant pan-Slavist doctrine to audiences in Moscow and Paris, advocating a Franco-Russian alliance.

The enthusiastic response in Russian military and aristocratic circles in 1886–7 to the rise of General Boulanger in France seemed to presage a coalition of militant pan-Slavism in Russia with revanchism in France. Boulanger's posture as an ardent patriot in the spring of 1887 won him some cheap popularity and the backing of the boulevard press and French nationalists, whose cries of 'vers le rhin' alarmed not only Bismarck but also the cautious Republican leaders in France. However, Boulanger's remarkable by-election victories in 1888 were more a reaction against the drabness and shortcomings of Republican rule, aggravated by an economic recession, than a desire for war with Germany. Public opinion was nevertheless inflamed from time to time by the sensationalist press.

Bismarck's overt response to Boulangism was to exploit it for his own political purposes in the elections of February 1887 and in the subsequent debates on the German Army Bill. Significantly, his response to the tsar's refusal to renew the *Dreikaiserbund* was to negotiate a secret treaty with Russia in June 1887. The tsarist regime thereupon began to restrain the pan-Slavist campaign and to curb the enthusiasm of the Russian press for the Boulangist cause in France.

Consequently, the main danger Bismarck had to fear from Russia after the alliance of June 1887 was the uncertainty of its reaction to a possible Franco-German war, arising perhaps from an initial Italo-French conflict. The latter was a more likely scenario than a direct French attack on Germany, inspired by Boulangist and revanchist sentiments. Although Bismarck could legitimately fear that Boulangism was an unpredictable force which might be a threat to Germany' security, modern historians tend to dismiss the Boulanger crisis in France as something of a nine days' wonder. Indeed, a recent 'Gaullist inspired' reappraisal of Boulangism has emphasized the genuineness of the General's Republican credentials and his intent to restore stability to the governmental system through peaceful and legal means.

Although the pan-Slavist agitation in the mid–1880s and its flirtation with Boulangism were somewhat ephemeral, some historians see it as having had a significant effect on the attitude of Bismarck and other European leaders towards Russian foreign policy. Foreign observers were understandably puzzled at the licence allowed to Katkov and others to print such strong criticisms of tsarist foreign policy and to voice their anti-German sentiments. Bismarck's conclusion seems to have been that the anti-German press campaign indicated an impending change of course in Russian policy towards an alliance with France. It has also been suggested that the ultimate significance of pan-Slavism was to persuade Bismarck in the late

1880s that the Russo-German entente could not be more than a short-term solution to the problem of Germany's security.

THE BULGARIAN CRISIS OF 1885–1887 AND THE BISMARCKIAN SYSTEM

The revival of Austro-Russian tension during the Bulgarian crisis of 1885–7 destroyed the *Dreikaiserbund* and shook Bismarck's alliance system to its foundations. In response, Bismarck created a new alliance with Russia, while encouraging the formation of a tripartite alliance between Austria, Italy and Britain to act as a check on Russia in the Near East.

The crisis over Bulgaria, which went through several phases, caused great offence and anger in St Petersburg and seemed likely to end in hostilities when the Austrians opposed Russian intervention in Bulgaria.

The crisis began with a revolt in Eastern Rumelia in September 1885, with demands for union with Bulgaria. Alexander of Battenberg, Russia's protégé as prince of Bulgaria since 1879, was soon forced by popular pressure to take over the leadership of the movement, but this move was wrongly interpreted as the culmination of a series of anti-Russian actions taken by the prince since the early 1880s. The fundamental reason for Russia's hostility to the prince was the tsar's insistence that the unification of the two Bulgarias, whose separation had been forced on Russia in 1878, should be accomplished under Russian auspices. The first phase of the crisis was further complicated by Serbian and Greek demands for compensation for the aggrandizement of Bulgaria. Furthermore, the Russians mistakenly assumed that Serbia's pre-emptive strike against Bulgaria had been prompted by the Austrians. The unexpected rout of the Serbian forces at Slivnitsa in November 1885 did, in fact, induce the Austrians to intercede, but only to prevent the total humiliation of their Serbian protégé. But this naturally tended to confirm Russian suspicions of Austrian collusion with Serbia.

As far as the great powers were concerned, the main issue to be determined at the Constantinople Conference in late 1885 was how to rescind the recent union of the two Bulgarias. The Russians demanded a return to the *status quo ante*, insisting, quite rightly, that the union was a violation of the Treaty of Berlin. With Germany backing Russia, the Austrians reluctantly decided to follow suit. The unity of the *Dreikaiserbund* was thereby preserved. The Turks, however, refused to employ force to return Eastern Rumelia to Turkish suzerainty, the only solution acceptable to Britain. The deadlock at the conference worsened when the British government subsequently decided to back the Bulgarians, once the realization dawned that they were no longer a Russian puppet. In the following spring Russia reluctantly accepted the British proposal, supported by France and Italy, for the creation of a 'personal union' of the two states with Prince Alexander as governor-general of Eastern Rumelia.

This solution pleased the Austrians, whose policy during the crisis had been constrained by Berlin's insistence on loyalty to the *Dreikaiserbund*. Russia's restraint in accepting the British proposal owed much to its economic and military weakness, exemplified by a large reduction in military expenditure in 1882. The government was none the less under great pressure from the press to intervene, especially after the failure of the Constantinople Conference. But this policy of restraint implied that the sacrifices made by Russia on behalf of Bulgaria in 1877–8 had been in vain. It was hard for both the government and public opinion to face up to the fact that Bulgarian gratitude had been so rapidly forfeited by the clumsy and insensitive behaviour of Russia's military and civilian agents, two of whom held posts in the Bulgarian government. Nor was there any prospect of increasing Russian influence through economic links, since Russia could not compete successfully in commercial matters even against the Austrians.

The tsar's determination to replace Alexander with a more compliant ruler as a way of reasserting Russian influence in Bulgaria provoked strong protests from Austria at the unorthodox methods employed. Prince Alexander was forcibly abducted in a conspiracy mounted by pro-Russian army officers. After a counter-coup, he decided that without the tsar's approval the role of prince of Bulgaria was too hazardous for comfort and so resigned. In the power struggle that ensued between Stamboulov, the 'strong man' of Bulgarian politics, and Russia's uninvited agent, General Kaulbars, the tsar's aim was to create a pro-Russian regency which would ensure the election of his nominee as prince of Bulgaria. Kaulbars's heavy-handed interference in the politics of the Bulgarian capital, which earned him the title 'General Sofiasco', was a failure. His abrupt departure in November 1886 signified the severance of normal diplomatic relations between St Petersburg and Sofia. Consequently there was widespread expectation in the capitals of Europe that Russia would use force to establish a regime in Bulgaria that it found acceptable. In November 1886 the Austro-Hungarian foreign minister warned Russia that an attempt to occupy Bulgaria could result in war. This rebuke from an ally so incensed the tsar that he refused to consider renewing the Three Emperors' Alliance in the following spring.

Tension over Bulgaria arose for the third time in the summer of 1887, when the Bulgarian assembly elected Ferdinand of Coburg as its new prince. An Austrian army officer and a Roman Catholic, who was related to Queen Victoria, Ferdinand was anathema to the tsar. The Russians put enormous pressure on the Turks to evict him, but Britain and Italy gave strong diplomatic support to the Austrians in opposing this pressure at Constantinople. There was, of course, no prospect whatever of German support for Austria on this issue.

Bismarck had declared in January 1887 that it was 'a matter of complete indifference to Germany who rules in Bulgaria and what becomes of her'. By December 1887, however, the British government had been persuaded by Bismarck to extend its modest commitments in the Mediterranean, undertaken in the spring, to cover the independence of Bulgaria. Russia's eventual recognition of the fact that it could not get its own way over Bulgaria brought the crisis to an end, though it was not until 1896 that Russia agreed to recognize Ferdinand as prince of Bulgaria.

Bismarck may well have felt that the Bulgarian crisis had created the most dangerous situation for Germany since 1870–1, threatening his whole alliance system. The overt clash between Austria and Russia in late 1886 was followed by the tsar's refusal to renew the *Dreikaiserbund* in the spring of 1887. To add to Bismarck's troubles, Italy was demanding better terms as the price of renewing the Triple Alliance, which expired in May 1887, while revanchist agitation in France, aroused by Boulanger, coincided with pan-Slav pressures for a Franco-Russian alliance. On top of this, tariff quarrels exacerbated both Russo-German and Franco-Italian relations in the course of 1887–8.

Bismarck's initial response to the Bulgarian problem was the classic one of imposing restraint on Austria while encouraging Britain to take the lead in confronting Russia, as in 1878. Britain's stand on 'personal union' at the Constantinople Conference in 1885 certainly drew Russia's ire, but Kalnoky's warning to the Russians not to transgress the limits of acceptable behaviour in Bulgaria infuriated the tsar. Bismarck, seemingly unaware of Russia's military and financial weakness, was anxious to prevent a breach in Russo-German relations which might well result in a Franco-Russian alliance.

Hence the secret Reinsurance Treaty concluded with Russia in June 1887. Germany recognized Russia's right to a preponderant influence in Bulgaria and also promised diplomatic support if Russia should need to assert its control over the Straits. In more general terms, the allies agreed to observe benevolent neutrality if one of them was at war with another great power, except in the case of a Russian attack on Austria or a German attack on France. By this proviso Germany forfeited the free hand it had enjoyed since 1881 to attack France without fear of Russian intervention.

As a temporary stop-gap to avoid the perils of Russian resentment and as a way of shoring up the crumbling edifice of the Bismarckian system, the Reinsurance Treaty had its value. But there is little doubt that the promise of Germany's diplomatic support for Russian interests in the Balkans and the Straits conflicted with the spirit, if not the letter, of the Dual Alliance of 1879. It was also totally at variance with the objectives of the agreement between Austria, Italy and Britain, made in December 1887 with Bismarck's encourage-ment, to defend the *status quo* in Bulgaria and the Straits.

BRITAIN AND THE TRIPLE ALLIANCE

The most useful role that Britain could play in international affairs, in Bismarck's view, was as a check on Russian expansion in the Near East. This would lessen Austrian anxieties about Russian aims in the Balkans, enabling Bismarck to preserve harmony within the *Dreikaiserbund*, the lynchpin of his 'system'. From the viewpoint of London, however, this scenario placed far too great a burden on Britain, which regarded the defence of Turkey-in-Europe as a matter of concern to other powers as well, especially Austria. In 1887, with the *Dreikaiserbund* in ruins and Italy demanding concessions in return for renewing the Triple Alliance, Bismarck was keen to encourage the British government's hesitant steps towards an under-standing with Austria and Italy to cover the Mediterranean and the Near East.

The Mediterranean Agreements, concluded in the spring and winter of 1887, are sometimes regarded as the obvious British response to its difficulties with France over Egypt and its fears of a further confrontation with Russia over Bulgaria. Faced with the prospect of French and Russian hostility, Britain seemingly sought refuge in an association with the Triple Alliance powers, which was, in the view of Lord Salisbury, the Conservative premier and foreign secretary, 'necessary to avoid serious danger'. In the first agreement, concluded with Italy in February 1887, to which Austria acceded in March, the signatories promised mutual support for the defence of the *status quo* in the Mediterranean region, including Egypt and Constantinople. In the much more specific tripartite treaty signed in December 1887, the allies committed themselves to the defence of peace and the *status quo* in the Near East, including Bulgaria and the Straits.

There is thus a simple logic behind Langer's view that the agreements of February/March were directed against France, while that of December 1887 was aimed at Russia. The weakness of this interpretation of the origins of Britain's association with the Triple Alliance, however, is that it over-simplifies a complex and changing diplomatic situation.

In the first place, it is clear that the initiative for both agreements came not from Britain but from Italy, with some pressure behind the scenes from Bismarck. In the negotiations for the renewal of the Triple Alliance in the spring of 1887 Italy, on bad terms with France and with aspirations to play a role as a Mediterranean power, with particular ambitions towards Tripoli, was demanding greater recognition of its interests. Although Germany was willing to guarantee Italy's security against France and Austria reluctantly agreed to compensation for Italy for any future territorial changes in the Near East, support for Italian aspirations in the Mediterranean could best be provided by Britain, the leading naval power. By February 1887 Bismarck had become quite open in his warnings of Germany's hostile reaction if Britain failed to respond to Italy's overtures.

In the case of the second agreement concluded in December 1887, the initiative was once again taken by the Italians, in particular by Crispi, the premier and foreign minister, who in Salisbury's view was intent on 'some splashy interference in Bulgarian affairs'. Crispi's idea of extending the Mediterranean Agreement to include Turkey was warmly supported by Kalnoky, irritated by Bismarck's siding with Russia against the Coburg candidature for the Bulgarian princedom. The British response to Crispi's idea was, by contrast, distinctly cool and it required Bismarck's strong recommendation to persuade the British cabinet that it should take on the commitments outlined in the Austro-Italian proposal. In Salisbury's view, the second agreement was simply the lesser of two evils, the alternative being that Britain would once again find itself isolated.

The perils of isolation had been dramatically revealed in the spring of 1885, when the other powers had combined to persuade the Turkish sultan not to allow Britain to send a naval force into the

Black Sea as a riposte to Russian action at Pendjeh, on the Afghan frontier in central Asia. However, the focus of contention between Britain and Russia from September 1885 to December 1887 was once again the Balkans and the Straits, while Egypt remained the main point at issue between Britain and France.

The most obvious danger to British interests at this time seemed to be a Franco-Russian coalition, designated in a military intelligence report of April 1887 as 'the worst combination we have any reason to dread'. However, what Salisbury seems to have feared most after 1885 was the hostility of *either* France *or* Russia, backed by the Triple Alliance. Hence his readiness to negotiate with Italy and Austria in the early part of 1887, since, as the Italians pointed out: 'England would be once more linked to the central powers.' Although the Bulgarian crisis and French hostility to the continuing occupation of Egypt by Britain remained major issues in British policy between 1885 and 1887, the fluidity of both of these situations undermines the attractively simple logic of Langer's interpretation of the origins of the Mediterranean Agreements – that the first was directed against France and the second against Russia.

As regards Egypt, relations with France remained quite cordial for as long as British assurances of their intent to withdraw from Egypt retained some credibility; that is, until May 1887. Despite the lack of progress over Egypt, the French government forbore to cooperate with Russia over Bulgaria in the hope of a direct settlement with Britain. There was therefore no reason why Salisbury should seek Italian or Austrian support against France in February/ March 1887. In fact, the main value to Britain of diplomatic support from the Triple Alliance lay in Constantinople, where renewed negotiations with the sultan about the terms for Britain's withdrawal from Egypt were under way. The Alliance's support increased the chances of a settlement of the Egyptian question, which would not only improve relations with France but Anglo-Turkish relations as well. The failure of the Drummond-Wolff negotiations at Constantinople in May 1887 was primarily caused by France's decision to join with Russia in putting pressure on the sultan to reject the British proposals, in the mistaken belief that the French could secure better terms for Britain's withdrawal.

This fateful miscalculation relieved the British government of a moral obligation to evacuate Egypt in the near future. It did not signify a need for diplomatic support against France, which had ruined its own case over Egypt. Similarly, the renewal of the Bulgarian crisis in July 1887 with the election of the pro-Austrian

Coburg prince did not produce a strong desire for diplomatic support against Russia. This was because Ferdinand of Coburg was not highly regarded by the British government, which was, in any case, hoping for a peaceful resolution of the crisis. However, once Kalnoky had responded warmly to Crispi's idea of extending the Mediterranean Agreement to include Bulgaria and Turkey, Britain was left in a quandary.

The problem was that if Britain refused to participate in this plan the Austrians, already aggrieved by Germany's support for Russia in Bulgaria, might decide that their only course was to seek a *rapprochement* with Russia. Britain would then be left once more without allies among the great powers. What seems to have clinched the argument with the waverers in the British cabinet was Bismarck's strong support for Britain's adherence to the Austro-Italian agreement. By an exchange of notes, which avoided the parliamentary approval necessary for a formal alliance, the government committed Britain to the defence of peace and the *status quo* in Bulgaria, the Straits and Asia Minor and to the independence of Turkey. This agreement, made in December 1887, which was tantamount to an alliance since it envisaged the use of force, secured for Britain the cooperation of the Triple Alliance that Salisbury had been seeking as a means of defending British interests in the Near East and the Mediterranean since 1885. It remained the basis of British foreign policy for a decade, and in conjunction with the strengthening of the navy by the Naval Defence Act of March 1889 provided, in Salisbury's view, adequate protection for British interests.

Salisbury was therefore able to decline Bismarck's offer of an alliance directed primarily against France in early 1889. Not only did the British premier dislike this aspect of the proposed alliance, he also feared it would make Britain dangerously dependent on German goodwill. After the accession in 1888 of Wilhelm II, noted for his erratic behaviour, such goodwill was an even more uncertain factor. Salisbury's decision to leave Bismarck's alliance offer 'on the table' was also influenced by two other factors. First, the government relied on support from the Liberal Unionists, who were anti-German and averse to firm commitments to the continental powers. Second, Crispi's belligerent stance towards the French made a war against France seem possible, which Salisbury had no wish to encourage by too close a tie with the Triple Alliance.

THE DECLINE OF THE BISMARCKIAN SYSTEM

The shifts and evasions in Bismarck's diplomacy between 1887 and 1890 have naturally led historians to question the viability of the 'Bismarckian system', whose inconsistencies grew apace. For example, only a few months after signing the Reinsurance Treaty, Bismarck sought to weaken Russia by depriving it of credit. The so-called *Lombardverbot* has been explained by Gall as an attempt to 'combine the apparently incompatible'. By creating financial difficulties for Russia, the measure was supposed, according to Bismarck's son, 'to bludgeon the tsar into seeing where his interest lies'. Simultaneously it was intended to placate German military circles, who feared the growth of Russian power, but without resorting to the sort of overt political or military action which would irrevocably destroy the Russo-German entente. Similarly, the raising of tariffs against Russian exports to Germany was designed to placate German economic interests in order to ease Bismarck's domestic political difficulties, while also serving to retard Russia's economic growth.

As Geyer has shown, Bismarck's actions in 1887 almost destroyed the economic underpinning of the Russo-German entente, which had already been declining for some years. The mutually beneficial exchange of Russian grain for German manufactures, dating from the early 1870s, was weakened by changes in tariff policies and by Russia's attempt to expand its own manufacturing base. Germany played a vital role in the Russian economy both as a supplier of capital and as a consumer of Russian grain, the earnings from which helped to finance railway construction and industrialization.

Bismarck's switch from free trade to protectionism in 1877–9 had a harmful effect on Russo-German relations, but the real crisis came in 1885–7 when both states raised their tariffs sharply. In Russia's case, the increases were intended to ease the chronic balance-of-payments deficit and to protect its infant industries, whose cause was championed by the anti-German lobby, including Katkov. In the case of Germany, the tariff issue had more overt political overtones. Although German exports to Russia had declined by about a third in value during the 1880s, the German economy was inherently strong while that of Russia was weak. In short, whereas Russian economic policy was dictated by severe financial pressures, Bismarck deliberately chose a collision course in 1887 in order to ease domestic political tensions, by trying to placate not only industrialists and the agrarian interests but also the groups advocating a preventive war against Russia.

The *Lombardverbot* misfired, however, since it created an opportunity for France to replace Germany as Russia's main source of credit. The war hysteria against France during the Boulanger affair also backfired by prompting a French request for Russian military support if France were attacked by Germany. Bismarck's own actions in 1887, therefore, contributed to the development of the subsequent Franco-Russian alliance – the very coalition he had been most anxious to avoid.

In the two years prior to his resignation in 1890 Bismarck himself was becoming pessimistic about the future as German opinion veered towards an aggressive, expansionist policy. He remarked to a General in December 1887: 'the task of our policy is, if possible, to prevent war entirely and if that is not possible, at least to postpone it.' Bismarck himself was well aware of the fragility of the whole structure he had created in central Europe, but he seemed to have few creative ideas for replacing it. Although he contemplated a firm alliance with one of the 'flanking powers', Russia or Britain, he did not pursue the idea with much zest. His approach to Britain in January 1889, for example, contained detailed proposals but he seemed unmoved by the non-committal nature of the British response. Temperamentally, Bismarck seemed too attached to the 'free hand', to retaining for Germany the independent and semi-hegemonic position between the other powers that it had enjoyed since 1871.

In seeking security for Germany by preserving peace in Europe and by preventing the formation of hostile coalitions, Bismarck was undoubtedly successful in the short term. Austro-Russian rivalry in the Balkans was kept within bounds and Britain was persuaded to play a lead role in opposing Russia, since it was not Germany's responsibility, in Bismarck's view, to keep the Russians out of Constantinople. The possibility of a Franco-Russian alliance, a danger he greatly exaggerated, was avoided by timely negotiations to placate the tsar and his conservative ministers. Bismarck, the troublemaker of Europe from 1865 to 1875, became the 'troubleshooter' in the late 1870s and 1880s, when Berlin acted as the pivot of European diplomacy.

His policy of a balancing of discontents, on the other hand, was an essentially negative approach which, Simon suggests, seemed to require ever more ingenious expedients to deal with the desperate situations that arose. Hence, although Bismarck reflected at length on the international situation in the Kissingden Dictate of June 1877, it may be questioned whether Bismarck's 'system' amounted to much more than a preference for alliances with other conservative states, supplemented by exercises in 'crisis management', as Gall puts it, when the unresolved tensions became acute.

Bismarck's professed objective, revealed at Kissingden, was 'an overall political situation in which all powers except France have need of us and are, as far as possible, kept from forming coalitions against us by their relations with one another'. Whether this required an elaborate system of alliances is not altogether clear. Arguably, the animosities between Russia and Austria, and between Russia and Britain, impelled these three powers to seek Germany's goodwill. If the experience of 1878 disillusioned Bismarck with regard to the advantages of adopting a passive role during a crisis, then his change to a system of commitments makes obvious sense. But it is not altogether clear whether Bismarck himself regarded the alliances made between 1879 and 1882, not to mention the 1887 treaty, as constituting a 'system' with long-term aims, as most historians have tended to assume, or whether they were, as Gall suggests, a series of 'stop-gaps' created on an *ad hoc* basis, as new problems or threats to Germany's security arose. With hindsight, it might be said that Bismarck worried too much about Russia and the danger of the tsarist regime allying with republican France. Like most of his contemporaries, he failed to appreciate the gravity of Russia's internal weaknesses, which limited that country's ability to act as a formidable force in European affairs.

The question remains whether any alliance system could effectively have 'squared the circle' of Austro-Russian rivalry in the Balkans. Although the *Dreikaiserbund* of 1881 fulfilled the aim of Germany being 'one of three in an unstable equilibrium of five powers', it disintegrated under the strain of the animosity provoked by the later stages of the Bulgarian crisis.

Finally, one other limitation of Bismarck's statesmanship was, Gall suggests, his predominantly Eurocentric view of international relations at a time when great power rivalries were becoming global, as they did in the 1880s. A greater awareness of this change might, perhaps, have led him to re-evaluate the potential value of an Anglo-German alliance as a means of breaking the deadlock that his preoccupation with a central European bloc had created by 1890.

SOURCES AND FURTHER READING

Bridge, F. R., *From Sadowa to Sarajevo. The Foreign Policy of Austria-Hungary 1866–1914*, London, Routledge & Kegan Paul, 1972.

Bridge, F. R. and Bullen, R., *The Great Powers and the European States System 1815–1914*, Harlow, Longman, 1980.

Crampton, R. J., *A Short History of Modern Bulgaria*, Cambridge, Cambridge University Press, 1987.

Dorpalen, A., 'Tsar Alexander III and the Boulanger crisis in France', *Journal of Modern History*, 1951, vol. 23(2): 122–36.

Gall, L., *Bismarck. The White Revolutionary*, vol. 2: *1871–1898* (transl. J. A. Underwood), London, Allen & Unwin, 1986.

Geyer, D., *Russian Imperialism 1860–1914* (transl. B. Little), Leamington Spa, Berg, 1987.

Jelavich, B., *St Petersburg and Moscow. Tsarist and Soviet Foreign Policy, 1814–1974*, Bloomington, Ind., Indiana University Press, 1974.

——, *History of the Balkans*, vol. 1, Cambridge, Cambridge University Press, 1983.

Langer, W. L., *European Alliances and Alignments 1871–90*, New York, Knopf, 1950 (2nd edn).

Lowe, C. J., *The Reluctant Imperialists. British Foreign Policy 1878–1902*, vol. 1, London, Routledge & Kegan Paul, 1967. (Chs II and IV.)

Medlicott, W. N., *Bismarck and Modern Germany*, London, English Universities Press, 1965.

Medlicott, W. N. and Coveney, D. K. (eds), *Bismarck and Europe*, London, Arnold, 1971.

Pflanze, O., *Bismarck and the Development of Germany*, vol. 2: *1871–1880*, vol. 3: *1880–1898*, Princeton, NJ, Princeton University Press, 1990.

Simon, W. M., *Germany in the Age of Bismarck*, London, Allen & Unwin, 1968.

Taylor, A. J. P., *The Struggle for Mastery in Europe 1848–1918*, Oxford, Clarendon Press, 1954. (Chs XI, XII and XIV.)

The 'Bismarckian system' is fully discussed in volume 2 of Gall's impressive work. Otto Pflanze's recently completed biography is another major study. Useful brief accounts of Bismarck's aims and policies can be found in Medlicott (an expert on the Balkans in 1878) and Medlicott and Coveney (with interesting documentary extracts), supplemented by W. M. Simon's short study (also with documents).

The objectives of Austrian diplomacy are skilfully illuminated in F. R. Bridge's detailed work, while Geyer has much of interest on Russian policy and pan-Slavism. So also does Jelavich in her outline treatment of Russian diplomacy. The brief flirtation between pan-Slavism and revanchism is explored in the article by Dorpalen. British policy is succinctly treated by C. J. Lowe.

The tangle of Balkan politics is unravelled in Jelavich's *History*, as well as by R. J. Crampton.

This period is well covered by general diplomatic histories. Bridge and Bullen's is brief and modern; Langer's is a classic; Taylor's is authoritative.

3 Imperial rivalries in Africa, 1875–1898

THE DEBATE ON IMPERIALISM

Imperialism is a complex phenomenon. Few modern historians would be satisfied with a definition that related only to the acquisition of overseas territory, which has been likened to 'judging the size and character of icebergs solely from the parts above the water line'. Yet it is not clear that the economic relationship between European states and the rest of the world was necessarily an imperialistic one. While 'economic imperialism' seems an appropriate enough term in the case of China, it seems less adequate as a description of the complex situation in Latin America. Most modern writers therefore use the word 'imperialism' in the broad sense of the assertion of European political influence or control over other territories, especially in Africa and Asia, involving some measure of economic exploitation. In other words, imperialism is a somewhat elastic term unless you opt for the rather dated Leninist definition of it as a specific phase in the development of capitalism.

One problem in seeking an explanation of the remarkable expansion of European influence overseas in the later nineteenth century is that no European empire seems to have served any definable purpose. The British empire alone was a curious hotch-potch of crown colonies, protectorates and self-governing dominions, scattered across the whole globe. By about 1900 the French empire included vast (and unproductive) tracts of west Africa, some more valuable lands in north Africa, and Indo-China. The Germans, who ruled over a disparate collection of territories in Africa, as well as a few Pacific islands, were unsure whether their colonies should serve as areas of white settlement or as regions for economic exploitation. Russia's conquest of central Asia gratified the tsar's pride as the ruler of a vast land-based empire, but its economic value was problematic. The very diversity of the empires of the great powers in itself suggests that a multi-causal explanation of imperialism is more appropriate than a reliance on 'simple universal economic forces'.

Another problem that has attracted considerable attention, particularly from British historians, is the question of continuity or discontinuity in Britain's imperial policy in the nineteenth century. The term 'new imperialism', although widely used as a convenient shorthand for the period of rapid imperial expansion after about 1870, consequently remains controversial; thus its usage is not, strictly speaking, entirely neutral.

Most of the traditional explanations of this 'new imperialism' have naturally stressed the importance of economic factors, such as the demand for raw materials and the quest for markets for manufactures, together with opportunities for investment. Since the late 1960s, however, more emphasis has tended to be placed on political factors, including great power rivalries, prestige, and the growth of nationalism and the popular press. Both of these approaches are essentially Eurocentric. This preoccupation with pressures emanating from within Europe has been regarded as deficient in not taking into account those 'complex situations in the non-European world' where significant political and economic changes were also taking place. It is now thought necessary to see imperialism as an interaction between developments within the European states and changing conditions in the so-called 'periphery'.

The fact that European (mainly British) investment overseas increased enormously at about the same time as the annexation of territory in Africa and elsewhere by Europeans, naturally suggests there was a causal connection between them. Hobson, an English radical or socialist writing in 1902, made this connection explicit by asserting that Britain's recent foreign policy had largely been a struggle for profitable investment markets. In his view the beneficiaries of British imperial growth were 'sectional interests', especially the great financial houses who manipulated the patriotic forces in society and exercised a sinister influence over politics for their own advantage.

Hobson's conviction that 'surplus capital' rather than 'surplus manufactures' was the driving force behind the new imperialism was elaborated by Lenin, who equated imperialism with a particular phase in the development of capitalism, which he called monopoly finance capitalism. Since Lenin dated this phase as beginning in about 1900, his definition does not relate directly to the main period of imperialist annexations in the 1880s and 1890s, when capitalism was in a 'transitional' phase. Lenin's views may therefore have more relevance to the activities of multinational corporations after the First World War, even if they constitute a rather simplistic explanation of the war's origins, seemingly his main objective when writing his pamphlet in 1916. The persisting influence of Hobson's and Lenin's views on imperialism may owe more to their skills as publicists than to the novelty, and perhaps validity, of their ideas. Many of these can be found in less persuasive form in works by earlier writers and constitute part of a long tradition of essays on political economy, dating back to Adam Smith's *Wealth of Nations*, published in 1776.

The fallacies of the 'surplus capital' explanation of imperialism have been exposed for many years. Modern statistical studies and analysis of overseas investment in the period before 1914 have shown that only a small proportion of the capital was invested in the newly acquired tropical or subtropical territories in Africa and Asia. Although about half of British capital exports in 1914 went to the empire, the vast bulk (about £1,680 million) was to the older colonies, especially the Dominions and India, while less than £100 million went to the newer colonies such as west Africa. Non-colonial territories, including the United States and Latin America, accounted for about £1,880 million. None of the other European powers invested much capital in their overseas possessions. For France, the average was about 10 per cent of its foreign investment, while the Germans invested a puny 2 per cent in their colonies. Furthermore, imperialist Russia had to import capital to finance its own industrialization and railway expansion. The conclusion seems inescapable that the correlation between the destination of capital exports and the colonial territories newly acquired in this period is almost nil. In the 1980s, interest in overseas investment tended to focus more on the complex issue of the profitability of overseas colonies. Critics of some recent work in this field have suggested that the statistical problems encountered by cliometricians in drawing up a balance sheet of empire tend to induce 'decimal dementia'!

Although the case for 'surplus capital' providing the motive force behind imperialism no longer carries much weight, this does not exclude the possibility that financial interests were able, at times, to influence the nature and direction of overseas expansion in this period. Nor is the reliability of the statistics for capital exports universally accepted, let alone the interpretation of them. Despite these reservations, the insistence of some Marxist or neo-Marxist writers that imperialism was the product of the 'imperative necessities of advanced capitalism' is not very convincing. In the early 1990s it seems unlikely that the aura of perceived truth that has long enveloped Marxist-Leninist interpretations of imperialism will be able to survive the collapse of communism as an economic and political system in central and eastern Europe. While the ideology on which those regimes were purportedly based has been discredited, the power of nationalism as a popular force has been dramatically underlined. This does not mean that all economic interpretations of imperialism can be consigned to the lumber room of history, but it may further undermine Hobson's and Lenin's case that the 'super-abundance of capital' was the key motive force behind it.

The connection between trade and imperial expansion, on the other hand, seems to be more convincing, but not in the sense of 'trade follows the flag'. The reality was, as Baumgart has asserted, that trade followed the price-tag. This is not to pretend that there was much trade to be had with the 'malarious swamps and barren deserts' which made up a fair part of France's African empire, whereas a lucrative trade was conducted with states that were independent of European control. In some cases, such states subsequently became colonies of one of the great powers – an example of the flag following trade.

In the case of Britain, there is much evidence that the pressure of foreign competition for markets for its manufactured goods had become quite strong by the 1880s. Industrialization on the continent severely reduced Britain's earlier advantages as the first industrial nation. It was becoming more difficult for British manufacturers not only to sell their products in Europe but also to retain their quasi-monopoly in world markets. Historians such as P. J. Cain have argued that the relative failure of the British economy after 1870 was a major force behind imperial expansion. The so-called Great Depression of the 1870s and 1880s intensified the competitive struggle, creating fears among industrialists all over Europe of a crisis of over-production.

Serious though these problems were, the factor which seems to have caused the most alarm to British manufacturers was the growth of protectionism, leaving Britain almost alone in clinging to the principle of free trade. Although quite moderate in the early 1880s, protectionist tariffs were raised sharply in the 1890s, especially by the Americans and by the French, who extended them to their overseas territories. Hence Platt has argued that British fears of being excluded from markets in China and Africa by tariffs, differential duties and exclusive concessions led to a determination to safeguard British commercial interests through the exercise of political influence. In China this took the form of demands for 'counter-concessions'. In Africa it led to pre-emptive annexations, which Lord Salisbury justified on the grounds that 'we only desire territory because we desire commercial freedom.'

Platt's case has been reinforced by Hynes's evidence of changing business attitudes towards government support for commercial enterprise in Britain between 1870 and 1890. When the search for new markets in Africa and Asia, prompted by the depression, was impeded by French tariffs and differential duties, British traders abandoned their hostility to government 'interference' in regions such as west Africa and became champions of a 'strong imperial policy'. There is considerable evidence that the combination of the trade recession with discriminatory practices by competitors, leading to what Curzon called in 1892 'the furious commercial competition that now rages' provided some of the impetus behind the new imperialism of the period.

A variant of the economic argument relating directly to Germany's overseas expansion is Wehler's concept of 'social imperialism'. He argues that Bismarck adopted an imperialist policy in 1884 as 'the alternative to the stagnation of economic life which would have entailed severe class conflict'. This constitutes 'social' imperialism, since the aim was to preserve the supremacy of the traditional ruling elites and the authoritarian power structure within the so-called *Kaiserreich*. However, Wehler's critics have drawn attention to the fact that Bismarck's colonial enthusiasm was remarkably short-lived for such a drastic remedy for Germany's supposed ills. They also note the indifference of German capitalists to overseas ventures, while stressing the many short-term political advantages that Bismarck could hope to derive from pursuing a colonial policy in 1884–5. Attempts to apply the concept of social imperialism to France and Britain have also been largely unsatisfactory.

Political explanations of imperialism derive a certain plausibility from the fact that governmental decisions to assert influence or control over an overseas territory can be directly related to a calculation of anticipated benefits. This at least has the advantage of not automatically equating the outlook and motivation of political leaders with those of business or financial circles. The variety of political factors adduced also avoids a mono-causal explanation, while not denying the influence of economic considerations as one of several factors in the formulation of imperial policy.

By relating imperial expansion to great power rivalries, historians such as Baumgart have emphasized the role of prestige in an era when colonial empires came to be regarded as status symbols, in addition to the traditional gauges of military and naval strength and industrial power. Hence, for example, Gambetta's declaration after the occupation of Tunis in 1882 that 'France is recovering her position as a great power' and Caprivi's suggestion that many Germans believed that 'once we come into possession of colonies . . . we would become a great people.'

A key characteristic of the new imperialism, in Baumgart's view, is that a pluralistic and universal rivalry developed among the leading great powers on a global scale, replacing the simple Anglo-French rivalry that had been largely confined to west Africa. This intensified form of great power rivalry gave a momentum to the acquisition of colonies, expressed in terms such as 'the race for Africa'. It resulted in pre-emptive annexations, especially in the 1890s, summed up in the oft-quoted phrase 'pegging out claims for the future'. In fact Lord Rosebery regretted the phrase, since he held an essentially defensive and consolidationist view of the British empire. The real enthusiasts for expansion were army commanders in regions such as central Asia or west Africa who were in search of the perfect frontier, which was always 'somewhat further off'.

Strategic considerations naturally loom large in what Robinson and Gallagher have termed the 'official mind'. Their explanation of Britain's role in the partition of Africa highlights the crucial importance of the concern of successive governments for the security of the routes to India via Suez and the Cape. Although their notion of a 'chain reaction' sparked off by the British occupation of Egypt in 1882 is flawed, their argument that the government was more concerned to stake a claim to east Africa, where British trade was minimal, for strategic reasons, is better founded. The need to defend 'the imperial factor' at the Cape also makes sense of the complex politics of southern Africa in the 1880s and 1890s. For the other great powers, however, strategic considerations were not a motive for becoming involved in the partition of Africa.

The governments of most of the great powers were bombarded with demands for action from a variety of pressure groups, colonial societies and the press. Missionary societies and the humanitarian lobby in Britain were vocal in their requests for protection for their activities, successfully in cases such as Uganda and Nyasa. The Union Coloniale and Comité de l'Afrique Française were matched by the Kolonialverein and the British Empire League. More specific pressures were exerted by commercial interests, ranging from chambers of commerce to the British (or German) East Africa Companies. A pressure group's chances of persuading a government to act were, of course, greatly enhanced if it secured the backing of the press. A well-documented example of this was the French government's volte-face in ratifying de Brazza's dubious treaties in the Congo in 1882, following an energetic press campaign. By 1900 popular newspapers in Britain, such as the *Daily Express* and the *Mail*, had become outspokenly imperialist in sentiment, but well before then British and French governments had had cause to fear the reaction of the press to possible clashes between their military forces in the hinterlands of west Africa.

The power of the press to influence imperial policy depended, of course, on the response of public opinion. Some historians have argued that by the 1890s, if not earlier, imperialism had become a projection of nationalism beyond the boundaries of Europe or even, as Fieldhouse puts it, 'the product of a national mass hysteria'. Even in France, where public interest in colonial affairs was fitful, it is said that nationalism made many French people imperialists in the wake of Anglo-French rivalry in the 1890s and the later Franco-German clashes over Morocco. One testimony to the influence of the press is Salisbury's comment in 1901 that 'the diplomacy of nations is now conducted quite as much in the letters of special correspondents, as in the despatches of the foreign office.'

The jingoism of the popular press was to some extent complemented by the crude generalizations of social-Darwinist ideas which came into vogue in the late nineteenth century. The simplistic concept of 'survival of the fittest' could be used to justify the right of 'superior races' to lord it over indigenous societies in Africa and Asia. Similarly, the application of pseudo-Darwinist ideas to relations between nations called for policies which served the 'struggle for existence'.

Baumgart argues that Spain's defeat by the United States in 1898 appeared to confirm the existence of an 'inexorable law of evolution in the life of nations', posing the stark choice between expansion and decline. Jules Ferry had used such sentiments to justify his policies in 1885, warning that unless France engaged in colonial expansion 'we shall take the broad road leading to decadence'. Less dramatic but none the less significant was Salisbury's reference in a speech of 1898 to the 'living nations' and the 'dying' nations. Britain's leaders, conscious of the problem of the country's overstretched resources, took comfort from its acknowledged claim to be one of the three world empires of the era, alongside the United States and Russia. Germany's aspirations to join the ranks of the world empires prompted, in the view of some historians, its desire for a broader power base in Europe through the *Mitteleuropa* scheme and a larger overseas empire – the *Mittelafrika* policy.

How far these various political factors acted as the motive force behind the new imperialism is obviously a matter of debate. However, most modern historians accept that they played some part in influencing the policies of most, if not all, of the great powers, even though their influence was at its height in the 1890s, when much territorial annexation had already taken place.

An interesting challenge to the Eurocentric nature of both the economic and political explanations of the new imperialism emerged in the 1970s, when several historians drew attention to the role of 'peripheral' factors. In Fieldhouse's words, 'Europe was pulled into imperialism by the magnetic force of the periphery.' The key changes that account for the expansion of empire in the 1880s, he suggests, took place overseas, not in Europe; sometimes in the form of local crises. These changes were of three different kinds.

The most significant was the erosion of stable indigenous societies, resulting from the cumulative effects of decades of contact with the west, in the form of trading companies, European finance and investment, or perhaps missionary activity. Faced with the inability of traditional rulers to maintain reasonable conditions for trade and/or financial operations, European governments were persuaded to assert some measure of political influence or control over the region. The second type of change was caused by a form of 'sub-imperialism' in which an existing European colony, such as Algeria or the Transvaal, encroached on neighbouring communities for the sake of more land, cheap labour or frontier security. The third category embraces a variety of factors capable of causing local crises which led to the breakdown of the existing relations between Europeans and 'native' societies. A good example of the crucial role played by 'the politics of the periphery', as Schreuder calls it, can be found in the 'scramble' for southern Africa.

Fieldhouse's stress on peripheral factors has similarities to Robinson's theory of collaboration. The latter suggests that 'native' elites which had adjusted to a European presence found compliance with the growing demands made upon them increasingly difficult to bear. The resultant breakdown of collaboration or cooperation usually led to the imposition of a more overt and formal type of European control over the region.

Awareness of the periphery has added an extra dimension to the discussion of imperialism, particularly by its stress on the interaction of Europeans and indigenous societies. But its critics have not been slow to point out that too much emphasis on changes in the periphery can lead to a neglect of the important changes that were taking place within Europe itself – changes which, by themselves, provided a powerful impetus to the new imperialism.

THE SCRAMBLE FOR AFRICA

In explaining the European colonization of Africa, some of the more recent general interpretations of imperialism are of more relevance than the older theories based on the concept of 'surplus capital'. Whereas 'white elephants' were to be found in abundance in Africa, there were relatively few 'glittering prizes' to satisfy the colonial appetites of the European powers. To make sense of the partition of Africa, therefore, it may be necessary to regard the activities of the Europeans there, and the economic exploitation that unquestionably took place, as being in some respects quite separate from the diplomacy of the great powers during the twenty-odd years of the 'scramble'.

Contact between Europeans and Africans was nothing new in the later nineteenth century. However, the difficulty of transporting goods over vast distances into the interior acted as an impediment to the expansion of trade. Nevertheless, well before 1870 many parts of Africa had encountered traders carrying European cotton goods, firearms and spirits, or even Indian or American textiles. As a result of growing economic penetration some parts of Africa had become integrated into the international economy, but world trade had grown much faster than had the African economy in the period 1815–70. Consequently there was a major imbalance in economic terms, as well as politically and militarily, between Europe and Africa.

Africa was not, of course, a single economic unit. Enormous disparities existed between its various regions in terms of their level of economic development as well as their commercial potential. The diversity between north and south was striking, but it was no more so than that between west and east. Muslim north Africa, for centuries an outpost of the Ottoman empire, was closely involved in trade with Turkey and Europe. South Africa, dominated by Boers and British settlers, experienced a steady, if unspectacular, growth in trade until the discovery of gold and diamonds in the 1870s and 1880s revolutionized its economy. Meanwhile west Africa, after the suppression of the slave trade, developed a flourishing trade in tropical products such as palm oil, vegetable oils, timber, ivory and gum. East Africa's development, on the other hand, awaited substantial investment in its economic infrastructure, especially transport facilities.

The growth of trade between Africa and Europe does not, by itself, explain the rapid extension of European political control over most of Africa between 1875 and 1895. Rather than 'trade follows the flag', it was a case of the flag being used to defend trade because of the nature of the commercial rivalry prevailing in regions such as west Africa and the Congo. One reason why the French annexed African territory was to facilitate the creation of a tariff regime to prevent cheaper British goods from competing with French exports. As a consequence, a British spokesman asserted: 'we are forced to extend our direct political influence over a large part of Africa to secure a "fair field and no favour" for our commerce.' Overall, a good case can be made that trade, coupled with fears of tariffs and discriminatory duties, was a significant factor in the scramble for Africa. Chartered companies played a role in this as well, since in many instances the profitablity of their commercial activities depended on securing exclusive rights in the area of their operations, as in the case of the Niger Company.

Political factors are also relevant to the 'scramble'. The tendency towards pre-emptive annexations to shut out rivals was quite marked in the 1890s, by which time colonial acquisitions had become prestige symbols for the great powers. Certain aspects of the 'scramble' could even be regarded as a manifestation of irrational nationalism, not to say sheer lunacy, on the part of some leading political figures, pressure groups and public opinion. There were occasions, on the other hand, when the partition was influenced by rational calculation. For example, Bismarck rejected the exaggerated claims to east Africa made by German adventurers and colonial enthusiasts on the grounds that they would upset diplomatic relationships in Europe.

The partition also illustrates the influence of peripheral factors on the policies of the great powers. The role of 'local crises', sometimes political, sometimes economic, in drawing European governments into asserting political influence over parts of Africa was quite significant. In this sense, imperialism was partly the product of an interaction between Africans and Europeans, as opposed to the older notion of a passive Africa being shaped by the will of Europeans. Perhaps an important distinction between the two cultures was that Europeans could conceive of Africa as an entity, as shown by their ambitious railway projects (for example, Cecil Rhodes's idea of a Cape-to-Cairo link).

Studies by African historians have also created a greater awareness of the so-called 'African partition of Africa', effected by powerful native dynasties and tribal supremacies in both northern and southern Africa. Muslim *jihads* (holy wars) and Zulu *mfecane* established paramountcies over parts of the 'dark continent' that had important repercussions on the African scene before the European partition began. For one thing, the maltreatment of the defeated tribal groups by the victors could make European rule seem, by comparison, as benign as a vicarage tea party.

The timing of the partition was probably more closely related to specific political events than to economic trends which lack a precise chronology. One of the most plausible political explanations of the timing is the one advanced by Sanderson in terms of the decline of British 'paramountcy' in the early 1880s. Britain's success in maintaining its informal influence over most of sub-Saharan Africa into the 1870s was due to respect for its naval power and the preoccupation of other powers, especially France and Germany, with more pressing concerns in Europe. However, Sanderson argues that evidence of British military weakness, coinciding with a decline in its naval strength relative to other maritime states, suggested to Bismarck that Britain's ill-defined claims to influence over sub-Saharan Africa were vulnerable to concerted pressure. Britain's acceptance of Franco-German demands for an international conference in 1884 marked the end of British 'paramountcy', but its sudden collapse left a void which was quickly filled by rival claims to African territory. By attempting to adjudicate on these competing claims, the Berlin West Africa conference of 1884–5 signified the start of the partition of Africa by the European powers.

Oddly enough, this seems not to have been the intention of the delegates at Berlin. According to recent work on the subject, they were more concerned with affirming the principle of free trade in Africa than with territorial occupation. But, by drawing lines on maps in ignorance of the topography, 'partition stimulated the territorial rivalries it was intended to prevent' when the powers subsequently began to define the limits of their spheres of influence on the ground. Furthermore, the costs of 'pacification' ate into the profits of commerce, with the result that the conference's free-trade zones became economic monopolies in order to make them pay. Hence the paradox of a European conference which seemingly adopted an 'anti-colonial' approach to partition, for the sake of giving priority to keeping Africa open to free trade, but which actually resulted in a 'proto-colonial' partition, in which Africa was staked out for future occupation by the European powers.

ANGLO-FRENCH RIVALRY OVER EGYPT AND WEST AFRICA IN THE 1880s

The British occupation of Egypt in 1882 has been accorded too much importance as a catalyst to the partition of tropical Africa, but its impact on Anglo-French relations for the next twenty years was undoubtedly very great. French pique at their own lack of decisiveness during the Egyptian crisis was reinforced by resentment at Britain's refusal to restore the former partnership in Egyptian affairs. Thereafter, the only thing that would mollify the French was Britain's withdrawal from Egypt but, as noted above, they perversely frustrated British proposals in 1885–7 to bring the occupation to an end. The resultant estrangement between France and Britain was, in itself, an unwanted development, but it became a serious bugbear when Britain subsequently became unable to govern Egypt effectively without Germany's goodwill.

European interference in the internal affairs of Egypt arose from an attempt to supervise Egypt's finances through a Commission of the Public Debt, set up after the khedive's virtual bankruptcy in 1876–9. From the outset, the system of dual control established by France and Britain was an uneasy arrangement. The Conservative government in London regarded cooperation with France as a necessary evil to ward off interference by the other powers, but it disliked the 'partnership with bondholders' that seemed to motivate the government in Paris. Although the financial problem itself was ostensibly settled by the Law of Liquidations of July 1880 (to the satisfaction of the bondholders at least, who were mainly French), its repercussions had created serious unrest in Egypt by 1882. European intervention had not only virtually destroyed the khedive's precarious authority, it had also fostered the growth of an anti-foreigner movement, led by an army officer named Arabi Pasha.

By the summer of 1882 Gladstone's government was faced with 'nothing but bad alternatives to choose from', as the Liberal foreign secretary lamented. Pushed into a confrontation with the 'Egyptian movement', initially by the French but subsequently by the British consul-general's misleading reports of the situation and Admiral Seymour's reckless bombardment of Alexandria, the British government faced a stark choice. Gladstone had to decide between abandoning British influence over Egyptian affairs, including its finances, or intervening by force to destroy Arabi Pasha and the nationalists.

In 1882, as in 1956, London took the wrong decision for the wrong reasons but, unlike in 1956, without French assistance and with a different outcome. Arabi's forces were destroyed at Tel-el-Kebir in September 1882, an action defended on the grounds of 'so securing to ourselves such a position in Egypt as to secure our Indian Dominions and to maintain our superiority in the East'. The moral of 1956 seems clear enough. The paradox of 1882 was that an irresolute Liberal government with genuine 'anti-imperialist' credentials was misled by the 'men on the spot' into opting for military intervention to preserve European financial interests (mainly French) under the impression that this action was needed to safeguard the Suez Canal.

The decision to remain in occupation of Egypt was almost inevitable after the defeat of Arabi and the undermining of the khedive's authority, since there was no one to whom power could now be transferred. But the decision not to revive the dual control came as a rude shock to French opinion which, a French historian has observed, found it difficult to pardon the British for not having shared their pusillanimity at the height of the crisis. The exclusion of France, for the sake of 'freedom and self-development, as far as may be, for Egypt' was a serious affront to French pride. Historic ties dating back to Napoleon I had been reinforced by commercial and financial links, as well as by cultural ties in the form of schools and institutes, not to mention de Lesseps and the Suez Canal.

Although a diplomatic circular in January 1883 proclaimed the temporary nature of the British occupation (the first of sixty-six such communications), the chances of an early British evacuation were shattered by a crisis in the Sudan, an Egyptian dependency. An Egyptian army led by Hicks Pasha was routed by the forces of the Mahdi in November 1883. This disaster had important consequences. Not only did it leave Egypt itself vulnerable to attack from the Sudan but it also destroyed the already precarious finances of the Egyptian government. The problem was compounded by Gladstone's failure to create a satisfactory framework for overseeing Egypt's development, despite his commitment to its reconstruction under Britain's moral tutelage until political and financial stability had been restored.

By refusing to annex Egypt, but consenting to international control of the Caisse de la Dette Publique which supervised the Egyptian finances, Gladstone ensured that 'the government of Egypt is now impossible', as the British administrator (the future Lord Cromer) complained. With France and Russia constantly in opposition to Britain and Italy on the public debt commission of the six powers, Germany held the trump card, which Bismarck was able to exploit quite shamelessly. By threatening to cast Germany's vote against British proposals for reform in Egypt, Bismarck could extract concessions from Britain elsewhere – the so-called Egyptian lever. Bismarck's use of the *bâton égyptien*, coupled with Salisbury's doubts about Egypt's importance to Britain's strategic interests, prompted the attempt to secure the sultan's agreement to the British terms for evacuating Egypt, of which he was the nominal suzerain. The failure of the Drummond-Wolff negotiations of 1885–7 ensured that Egypt remained a contentious issue in Britain's relations with both France and Turkey. It also meant that sooner or later the British government would have to face up to the problem of the Sudan, whose evacuation in 1884 had been bungled in dramatic fashion by God-fearing General Gordon, culminating in the fall of Khartoum to the forces of the fundamentalist Muslim, the 'mad' Mahdi.

In west Africa, France's latent rivalry with Britain developed into an active challenge to Britain's informal influence in the region in the 1880s, but the change was not due to French resentment over Egypt, as Robinson and Gallagher believed. Studies of French imperialism in the western Soudan have established that the impetus to expansion existed before 1882 and that its implementation was the product of factors unrelated to the situation in Egypt.

The expansionist dreams of governors of Senegal, such as Louis Faideherbe in 1863 and Brière de l'Isle in 1876, had hitherto encountered an insuperable obstacle. The French government could not be persuaded to provide the funds for what seemed to be, from the perspective of Paris, an expensive and hazardous enterprise of dubious utility. The crucial factor, therefore, in giving the green light to the conquest of the western Soudan in the 1880s was a sudden change of attitude in Paris. When Freycinet, a former minister of public works, became premier in 1879 with a like-minded colleague at the Ministry of Marine (which dealt with colonial affairs), the Senegalese imperialists had found a receptive audience for their schemes.

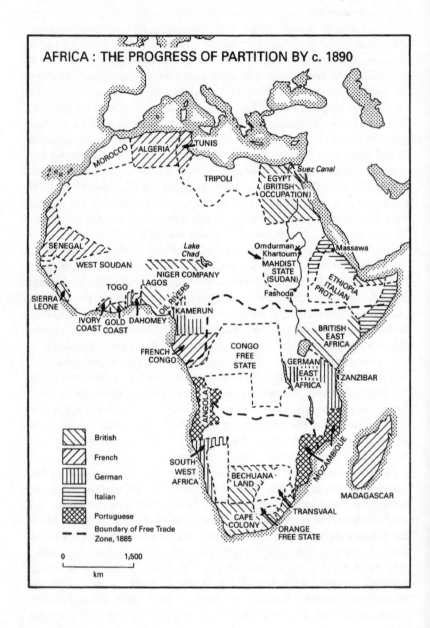

AFRICA : THE PROGRESS OF PARTITION BY c. 1890

MOROCCO

ALGERIA

TUNIS

TRIPOLI

Suez Canal

EGYPT (BRITISH OCCUPATION)

SENEGAL

Lake Chad

Omdurman
Khartoum

Massawa

WEST SOUDAN

NIGER COMPANY

MAHDIST STATE (SUDAN)

ETHIOPIA ITALIAN PROT.

TOGO

LAGOS

Fashoda

SIERRA LEONE

OIL RIVERS

IVORY COAST

GOLD COAST

DAHOMEY

KAMERUN

BRITISH EAST AFRICA

FRENCH CONGO

CONGO FREE STATE

GERMAN EAST AFRICA

ZANZIBAR

ANGOLA

SOUTH-WEST AFRICA

BECHUANA-LAND

MOZAMBIQUE

MADAGASCAR

CAPE COLONY

TRANSVAAL

ORANGE FREE STATE

British

French

German

Italian

Portuguese

Boundary of Free Trade
Zone, 1885

0   1,500

km

Expansion in west Africa was presented as 'une oeuvre pacifique et civilisatrice', in which the state should play an active role through the creation of railways – one of Freycinet's pet projects. The plans included linking Senegal with the Niger and an even more ambitious trans-Saharan scheme from Algeria to west Africa. To persuade the deputies to vote the necessary funds, much was made of the supposed economic potential of the western Soudan both as a market for French exports and as a source of raw materials. Forecasts of generating a trade worth 100 million francs a year proved to be wildly exaggerated. The reality was that after twenty years the annual value of the exports of the region amounted to a mere 3 million francs, about 0.07 per cent of France's total imports.

French faith in the power of 'steam and iron' to work miracles in Africa was shared by many Europeans. Where the French government miscalculated was in its assumption that the engineers surveying the routes for railways would be regarded by the local population as heralds of French civilization and so would be able to carry out their mission in safety. Although the need for military 'pacification' led to disenchantment in Paris, expressed in a marked reluctance to vote further funds for the projected railways, this did not bring to a halt the conquest begun by the *officiers Soudanais* of the French colonial army. Funds intended for railway construction were seemingly appropriated to finance further military operations, which developed a momentum of their own, regardless of orders from Paris. This momentum was, in turn, sustained at critical moments by the government's sensitivity to the need to defend France's honour and prestige in Africa. As a result, the colonial army's 'determined bid for territory', as Kanya-Forstner calls it, was not even halted by military reverses.

French activities in west Africa had a major impact on the attitude of British traders and the government. Until the 1880s Britain had exerted an informal influence over the Oil Rivers region (the Niger delta) for three decades at little cost to the taxpayer, thanks to the skill of British consuls. But the intrusion of two French companies and the appearance of French warships along the coast suddenly threatened the near-monopoly of British commercial houses, which had built up a lucrative trade in palm oil in exchange for cheap cotton goods, hardware and firearms. In response to this challenge, British companies attempted to preserve their favoured position by treaty-making with local chiefs. The dubious legality of these company treaties, however, induced the British government to reinforce its consular service, so that by the mid–1880s Britain had established a virtual protectorate over the Niger region. It was the sudden increase in French activity in west Africa, therefore, which was a major factor in provoking Britain into asserting formal claims to territory in a region where it had previously been content to exercise an informal influence.

Commercial rivalry between France and Britain also intensified along the whole west African coast from Sierra Leone to the Congo. One sign of this was the revival of a French protectorate over Porto Novo (Dahomey) in 1883, designed to prevent Britain from establishing a continuous sphere of influence from Lagos to the Gold Coast.

Competing claims to the Congo gave a new twist to the Anglo-French rivalry and led Britain into a dispute with other European states. The International Association, a bogus humanitarian front created by King Leopold of the Belgians to conceal the ruthless exploitation of the Congo's resources of ivory and rubber, claimed sovereignty over the region. Its claim was based on treaties, ostensibly commercial in nature, which had been concluded with local chiefs. But Leopold's rights were challenged by the French explorer de Brazza, who asserted a French territorial claim to part of the Congo, which the government in Paris was reluctantly obliged to support.

The British government, which regarded French claims as a much greater threat to British commercial interests than Leopold's, attempted to negate them by concluding a treaty with Portugal, recognizing the ancient, if somewhat shadowy, Portuguese claims to jurisdiction over the mouth of the Congo. This dubious strategem turned out to be a complete failure. Commercial groups in Britain protested loudly against the actual terms of the agreement with Portugal, while France and Germany understandably objected to the treaty as a whole as a ruse to exclude them from the Congo. Under pressure, the Portuguese government was obliged to submit the issue to the scrutiny of an international conference held at Berlin from November 1884 to February 1885. The outcome of the conference, however, served British interests well enough. In the Congo Free State the principle of freedom of commerce was established, while Britain secured recognition of its predominance at the expense of French claims in the Niger region – the only area in west Africa with commercially viable prospects.

CONFRONTATION ON THE NIGER AND THE NILE IN THE 1890s

Anglo-French rivalry in west Africa intensified in the 1890s as both sides attempted to stake out territorial claims based on dubious treaties concluded with local chiefs. The comic absurdity of rival missions hoisting the Union Jack or *tricolore* over tracts of seemingly worthless territory nevertheless had a serious side to it. French expansion from Senegal to the east and south-east threatened to deprive the British coastal settlements of the 'hinterlands' that had become essential to their economic viability. Despite tentative boundary agreements in 1890, sufficient vagueness remained to allow scope for energetic action by the 'men on the spot' to secure trade routes and communication centres. This sort of rivalry became increasingly dangerous in the 1890s, when clashes between zealous commanders became more frequent. A state of 'suspended war' all but developed in the region when the Niger Company's West African Frontier Force under Captain Lugard attempted to preserve northern Nigeria from the clutches of the French military, whose easterly drive along the Upper Niger took them to Lake Chad, over 1,800 miles from Senegal, by 1900.

Although neither London nor Paris regarded west Africa as worth a conflict, public opinion, aroused by the press, had become unduly sensitive to an affront to national honour. The appointment of Joseph Chamberlain as colonial secretary in 1895 aggravated the situation because of his insistence on 'reciprocal concessions' when negotiating with the French, which delayed a final settlement until 1898. Salisbury, the prime minister and foreign secretary, regarded the disputed territory as a 'light soil' region and would have given ground quite willingly in west Africa in return for an agreement with France on Egypt and the Nile.

In 1898 the tension between France and Britain over Egypt came to a head in the Fashoda crisis. The arrival on the Upper Nile of a French mission led by Captain Marchand was rightly interpreted in London as a deliberate challenge to the British position in Egypt. However, the timing of Marchand's arrival at Fashoda in July 1898, more than two years after he had set out from the Congo, was doubly unfortunate for France. Whereas the hand of the British government had just been strengthened by a great victory in the Sudan, the French government was weakened by the furore over the reopening of the Dreyfus case, a *cause célèbre* of espionage and mistaken identity.

The Fashoda expedition was bound to have a serious impact on Anglo-French relations. Despite this it was authorized because weak, short-lived governments in France in the 1890s failed to exercise proper control over madcap schemes approved by the colonial ministry. It was believed that once the *tricolore* was flying over Fashoda, Britain would have to agree to an international conference on Egypt and the Sudan, which would, in France's view, insist on British withdrawal from Egypt. There was also a curious notion going the rounds in the French colonial ministry that a French expedition could somehow either divert or dam the waters of the Nile. The resultant havoc in Egypt would then oblige the British to evacuate the country.

Ironically, this was supposed to inaugurate a new era of harmony in Anglo-French relations. Such was the strange logic of Delcassé, the colonial minister in 1894 who, by a neat twist of fate, had to face the outcome of the Fashoda project as the foreign minister of France in 1898.

The British government's demand that Marchand be ordered to leave Fashoda unconditionally was strengthened by General Kitchener's recent reconquest of the Sudan. After the defeat of the Dervishes at the battle of Omdurman in early September 1898 the status of the Sudan, abandoned since the time of General Gordon's death in 1885, ceased to be equivocal. French officials and ministers were taken aback by Britain's refusal to negotiate, since they had assumed that Britain would not risk damaging its commerce by resorting to war over such an issue. It was the British refusal to compromise that made the crisis over Fashoda so dangerous, at a time when the Dreyfus affair made the French government peculiarly sensitive to demands to defend the honour of France.

But Fashoda represented a challenge to Britain's prestige as well. It was widely perceived in Europe as a test of British power and greatness. Salisbury's government was also under pressure not to yield to what the press regarded as an underhand move by the French to rob Britain of the 'fruits of Omdurman'. This made it impossible for Salisbury to adopt his standard device of 'graceful concessions' as a means of settling colonial disputes. Not that he would compromise on the main issue – the abandonment of French pretensions to influence Egyptian affairs. The recommendation by the director of naval intelligence in November 1895 that Alexandria was essential as a naval base implied that Britain should 'hold Egypt against all comers'. This influenced Salisbury to make a firm decision in 1897 that it was necessary to 'strengthen our position on the Nile'.

Britain's determination not to yield over Fashoda was demonstrated by the decision to mobilize the fleet, which in 1898 was much superior to the French navy. The crisis eased in November when Paris ordered Marchand to withdraw from Fashoda, but it was not until the following spring that an Anglo-French agreement on the Sudan was concluded.

The Fashoda crisis was unusual in that the confrontation did not arise from the recklessness of the 'man on the spot' exceeding or contravening the instructions of the government at home, as was often the case in west Africa and elsewhere. The Marchand expedition to Fashoda, a feat of remarkable endurance and heroism, was a deliberate challenge to a rival imperial power at one of its most sensitive strategic spots. Despite the clear warning given in 1895 that the occupation of territory adjacent to the Sudan would be regarded as an 'unfriendly act', the Marchand mission was not countermanded, even if some political leaders in Paris hoped that it would not reach its destination. The French ended up with the worst of both worlds. They missed the chance of a generous settlement of their claims in west Africa and were forced to accept a humiliating climbdown over their Egyptian pretensions. There was therefore some truth in the admission of France's folly by the president of the Republic that 'nous avons été comme des fous en Afrique.'

BISMARCK'S BID FOR COLONIES, 1884–1889

Bismarck's sudden, but short-lived, enthusiasm for colonies in the mid–1880s secured a modest overseas empire for Germany in Africa and the Pacific. That his successors were dissatisfied with his colonial legacy is indicated by the subsequent assertion that Germany was entitled to 'a place in the sun'. Bismarck's failure to maintain the momentum of Germany's colonial drive is usually explained on the grounds of his disillusionment with the whole business of imperialism, once it had served its immediate purpose. It also reflected a serious decline in Germany's diplomatic position in Europe, resulting from a revival of tension in the Balkans.

The desire for overseas expansion clearly reflected Germany's sense of growing power and economic strength, which needed an outlet beyond the confines of the European continent. Imperialism was therefore an attribute of the 'German Problem'. But Bismarck's

A FIXTURE.

heavy-handed methods of pursuing his colonial policy created resentment among hitherto pro-German elements in Britain, thereby contributing to the growth of anti-German sentiment, which constituted another aspect of the 'German Problem' in the field of international relations.

Bismarck's alleged aversion to colonies was summed up in his comment of 1881 that 'as long as I am imperial chancellor we shall not pursue a colonial policy.' The sudden reversal of his anti-colonial stance in 1884–5, coupled with the marked anti-British emphasis of his colonial policy, bewildered the government in London at the time and has puzzled historians ever since.

The explanation offered by Wehler in the form of his theory of 'social imperialism' has been criticized by Gall on the grounds that a realist like Bismarck was unlikely to believe that he could concoct such a 'relatively fast-acting patent medicine for his domestic policy ills' from such a brief flirtation with imperialism. Kennedy's analysis of Bismarck's colonial policy is more convincing because he relates it to a variety of pressures and issues, external as well as internal. Furthermore, he presents Bismarck's policy as evolving over a period of several months and feeding off the public response to his early moves, rather than being determined from the outset by fixed objectives.

Bismarck's colonial ventures began at a time when Germany's diplomatic situation was very strong. With the conclusion of the Triple Alliance in 1882 and the renewal of the *Dreikaiserbund* in 1884, during a period of calm in the Balkans, Bismarck was able to feel unusually relaxed about Germany's security. The economic situation, on the other hand, was much less favourable. Falling demand for manufactured goods fuelled fears that Germany was in the throes of a crisis of 'over-production', which led to pressure to find new markets, or to expand existing ones, for German exports. It was thought that such markets would be more secure if the state increased its political influence in the region, if necessary through annexation. Nor were Germans more immune than other Europeans to the pipe-dreams of vast colonial riches to be won, as shown by their view of east Africa as a 'second India'.

Trading companies in Hamburg and Bremen, which already had well-established links with west Africa and Zanzibar, were also seeking more active support from the German government to protect their interests against possible French or British discriminatory practices or tariffs. If Bismarck yielded to this pressure from commercial interests, seconded by the newly founded German Colonial Union, it was partly because he hoped to secure a colonial empire 'on the cheap', through the agency of chartered companies rather than by direct administration from Berlin at the government's expense. According to Pakenham, this solution to Bismarck's misgivings about the costs of empire was suggested to him by von Kusserow, a colonial enthusiast in the Wilhelmstrasse. The influence of this official on German policy in 1884 was possibly quite considerable, since he was responsible, through a translation error, for creating a false alarm over a supposed Franco-British agreement to divide west Africa, which implied the exclusion of German traders from the region.

Political calculation, both long- and short-term, also influenced Bismarck's decision to embark on a colonial policy before the 1884 elections. Bismarck needed an issue that would reverse the election results of 1881 which had strengthened the left Liberals and Progressives, whose fusion had made them the largest party in the Reichstag, threatening Bismarck's control over it. It seemed that imperialism could well be such an issue, since his main supporters, the National Liberals and Free Conservatives, had declared openly in favour of colonies by 1883 whereas his opponents were anti-imperialist. Once it became clear that the mood of public opinion in Germany was favourable to overseas expansion, Bismarck could profit by playing the colonial card against his opponents in the Reichstag.

A more dangerous, though less obvious, threat to Bismarck's political ascendancy stemmed from the association of the heir to the throne with those groups who advocated the adoption of Gladstonian-style Liberalism in Germany, which was hardly compatible with Bismarckianism. By imparting an openly anti-British twist to German imperialism, Bismarck could hope to weaken the influence of the 'English party' in German politics. Given the extent of British claims to informal influence over much of Africa, the chancellor had no difficulty in steering Germany's colonial policy in an anti-British direction.

Bismarck's task was certainly made easier by Britain's weak diplomatic position in 1884–5, as well as by the bungling and miscalculations of Gladstone's government. The worsening financial situation in Egypt, following the fiasco in the Sudan in late 1883, made Britain very vulnerable to pressure from France and Germany, who demanded that the Egyptian debt be placed under the control of an international commission. The fact that the Egyptian government needed to obtain the approval of the commission for some types of expenditure, coupled with certain French hostility to any British proposals, enabled Bismarck to wield the *bâton égyptien* to Germany's advantage. Not that the Liberal government had any desire to block German aspirations for overseas possessions. But Bismarck's own deviousness, compounded by the incompetence of both the foreign and colonial ministers in London, led to misunderstandings about the chancellor's real intentions. He was therefore able to present Britain to German public opinion as a barrier to Germany's overseas ambitions.

In the autumn of 1883 Berlin began to make enquiries about the status of south-west Africa, where a German trader had set up a commercial operation at Angra Pequena. Much to Bismarck's annoyance, these enquiries failed to elicit either a prompt or a clear reply from London for several months. But, contrary to Bismarck's belief that this was an attempt to exclude German influence from south-west Africa, the Foreign Office mistakenly believed that Bismarck's objective was to secure British protection for German traders in the region, not to establish a German colony.

Further delays in responding to Berlin's enquiries arose from prolonged 'buck-passing' between London and Cape Town. Although the colonial government wanted to keep the Germans out, it was no more willing than the government in London to take on the trouble and expense of administering south-west Africa. By the time the Cape government eventually annexed it, Bismarck regarded the territory as already under Reich protection and made a strong protest to London in June 1884. Threatened with the *bâton égyptien* the British government meekly accepted not only Bismarck's proposal to proclaim south-west Africa a German colony, but German protectorates over Togo and the Kameruns in west Africa too.

Bismarck was also able to play the colonial card over the Congo (where Britain had tried to use Portugal as the watchdog of free trade against France) by refusing to recognize the Anglo-Portuguese treaty and demanding an international conference. By late September 1884, if not earlier, Bismarck was confident of French support in opposing Britain not just in Egypt, but also in the Congo and west Africa, especially the Niger. Despite the formation of this Franco-German front, Britain came out of the Berlin West Africa conference, which met from November 1884 to February 1885, with its main interests in Africa unharmed. Since Bismarck's demands over the Congo had been conceded he had no reason to challenge British claims to the Lower Niger, especially as Germany had already staked its claims in west Africa and subsequently secured its interests

THE "IRREPRESSIBLE" TOURIST.

B-sm-rck. "H'M!—HA!—WHERE SHALL I GO NEXT?"

in New Guinea. Furthermore, the Germans suddenly woke up to the fact that France was not a very congenial partner in colonial matters, given its addiction to tariff regimes. Consequently Bismarck abandoned his campaign against Britain and accepted the British proposals for dealing with the problem of Egypt's finances in early 1885, with the comment: 'Egypt . . . is merely a means of overcoming England's objections to our colonial aspirations.'

Bismarck's enthusiasm for an active colonial policy was short-lived. Although Kennedy has demonstrated that Bismarck continued to support German claims in places such as Samoa and east Africa with some vigour after 1885, by 1889 he was complaining of being 'sick and tired of colonies'. What caused the Reich chancellor to become disillusioned with colonies so rapidly?

One obvious explanation is that the acquisition of an overseas empire in parts of Africa and the Pacific had fulfilled the domestic political objectives, including a satisfactory outcome to the 1884 elections, which may have been one of his principal motives for embarking on colonial ventures in the first place. In the process, he had derived great satisfaction from inflicting a series of humiliations on 'English Liberalism' in the form of Gladstone's government, which he had been anxious to discredit. The return to power of the Conservatives under Lord Salisbury in June 1885 and again, after a brief Liberal interlude, in August 1886 eliminated the anti-Gladstone factor in Bismarck's diplomatic calculations. Bismarck loathed Gladstone and the values he stood for. The difference this made to German attitudes towards the British government and colonial issues is shown by Holstein's comment concerning east Africa in 1889 that Germany 'should conciliate the English where they have . . . claims. Salisbury's preservation in office is more important than the possession of Witu.'

A second reason for Bismarck's disenchantment with colonies was that his expectations of an 'empire on the cheap' were unfulfilled. Chartered companies were either unwilling or unable to bear the expense of administering protectorates, while the big banks and industry showed little interest in investing in tropical territories. Hence Bismarck's angry comment that 'if commerce has no interest in keeping the colonies, then neither have I.' Worse still, insensitive treatment of local interests by consular officials and others provoked serious uprisings against German rule in east Africa and some other colonies in the late 1880s. Not only was this damaging to Germany's prestige but the cost of pacification was an additional burden on the imperial Treasury.

A final reason for Bismarck's change of attitude was the deterioration in Germany's previously strong diplomatic position which was evident in 1886–90. Both the Boulangist agitation in France and the growth of Austro-Russian tension over Bulgaria meant that Germany had need of Britain's goodwill, perhaps its support. Bismarck was reported to have emphasized in December 1888 that 'a good understanding with England means much more to him than the whole of east Africa.' The dangers to Germany's security arising from its unsatisfactory relations with France and Russia, highlighted by Boulangism and pan-Slavism, seemed real enough. There were therefore good grounds for Bismarck's curt rejoinder to pressure from the colonial propagandist Karl Peters for a more aggressive stance towards British claims in east Africa, in the oft-quoted phrase 'my map of Africa lies in Europe'.

GERMAN DIPLOMACY IN AFRICA, 1890–1898

The period between Bismarck's resignation in 1890 and the inauguration of the era of *Weltpolitik* ('world policy') in 1897–8 seems to constitute a sort of interlude, when German diplomacy lacked a clear sense of direction. However, it was the confusion of methods employed, rather than the absence of objectives, that makes German policy seem inconsistent. During this period Bismarck's successors were conducting a 'love-hate' relationship with Britain, using Africa as the chief terrain for their diplomatic manoeuvring. This enabled them to offer colonial concessions as a 'sweetener', but it also meant that they could exploit Britain's difficulties in Africa to put pressure on London to adhere to the Triple Alliance.

The main diplomatic concern of Germany's new leaders, the chancellor Caprivi, foreign minister Marschall and Holstein, a senior Foreign Office counsellor, was to strengthen Germany's security in Europe after the alliance with Russia had lapsed. This anxiety naturally increased following the signing of the Franco-Russian military agreement of 1892, which became a political alliance in 1894. One possible solution, a *rapprochement* with Russia, a recurrent theme in German diplomacy for the next twenty years, was hindered at times by a clash of economic interests, especially tariff policies. Another obstacle was Russia's desire to maintain its links with France, a desire strengthened by Russian dependence on French loans for its modernization programme. The main object of German foreign policy in the early 1890s, therefore, was to persuade or cajole Britain into joining the Triple Alliance, as a means of bolstering Germany's security in Europe.

The relationship between the two powers was complicated by several factors in this period. One of these was Berlin's preference for Lord Salisbury's presence at the Foreign Office, rather than that of the Liberal Lord Rosebery. Another was the personality of the Kaiser, Wilhelm II, whose moods fluctuated wildly betwen admiration and envy of the British empire. A third factor was the influence of the press and public opinion in Germany, whose heightened awareness of imperialism in the 1890s made them critical of government attempts to make concessions to Britain in colonial disputes.

Britain's reasons for resisting both blandishments and threats from Berlin were threefold. In the first place the government's freedom of action was becoming circumscribed, as it was in Germany, by the increasing attention paid by public opinion, the press and pressure groups to the defence of British commercial and imperial interests. In Chamberlains' view, 'nothing could be more unpopular than an uncompensated concession' to Germany in colonial matters. Second, Salisbury had doubts about Germany's reliability as an ally, given the alarming fluctuations in the Kaiser's moods. Third, neither Salisbury nor Rosebery could see much advantage for Britain in a formal alliance with Germany which would almost certainly preclude a *rapprochement* with France or Russia.

Anglo-German relations fluctuated greatly over African issues during this period. From a high point in 1890 at the signing of the Heligoland-Zanzibar treaty, they deteriorated during a quarrel in 1894 over the Anglo-Congolese treaty, to reach their nadir in 1896 during the Transvaal crisis. In 1898 relations improved aain with an agreement over the Portuguese colonies in Africa. If, in the early 1890s, German policy in Africa seemed to be almost a continuation of Bismarckianism (in its more benign form), it later degenerated into a policy of meddle and muddle that anticipated the worst features of *Weltpolitik*.

The fact that the partition of east Africa in 1890 was very favourable to Britain owed less to the merits of British claims than to Berlin's reappraisal of the value of colonies and the desire for an entente. This was only partly the result of Bismarck's fall in 1890. Although Germany had secured the lion's share of east Africa in the previous partition agreement in 1886, this reflected the lack of official British interest in the region at that time. Only a few years later, however, Salisbury had to contend with vociferous demands from commercial interests and the missionary lobby, backed by public opinion, to defend British claims against the erratic freebooting activities of Karl Peters. Before 1890 Bismarck himself had come to regard the expansionist ambitions of Peters and the DOAG (German East Africa Company) as a nuisance, prejudicing 'our good relations with England', and to recognize the need for a new agreement to put an end to the friction caused by the rivalry between German and British colonial activists, both in Africa and at home.

For Salisbury, the problem was how to make concessions to Germany without creating a storm of protest that might further weaken the position of the Conservative government, which still depended on Unionist support. An additional complication was that Britain's strategic interests lay to the north, in Uganda, where its claims were weakest. To keep the Germans out of Uganda concessions were necessary in the south, but this was the area (the so-called Stevenson Road) where British claims were strong and missionary interests well established. Furthermore, Britain wanted to end the unofficial condominium over Zanzibar itself, where Germany's brusque behaviour had deeply offended the sultan. Salisbury's solution to these difficulties was to offer to cede Heligoland, a strategically placed island off Germany's North Sea coast which had been British since 1815 – but was not inhabited by traders or missionaries.

Even so, it seems clear that the success of the negotiations in 1890 owed much to Berlin's desire to placate Britain and to keep Salisbury in power. In this respect, the men of the 'new course' – Caprivi, Marschall and Holstein – were following in Bismarck's footsteps when in June 1890 they stressed the need 'to lighten Lord Salisbury's task and to make possible his retention in office'. Similarly, the Kaiser was only echoing Bismarck's later sentiments when he told the British ambassador in May 1890 that 'Africa was not worth a quarrel between England and Germany.' Anglo-German relations were clearly very cordial in 1890.

By 1894, however, suspicion and distrust had soured these relations to such an extent that a warning was given to Berlin via Vienna that Britain would reconsider its commitments under the Mediterranean Agreements of 1887 if Germany persisted in siding with France in African questions. The dispute over the Anglo-Congolese treaty in 1894 illustrates the other side of the 'love-hate relationship'. Gladstone's return to power in 1892 affected Berlin's attitude towards Britain, despite Rosebery's 'reassuring presence' at the Foreign Office.

The object of Britain's ill-conceived treaty with Leopold of the

Belgians, *de facto* ruler of the Congo, was to deny access to the Upper Nile to French expeditions by tortuous, not to say underhand, methods which involved the lease of disputed territory. Further complications ensued when Rosebery's francophile cabinet colleagues objected to the secrecy clause, inserted into the agreement at Leopold's behest, on the grounds of the 'wanton provocation of France' which could seriously damage Anglo-French relations. Of more importance to the fate of the treaty, however, was Germany's decision to join France in opposing the revised – and no longer secret – Anglo-Congolese treaty. German objections were partly genuine, but also a matter of tactics. The Germans could reasonably object to a British right of way through Congolese territory as damaging to their trade prospects in German East Africa. However, the real reason for their threat to demand a new international conference on Africa (including Egypt) was, according to Gordon Martel, Rosebery's biographer, to demonstrate British dependence on Germany's goodwill to solve their imperial problems in Africa. Germany's subsequent offer of a compromise arrangement on the Congolese issue, after Rosebery's riposte to Vienna, demonstrates that the original objections were primarily tactical. Nevertheless, the abandonment of the Congolese treaty was a humiliating experience for Rosebery; he did not forgive the Germans, the tone of whose messages he found 'thoroughly insufferable'. When the Liberals came to power again in 1906, the memory of Germany's brusqueness still rankled.

Meanwhile, in 1896 German intervention in the affairs of the Transvaal provoked the most serious crisis in Anglo-German relations for thirty years. The external relations of the Boer republic, which had recovered its independence in 1881, were restricted by the Pretoria Convention. The Transvaal's relations with foreign powers was a sensitive issue for Britain because of Boer hostility to British rule in southern Africa. The creation of a German colony in south-west Africa in 1884 led to fears in London and Cape Town of German influence spreading eastwards towards the Transvaal and of an eventual territorial conjuncture between the two, if the Boers expanded westwards. These fears, much stronger in Cape Town than in London, prompted the proclamation of a protectorate over Bechuanaland in 1885 to satisfy demands that the Cape's route northwards into the interior was not blocked by Boer expansion.

Political and economic developments in southern Africa were bound to be of major concern to the British government because the maintenance of British influence at the Cape was seen as vital

to its imperial interests, especially the route to India. When, therefore, the discovery of gold and diamonds on the Rand in 1886
transformed the Transvaal from a poor, pastoralist Boer republic
into potentially the richest state in south Africa, the imperial implications were grave enough without 'the German inclination to take
the Transvaal under its protection', as a colonial secretary complained in 1894. Cape Colony, where the Cape Dutch constituted
about half the population, stood in danger of being absorbed into
a federation dominated by the Transvaal under its intransigent old
president, Paul Kruger.

This danger helps to explain how Cecil Rhodes obtained a royal
charter for his dubious British South Africa Company in 1889, after
the failure of attempts shortly before that to prevent the Transvaal
from securing its own rail outlet to Delagoa Bay. Rhodes claimed
that by the establishment of a British-dominated Rhodesia 'we shall
get the balance of Africa', in the sense of a loyal counterweight to
the Boer republic. Finally, when hopes that the *uitlanders* – the
foreign, mainly British, immigrants in the Transvaal – would bring
about Kruger's downfall were dashed by the denial of the franchise
to them, Rhodes, Chamberlain and others conspired to overthrow
Kruger by force.

The Jameson raid of December 1885, an armed invasion of the
Transvaal by Rhodes's company police to assist an anticipated *uit-
lander* rebellion against Boer 'oppression', ended in disaster. The
British government, which could plausibly pretend to have had no
foreknowledge of the plot, promptly disavowed it. It was therefore
improper of the Kaiser to congratulate Kruger on restoring peace
in the Transvaal 'without having to invoke the help of friendly
powers'. The British press reacted violently against what it regarded
as interference in Britain's imperial affairs and, according to the
German ambassador in London, 'the whole of public opinion'
would have been behind the government if it had decided for war
against Germany.

Germany's motives in provoking the crisis, to which Britain
responded by despatching a 'flying squadron' to south African
waters, are not altogether clear. Berlin was seemingly surprised by
the violence of the reaction of the British press to the Kruger
telegram, but it had been warned in advance that south Africa was
regarded as 'perhaps the most vital interest of Great Britain because
by the possession of it communication with India was assured'. The
two governments had also had quite pointed exchanges about the
fate of Portuguese East Africa and the Delagoa Bay railway, in

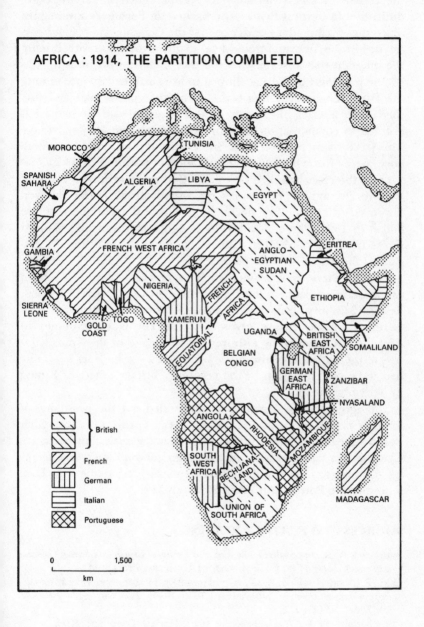

AFRICA : 1914, THE PARTITION COMPLETED

MOROCCO
TUNISIA
SPANISH SAHARA
ALGERIA
LIBYA
EGYPT
GAMBIA
FRENCH WEST AFRICA
ANGLO-EGYPTIAN SUDAN
ERITREA
SIERRA LEONE
NIGERIA
FRENCH EQUATORIAL AFRICA
ETHIOPIA
GOLD COAST
TOGO
KAMERUN
UGANDA
BRITISH EAST AFRICA
SOMALILAND
BELGIAN CONGO
GERMAN EAST AFRICA
ZANZIBAR
NYASALAND
ANGOLA
RHODESIA
MOZAMBIQUE
SOUTH WEST AFRICA
BECHUANA LAND
MADAGASCAR
UNION OF SOUTH AFRICA

British
French
German
Italian
Portuguese

0   1,500
km

the course of which Germany had made veiled threats to cause difficulties in Egypt if Britain encroached on Portugal's sovereignty. Since there is abundant evidence that the Germans knew that interference in the Transvaal would lead to a confrontation with Britain, the question that arises is what did they hope to gain from it?

One possibility is that they hoped to blackmail Britain into joining the Triple Alliance. Another is that if British imperial interests benefited from altering the status of the Transvaal the Germans felt entitled to compensation, possibly in Mozambique and/or Samoa. This was a claim, however, that British ministers would not countenance, partly for fear of sparking off another partition of Africa.

Once the crisis had died down, the German government reverted to its former attitude of cool reserve towards Britain. Relations even improved when London decided on a partial reconquest of the Sudan in 1896. The expedition to Dongola, by distracting Mahdist forces from the hard-pressed Italians at Kassala, was a friendly gesture to the Triple Alliance powers.

In 1898 there even seemed to be a prospect of 'a new era of Anglo-German cooperation' when the British cabinet insisted, despite Salisbury's reluctance, on negotiating an agreement with Germany on the future division of the Portuguese colonies in Africa. Germany thereby withdrew its patronage of the Transvaal – before the outbreak of the Boer war in 1899 – even if its neutrality had to be paid for again by the cession of Britain's share of Samoa in November 1899.

The agreement of August 1898 also ruled out the possibility of Franco-German cooperation in Africa directed against Britain, which would have been fateful during the Fashoda crisis. Furthermore, Chamberlain was convinced that German goodwill was worth securing as a means of resisting Russian expansion in the Far East, following the Port Arthur crisis of March 1898.

SOURCES AND FURTHER READING

Baumgart, W. R., *Imperialism. The Idea and Reality of British and French Colonial Expansion 1880–1914*, Oxford, Oxford University Press, 1982.

Cain, P. J. and Hopkins, A. G., 'Gentlemanly capitalism and British expansion overseas II: new imperialism, 1850–1945', *Economic History Review*, 1987, vol. XL(1): 1–26.

Chamberlain, M. E., *The Scramble for Africa*, Harlow, Longman, 1974.

Fieldhouse, D. K. (ed.), *The Theory of Capitalist Imperialism*, Harlow, Longman, 1967.

——, *Economics and Empire 1830–1914*, London, Weidenfeld & Nicolson, 1973.

Förster, S., Mommsen, W. J., and Robinson, R. (eds), *Bismarck, Europe and Africa. The Berlin Africa Conference of 1884–5 and the Onset of Partition*, Oxford, Oxford University Press, 1989.

Gall, L., *Bismarck. The White Revolutionary*, vol. 2: *1871–1898* (transl. J. A. Underwood), London, Allen & Unwin, 1986.

Gifford, P. and Louis, W. R. (eds), *France and Britain in Africa*, London, Yale University Press, 1971.

Hynes, W. G., *The Economics of Empire*, Harlow, Longman, 1979.

Kennedy, P. M., *The Rise of the Anglo-German Antagonism 1860–1914*, London, Allen & Unwin, 1980. (Chs 10–12.)

Lowe, C. J., *The Reluctant Imperialists. British Foreign Policy 1878–1902*, vol. 1, London, Routledge & Kegan Paul, 1967. (Chs 3, 6, 9.)

Martel, G., *Imperial Diplomacy. Rosebery and the Failure of Foreign Policy*, London, Mansell, 1986.

Newbury, C. W. and Kanya-Forstner, A. S., 'French policy and the origins of the Scramble for West Africa', *Journal of African History*, 1969, vol. 10(2): 60–75.

Owen, R. and Sutcliffe, R. (eds), *Studies in the Theory of Imperialism*, Harlow, Longman, 1972.

Pakenham, T., *The Scramble for Africa*, London, Weidenfeld & Nicolson, 1991.

Penrose, E. F. (ed.), *European Imperialism and the Partition of Africa*, London, Cass, 1975.

Platt, D. C. M., 'Economic factors in British policy during the "New Imperialism" ', *Past & Present*, 1968, no. 39: 120–38.

Porter, B., *The Lion's Share. A Short History of British Imperialism 1850–1970*, Harlow, Longman, 1975.

Robinson, R. and Gallagher, J., *Africa and the Victorians*, London, Macmillan, 1961.

Sanderson – see Penrose.

Wehler, H-U., 'Bismarck's imperialism, 1862–1890', *Past & Present*, 1970, no. 48: 119–55.

The motives for imperialism are lucidly discussed by Baumgart and also in the opening chapters of Fieldhouse's major work, *Economics and Empire*, the rest of which is devoted to case studies and the 'periphery' argument. The alleged links between capitalism and imperialism are shown in his wide-ranging edited selection of extracts. A broad range of Marxist and other views is presented in Owen and Sutcliffe. Wehler's 'social imperialism' thesis can conveniently be studied in his article. Trade as a factor in British imperialism is discussed at length in Hynes's book and more briefly in the articles by Platt and by Cain and Hopkins.

On Africa, M. E. Chamberlain is a good brief introduction, with some useful extracts and a helpful bibliography. By contrast, Pakenham is a long, action-packed narrative. Sanderson's views on the timing of the partition are lucidly presented in Penrose, but Förster *et al.*'s recent major work on the Berlin Conference and the partition is very detailed and something of 'a hard read'.

On British policy in Africa, Robinson and Gallagher is a mine of information but needs revision in places. A briefer treatment of British imperialism is to be found in the relevant chapters of Porter and of C. J. Lowe. Detailed studies of aspects of French and British imperial activities are contained in Gifford and Louis, with one by Kanya-Forstner, a contributor to an important article on French policy in west Africa.

4 The Far Eastern crisis of 1895–1905 and the ententes of 1904 and 1907

THE WESTERN POWERS IN CHINA

The fact that clashes of interest between the great powers in the Far East, a region so remote from Europe, could reach crisis proportions seems to reflect the global nature of imperial rivalries in this period. The crises were, however, largely an Anglo-Russian duel, with Japan playing the part of an increasingly concerned spectator, then participant. For the western powers, China hardly constituted an area of vital strategic importance. For them, the Far East was 'the end of the line', even if China persisted in regarding itself as the 'Middle Kingdom'. Still, China was coterminous with French Indo-China as well as British Burma, which bordered on India. Furthermore, both the British and the Russians regarded rivalry in China as an extension of the 'Great Game', a form of cold war bluff and intrigue, that was played from the Balkans to the Khyber Pass and beyond.

From the British point of view, uncertainty as to Russia's real intentions in China created a considerable amount of tension. Clearly, if Russia's interest in Manchuria was political as well as economic, St Petersburg could be aiming at the domination of the whole of northern China, including Peking. Such an increase in Russian influence and prestige would upset the global power balance. If, on the other hand, Russia's interest in Manchuria was only as a zone of economic exploitation for its backward industries, then Britain had less cause for concern.

This seems to have been the view of the ageing Lord Salisbury, who regarded Russian activities in the Far East as much less troublesome than in the Balkans or on the frontiers of India. The pressure for a more active British response to Russia came from the China lobby and from Salisbury's younger colleagues, notably Balfour,

Chamberlain and possibly Lansdowne, who took over the Foreign Office in October 1900. Significantly, the Germans shared Salisbury's view that Russian activity in China was relatively harmless, distracting Russia away from Germany's eastern frontier where, as the Kaiser aptly observed, no 'Chinese wall' existed to keep the Russians at bay. As regards the western powers, there is little evidence that they had serious territorial designs on China, though there were occasions when they infringed the country's integrity. The real threat to China in territorial terms came from Russia and Japan.

The activities of the western powers in China seem to represent a classic case of 'economic imperialism', in which the Europeans' technological superiority obliged a reluctant regime to grant them opportunities for trade and investment. The 'serene confidence of Confucian superiority', as Peter Lowe calls it, which led the Chinese authorities to resist the demands of the 'insolent barbarians' in the 1840s, was no match for the 'brash dynamism of the Industrial Revolution', backed by gunboat diplomacy.

Britain had taken the lead in opening up China to foreign trade through the system of treaty ports, numbering over thirty by the 1890s. By 1870 the British had acquired an undoubted predominance in China, enjoying about 70 per cent of China's external trade, and had a well-established position in the Yangtse region and in the International Settlement at Shanghai. But by the 1880s Britain was on the defensive, attempting to preserve its established position against French and German competition.

In retrospect, it hardly seems to have been worth all the trouble. In 1885 British trade with China amounted to little more than 1 per cent of total British trade. By the 1890s British exports to China had remained fairly constant for twenty years, while imports were declining. However, given the adverse trading conditions of the late nineteenth century, any trade was no doubt thought to be worth defending. But the real allure of China was its potential – the prospect of a market of 450 million people – provided one ignored the poverty and self-sufficiency of these potential consumers. Hence the contemporary references to China as 'the most hopeful place of the future for the commerce of our country' and the resultant determination to maintain the 'open door' for trade against the restrictive policies of Britain's rivals.

Opportunities for trade were not the only attraction of China for the western powers. In the 1880s China seemed ripe for modernization. With little in the way of railways, modern industries or public

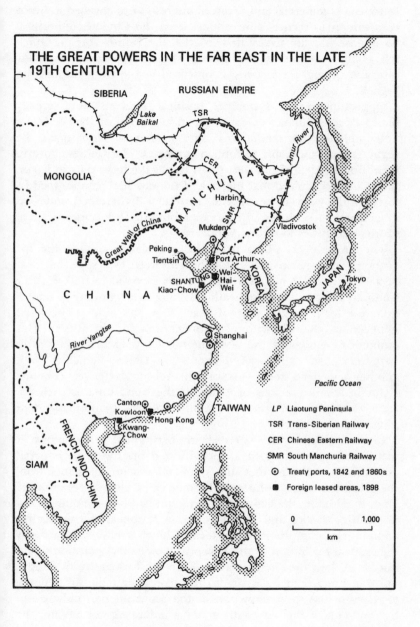

THE GREAT POWERS IN THE FAR EAST IN THE LATE 19TH CENTURY

SIBERIA

RUSSIAN EMPIRE

TSR

Lake Baikal

CER

MONGOLIA

M A N C H U R I A

Harbin

SMR

Mukden

Vladivostok

Great Wall of China

LP

Peking

Port Arthur

Tientsin

KOREA

SHANTUNG

Wei-Hai-Wei

C H I N A

Kiao-Chow

JAPAN

Tokyo

River Yangtse

Shanghai

Pacific Ocean

Canton

TAIWAN

Kowloon

LP   Liaotung Peninsula

Hong Kong

TSR Trans-Siberian Railway

Kwang-Chow

CER Chinese Eastern Railway

FRENCH INDO-CHINA

SMR South Manchuria Railway

⊙   Treaty ports, 1842 and 1860s

SIAM

■   Foreign leased areas, 1898

0   1,000

km

utilities, despite the projects of the 'self-strengthening' movement, European commercial and financial interests were engaged in fierce competition to secure 'concessions' from the Chinese authorities. So intense was the rivalry that in 1886 the British Foreign Office felt obliged to modify its hitherto strict rules against consular officials 'touting' for favours, as practised by the Germans and the French.

Opportunities for European business interests were greatly increased after China's defeat by Japan in the war of 1894–5. It was not simply that the revelation of the weakness of China made the regime more vulnerable to foreign pressures. The Chinese government now needed large loans, partly to pay the indemnity to Japan. But it also recognized that the lack of railways had handicapped its forces in the war with Japan. The years 1896–8, therefore, witnessed a 'midsummer madness' of concession-hunting by Europeans, some of which activities were utterly bizarre.

The pressure on China from the intensifying competition for economic concessions was suddenly reinforced by a spate of unexpected territorial demands by the European powers in 1897–8. After Germany's success in browbeating Peking into granting a ninety-nine-year lease on the port of Kiao-Chow, the other powers felt impelled to secure territorial compensation for themselves. This ominous development, the first time for fifty years that a European state had made territorial demands on China, coincided with another dangerous trend – that of demands for 'exclusive' economic rights in specific regions of China. If the trend towards exclusive 'spheres of influence' continued, China's survival as an independent state might be at risk.

China avoided Africa's fate of being partitioned partly because it was a unitary state, albeit a decentralized one, with an imperial government at Peking that still commanded some allegiance from the provincial viceroys who were, in some cases, the real power in the land. In addition, the Chinese government had become quite adept in delaying tactics and playing off one European power against another. However, the major factor in China's survival was probably the gradual realization by the European powers that partition would not be in their own best interests. Even the Russians, with designs on Manchuria, had no desire to provoke a scramble for Chinese territory before the completion of the Trans-Siberian railway and the build-up of their strength in the Far East. As for Britain, the prospect of being responsible for administering the vast central region of China, the Yangtse basin, held no attractions whatsoever.

Hence, with the only two 'plums' already spoken for, France and Germany came to realize that restriction of their activities to their probable spheres of interest (south China and Shantung) would not be to their advantage. If they needed convincing of the truth of this, the British government was eager enough to persuade them.

The idea of partition or exclusive spheres of influence was anathema to Britain, whose commercial interests extended throughout China. Consequently the British government negotiated agreements with Germany (September 1898) and France (October 1899) to check the trend towards exclusive rights. However, Salisbury's vigorous defence of the 'open door' policy, openly championed by the United States in the Hay Circular of September 1899, had only limited success with Russia. In the Anglo-Russian agreement of April 1899, the Great Wall of China was taken as delimiting their respective zones for railway concessions, terms which amounted to exclusive rights and were hardly consistent with Salisbury's other agreements.

During this period Europeans obtained from China rights to construct hundreds, if not thousands, of miles of railway track, most of which were not even begun a decade later. The point of the exercise was probably political, as a British minister conceded in his comment in 1898 that 'we are really fighting a battle for prestige rather than for material gain.'

British prestige in China had suffered a double blow from the Sino-Japanese war. The most obvious sign of this was Britain's non-participation in the 'Triple Intervention' of 1895, when Russia, France and Germany combined to force Japan to return the Liaotung peninsula to China. The failure to intervene on China's behalf to preserve Chinese territorial integrity, either during or after the war of 1894–5, undermined Britain's 'special relationship' with China. Although it was primarily Germany and the United States which had wrecked proposals for mediation by the great powers, Britain's reluctance to antagonize Japan implied that London no longer regarded China as Britain's 'natural ally' in the Far East. When the Chinese government needed a loan of £16 million it was negotiated by the three other powers, leaving Britain out in the cold. Britain's desertion of China in its hour of need gave Russia an excellent opportunity to step in and play the role of 'China's friend', against the Japanese.

RUSSIAN EXPANSION IN THE FAR EAST

The Russian decision in 1895 to exert diplomatic pressure on Tokyo to force Japan to relinquish its mainland gains testified to the ascendancy of Count Witte, the finance minister, in the tsarist government. Whereas the foreign minister and the forces' chiefs favoured a deal with Japan to secure an ice-free port for Russia in Korea, Witte insisted that the Japanese victory over China was a serious threat to Russia's interests in the Far East. In a sense Witte's decision prepared the ground for the Russo-Japanese war of 1904–5, just as Rosebery's decision not to oppose Japan's gains was a half-conscious foreshadowing of the Anglo-Japanese alliance of 1902.

Witte's policy in the Far East was based, ostensibly, on the 'peaceful penetration' of China by Russian industry and commerce, facilitated by the Trans-Siberian railway, which was begun in 1891. This 'event of earth-shattering importance', as Witte termed it, was intended to counteract Russia's industrial backwardness by giving it the advantage over the western powers of quicker land-based communications with China. However, the long-term viability of Witte's railway scheme depended, as Geyer shows, on the ability of the railway to promote an economic boom in Russia. This, in turn, depended on the success of stimulating the development of the thinly populated region of Siberia, rich in minerals, through which the railway passed *en route* to Vladivostok on the Pacific coast.

The concept of 'peaceful penetration' was also something of a chimera, since the long-term aim was to make Russian influence predominant in Peking by turning Manchuria and northern China into a Russian bastion. Hence 'trade and industry in the front, the army always in the rear' more accurately sums up Witte's plan for Russian economic expansion in the Far East.

The Sino-Japanese war gave Witte's policy of peaceful penetration an unexpected boost, since it provided Russia with the opportunity to pose as China's 'saviour'. The Chinese government's financial obligations to Japan were met by a Russian loan, with funds raised in Paris. In return, China agreed to the establishment of a Russo-Chinese bank in September 1895 which, not very surprisingly, secured a concession to construct the Chinese Eastern Railway across Manchuria. This concession, granted in August 1896, effectively shortened the Trans-Siberian route to Vladivostok by about 500 miles. To emphasize Russia's new role, a mutual assistance pact (the Li-Lobanov treaty) was concluded in June 1896. However, Witte's attempt to cultivate a 'special relationship' with China that seemingly eschewed threats or designs on Chinese territory, apart from the dubious concept of railway enclaves, was destroyed in 1897–8 by the Russian decision to occupy Port Arthur, in response to the German seizure of Kiao-Chow in November 1897.

The murder of two German missionaries in Shantung province provided the Kaiser with an excuse to occupy Kiao-Chow, coveted as a naval base. This seems like an example of *Weltpolitik*, the adoption of an expansionist overseas policy, but most historians now regard it as an aberration, a sort of *Flottenpolitik* to impress German public opinion. Many contemporaries, however, did regard it as a sign that 'the German Empire has at long last set foot firmly in Asia', as the Kaiser proclaimed, with all that that implied. The effect was to intensify the Far Eastern crisis by sparking off demands from the other powers for territorial compensation.

Russia was quick to react, sending warships to occupy Port Arthur in December 1897 and demanding, a few months later, a lease on the Liaotung peninsula. This was followed by pressure for a concession to construct the South Manchurian Railway to link Port Arthur with the Trans-Siberian line. The Russian response to Kiao-Chow, which represented a dramatic change in the policy towards China, illustrates the confusion that existed in policy-making in tsarist Russia. Despite Witte's strenuous opposition to occupying Port Arthur and against the Admiralty's preference for an ice-free port in Korea, the foreign minister, Muraviev, insisted on the need to make a demonstration of Russia's power in the Far East. The tsar eventually concurred, out of pique at the Kaiser's dramatic gesture. Muraviev then proceeded to warn Berlin that Russia now regarded Manchuria and Chihli province (including Peking) as an 'exclusive sphere of action', especially as regards political influence. The partition of China seemed to be beginning when Germany laid claim to Shantung province in January 1898 and France obtained a lease on Kwang-Chow in south-east China in April, while Britain, after much agonizing, secured Wei-hai-wei and a ninety-nine-year lease on the New Territories, opposite Hong Kong.

Why did Britain, whose avowed interests in China were commercial, not territorial, join in the scramble for a 'slice of the melon'? One answer is that one of the alternatives – insisting on Russia's withdrawal from Port Arthur – involved the risk of war. Negotiation seemed a wiser course but, by the time it became clear that Russia was intent on a permanent occupation, the resolve to challenge St Petersburg had weakened. Even so, Britain could have practised self-denial by sticking to its policy of the previous fifty years of respecting

China's integrity. But against this was the desire to preserve the 'European balance in Chinese waters' and the need to satisfy the appetite of British opinion for compensatory territorial gains to maintain Britain's prestige.

If Salisbury was disappointed at his failure to secure an understanding with Russia on Chinese affairs in 1898, the Japanese too had little cause for satisfaction at the outcome of their negotiations with the Russians. Japanese opinion was understandably incensed at the Russian takeover of Port Arthur, which they had been forced to relinquish in 1895. Once Russia's negotiations with China for the lease on the Liaotung peninsula were concluded, its attitude towards Japan hardened quite markedly.

Japan's proposal that St Petersburg and Tokyo should regard Manchuria and Korea as their respective spheres of influence (known as *Man-Kan kokan*) was rejected outright. The most that Japan obtained from the Nishi-Rosen agreement of April 1898 was recognition of its commercial and industrial interests in Korea. Russia would not concede any right to predominance in Korea to Japan, such as it was claiming for itself in Manchuria. In 1898 Japan's leaders opted for 'safety first' under the pro-Russian leadership of Ito, but some politicians and diplomats began to think of an alliance with Britain as a means of resisting Russia.

In London, however, British ministers were thinking in terms of an alliance with Germany as the best way to check Russian expansion. Chamberlain, in typical fashion, campaigned with great gusto in favour of the 'natural alliance' of the Anglo-Saxon and Teutonic nations, whose interests in China were allegedly 'absolutely identical'. Oblivious to the fact that his policy was based on false premises, as Salisbury correctly perceived, Chamberlain pursued the mirage of an Anglo-German alliance between 1898 and 1901. In a memorandum of September 1900, he suggested that 'both in China and elsewhere it is in our interest that Germany should throw herself across the path of Russia.'

The reality was that Germany's trade with China did not justify the risk of a clash with Russia, whose entanglement in the Far East was pure gain from Berlin's point of view. Moreover, the German Foreign Office based its response to Chamberlain on a miscalculation. Holstein believed that time was on Germany's side because the British empire would soon have to fight for its existence against Russia. This would enable Germany to dictate the terms of an alliance. Meanwhile Germany should 'keep hope shimmering on the horizon' by concluding an innocuous agreement with Britain on China in October 1900, which Berlin called the 'Yangtse' agreement.

The designation was significant, in that the two powers were only committed to defend the 'open door' in China 'as far as they can exercise influence' and to consult together if China's territorial integrity were threatened by another power. In Berlin's view there was no risk of a serious clash with Russia because the agreement did not envisage checking Russian economic activity in Manchuria and the tsar had disclaimed to the Kaiser any intention of annexing the province.

Chamberlain was not the only one to be duped by Berlin's response. The Japanese were also misled into thinking that Germany regarded the maintenance of the *status quo* in China as a serious issue. Consequently Kato, the foreign minister, was keen to adhere to the Anglo-German China agreement which, he hoped, would help to wean Germany away from Russia and lead to closer ties between Japan and Britain. However, the China (or 'Yangtse') agreement of October 1900 was soon found to be wanting when the Manchurian crisis arose in the spring of 1901, as a consequence of the Boxer rising of the previous summer.

THE BOXER RISING AND THE MANCHURIAN CRISIS

The Boxer rebellion became a serious threat to European lives and property in north-east China in the summer of 1900. The empress dowager skilfully deflected the anger of the insurgents, directed initially against the weakness of the imperial government, towards European missionaries in particular and foreigners in general. In areas where the local Chinese authorities failed to take timely action there were widespread attacks on Europeans and their property. The most dramatic episode of the Boxer rising, however, was the seven-week siege of the foreign legations in Peking. The strength of the Chinese forces acting at the instigation of the court delayed the advance on the capital of an international relief force, until reinforced by a contingent of 30,000 Japanese troops. Following the lifting of the siege in mid-August 1900, Peking was savagely pillaged and north China was subjected to punitive expeditions by European forces. The supreme commander, General Count von Waldersee, seemed to be out to justify his belated arrival by the severity of the reprisals.

Russia, however, dissociated itself from the actions of the other powers by withdrawing its troops from the Peking region within a fortnight of the ending of the siege of the legations and refusing to participate in the Financial Commission that followed the rising. By contrast, the forces of the other powers remained for a year, until the terms of the settlement of the Boxer rising were finalized in the Peking Protocol of September 1901.

Russia's policy towards China in the aftermath of the Boxer rising was ambivalent. On the one hand it sought to preserve its special relationship with China by not participating in either the punitive measures or the discussion of claims against the Chinese government. On the other hand, Russia required compensation for the damage caused by the Boxers in Manchuria, especially to the railway system, but was determined to exclude other powers from interfering in its negotiations with China. The attempt to secure a privileged position for itself in Manchuria led to the crisis of 1900–1.

The Boxer rising had caught the Russians off their guard and had caused enormous damage to the railway system and other commercial interests in Manchuria. Belated reinforcements brought the strength of the Russian forces to over 150,000 to deal with attacks by Chinese troops, Boxers and, subsequently, 'bandits'. The process of pacification, undertaken with the cooperation of reliable Chinese officials, was a slow business, arousing suspicions that Russia was deliberately prolonging its military occupation of Manchuria. It was certainly the case that Witte's policy of peaceful penetration suffered a major setback, which the military and the 'annexationists' capitalized on.

Mistrust of Russia's intentions was heightened by the publication in *The Times* in January 1901 of a version of the Tseng-Alekseyev draft agreement, concluded two months earlier. This agreement, although disavowed by both Peking and St Petersburg, seemed to represent recognition by China of a *de facto* Russian protectorate over Manchuria. Furthermore, in a secret draft treaty drawn up in February 1901, Russia seemed to be demanding substantial concessions from China as the price for the evacuation of its forces from Manchuria. However, any chance of the other powers mounting a concerted opposition to Russia in defence of the 'open door' principle was sabotaged by Bülow's announcement in the Reichstag in March 1901 of Germany's 'absolute indifference' to the fate of Manchuria. Britain and Japan, who believed that the China agreement committed Germany to oppose a Russian encroachment on Manchuria, were taken aback when they discovered that this was not the case.

Uncertainty as to Russia's real intentions towards China continued throughout the remainder of the year. This is not surprising, since the Russians themselves could not agree on their objectives. Not only was there the usual divergence of views between St Petersburg and the expansionist-minded military in the Far East, especially Admiral Alekseyev, but no consensus existed among the tsar's ministers either. Whereas Witte advocated a phased withdrawal of Russian troops in return for substantial mining concessions in Manchuria, Kuropatkin, the war minister, pressed for the retention of the northern region to strengthen the Sino-Russian frontier. Lamsdorff, Muraviev's successor as foreign minister from June 1900, reputedly counselled moderation but his pronouncements tended towards prevarication.

From the viewpoint of London and Tokyo, Russia's policy towards Manchuria seemed a threat to China's integrity as well as to their own commercial interests. Denied reliable information about Russia's proposals in the extended negotiations with China from February to December 1901, they tended to assume the worst. In Japan, anti-Russian agitation grew apace throughout 1901, putting pressure on an already divided government. Negotiations with the new Russian ambassador in Tokyo in early 1901 had been limited to a proposal for the neutralization of Korea, without reference to Manchuria. The visit of the elder statesman Marquis Ito to St Petersburg in late 1901 had also failed to persuade Russia to concede Japan's claim to political dominance in Korea. Unknown to Lamsdorff, this was Russia's last chance to forestall the conclusion of an alliance between Japan and Britain.

THE ANGLO-JAPANESE ALLIANCE OF 1902

That the British government took so long to see that an alliance with Japan was the obvious and logical solution to Britain's predicament in the Far East seems, in retrospect, quite surprising. The Kaiser clearly thought this when he commented, in 1902, 'the noodles have had a lucid interval at last!' Furthermore, Hayashi, Japan's ambassador in London in the early 1900s, had suggested as early as 1895 that 'Britain and Japan together can control China and ensure the maintenance of peace in the Orient.' Curiously, the Liberal foreign secretary, shortly before losing office in June 1895, wrote to the British ambassador in Tokyo, Sir Ernest Satow, that 'our policy ought to be a close alliance with Japan'. Evidence from recently published parts of Satow's diaries suggests that the Japanese were interested in such a possibility. But the diaries also reveal that at

"PAWS OFF!"

this time Salisbury distrusted Japan, suspecting that it would join with Russia and possibly France to dismember China.

Before the occupation of Port Arthur in 1897–8, however, Salisbury had not felt serious alarm at Russian policy in the Far East. Thereafter the problem was to divine just how far Russian ambitions towards China extended – a problem complicated, as noted above, by the existence of divided counsels in St Petersburg. In London, disagreements also abounded. Whereas Salisbury sought to reach an understanding with Russia on the basis of 'spheres of preponderance', Chamberlain favoured an alliance with Germany to keep Russia in check. Lansdowne had a foot in both camps. When his persistence in pursuit of an Anglo-German alliance bore no fruit, he made a final attempt for an understanding with Russia, albeit with little hope of success, in October 1901.

By the autumn of that year there was a danger that if Britain prevaricated much longer it would miss the opportunity of an alliance with Japan. Hence, building on the cordial relations which had developed between the two states in the course of a succession of crises since 1895 and the approaches made by Hayashi since March 1901, Lansdowne took the decision in October to seek cabinet approval for an alliance with Japan.

Two factors delayed the signing of the alliance until late January 1902. First, the Japanese ambassador was not empowered to negotiate until a final approach to Russia had been rejected. Second, when the attempt was made to formulate terms for an alliance, it suddenly became clear just how divergent British and Japanese interests in the Far East were. British ministers then had to face up to the risks involved in allying with Japan.

Britain's main concern over China was the preservation of peace and the *status quo*, which entailed defending China's integrity and the principle of the 'open door'. Russia's bid for economic predominance in Manchuria, however, was not seriously disputed – it was the threat of political control, endangering China's independence, that British ministers felt had to be resisted. The fate of Korea, on the other hand, was a matter of indifference to Britain, but Lansdowne was obliged to recognize its prime importance to Japan. Furthermore, he had to concede Japan's demand 'to keep for itself an absolutely free hand as to the pretexts upon which a quarrel might be fastened on Russia as to Korean affairs', as Lansdowne put it. This meant that Britain might well find itself drawn into a war against Russia and France, arising from Japan's expansionist aims in Korea over which Britain had absolutely no control. As Salisbury (who was not keen on the alliance) pointed out: 'There is no limit, and no escape. We are pledged to war.'

Despite some misgivings at the risks involved in the alliance, the British cabinet persisted with the negotiations. An important factor in their successful outcome was the powerful support Landsdowne received from the Admiralty. Selborne, the first lord, argued persuasively, if not altogether ingenuously, that an alliance with Japan would convert Britain's existing inferiority in battleships in Far Eastern waters, compared to those of France and Russia, into a comfortable preponderance of naval power.

The long delay in Japan's reply to Landsdowne's draft proposal of early November was a sign of the influence exercised in Tokyo by a powerful group of elder statesmen, the *genro*, many of whom favoured caution in Japan's policy towards Russia. How to respond to Russia's advance in the Far East had been a major problem for Japan's leaders since 1895. Anger and frustration at the loss of Japanese territorial gains because of Russian intervention after the Sino-Japanese war had necessarily been tempered by an awareness of Japan's relative military and financial weakness. But the best that could be achieved by negotiations with Russia, even after the latter's occupation of Port Arthur in 1897, was the Nishi-Rosen agreement of April 1898, which merely recognized Japan's commercial interests in Korea. This was a major setback for the policy of *Man-Kan kokan*. Even after their military occupation of Manchuria in July 1900, the Russians offered nothing more than the 'neutralization' of Korea. By the spring of 1901, the continuing Russian occupation of Manchuria had become a major issue in Japan's domestic politics as well as in its foreign policy.

Japanese resentment against Russia had grown to such an extent by the autumn of 1901 that it was doubtful if the new government in Tokyo would now regard *Man-Kan kokan* as the basis for a settlement with Russia. In August the prime minister, Katsura, was strongly in favour of an alliance with Britain, as was, of course, the war party in Japan led by Field Marshal Yamagata. However, their desire to open negotiations with Britain was held in check by the *genro*, particularly Ito, who clung to the policy of seeking an agreement with Russia. Ito's last-minute visit to St Petersburg in late 1901 to secure major concessions over Korea was a failure. This removed the last obstacle to the Katsura government's desire to pursue serious negotiations with Britain. Even so, disagreement over the terms of the alliance delayed its conclusion until the end of January 1902.

In its final form, the treaty recognized Japan's special interests in

Korea and its right to 'take such measures as may be indispensable' to safeguard them. Respect for the *status quo*, peace and the 'open door' in China and Korea also featured in the treaty. Britain's main 'let-out' from involvement in a Far Eastern war of no concern to its interests in China proper was the stipulation that the *casus foederis* only applied if one of the allies were attacked by two or more powers. While Britain was disappointed at Japan's refusal to include India within the scope of the alliance, the Japanese had to be satisfied with a formula that did not bind Britain to maintain its existing naval strength in the Far East.

Whether it was wise, in the long term, for Britain to side with the war party in Japan has been questioned ever since Pearl Harbor and the fall of Singapore in 1941. In the short term, the alliance was clearly a gamble that paid off in that Britain did not have to participate in the Russo-Japanese war of 1904–5, which effectively ended the Russian threat to China.

Whether the alliance of 1902 ended Britain's so-called 'splendid isolation' is not so clear. Britain certainly took on a military/naval commitment to fight in virtually unspecified circumstances, but the treaty with Japan was essentially a regional pact, confined to the Far East. It was an 'entangling alliance', but much less so than an alliance with Germany would have been; such an alliance, advocated by Chamberlain and Balfour, would have ruled out a *rapprochement* with France and Russia.

THE ANGLO-FRENCH ENTENTE OF 1904

Britain's alliance with Japan not only kept open the option on a *rapprochement* with France; it also, strangely enough, provided a powerful impetus to the conclusion of an entente in April 1904. Some historians go even further. A. J. P. Taylor, for example, asserts that 'The Far East, and the Far East alone, caused the Anglo-French entente.' Langhorne, more judiciously, suggests that 'The 1902 alliance was not the only cause of the Anglo-French Entente, but it was a very important one.' How could a colonial agreement, whose substance was a deal over Egypt and Morocco, be so closely related to the crisis in the Far East and the alliance with Japan?

Langhorne's explanation is relatively straightforward – it exemplifies the interlocking nature of international affairs in an age of global imperial rivalries. Taylor's is more complex, being based on Delcassé's miscalculation of the prospects of war in the Far East which, the French ambassador in London observed in something of an understatement, 'inspired in all a desire to limit the conflict'. The nightmare scenario of Britain and France having to fight against each other as the 'seconds' of their allies (Japan and Russia) was quite a powerful inducement to London and Paris to settle their own colonial quarrels so as to make an Anglo-French conflict unthinkable. In addition, both sides viewed the Entente Cordiale as a necessary preliminary to an Anglo-Russian understanding, which Delcassé was particularly eager to promote.

Curiously enough, this was perhaps the only common factor in the French and British strategies for reaching a colonial agreement. As Christopher Andrew's study of Delcassé shows, the French foreign minister was a very late convert to the idea that French pretensions towards Egypt would have to be sacrificed for the sake of France's aspirations in Morocco. Although leading French colonialists had come to this conclusion soon after Fashoda, Delcassé himself did not come round to it until February 1903.

Delcassé's original ideas on how to eliminate the friction arising from Britain's presence in Egypt were somewhat bizarre. After the foolhardy Fashoda expedition had failed to bring about Britain's withdrawal from Egypt, he resorted to plotting with Germany. Responding to Marschall's invitation 'to limit the insatiable appetite of England', Delcassé offered in February 1900 'not to hinder Germany in other parts of Africa where she may have ambitions'. The Kaiser's clever footwork over the proposed Continental League against Britain during the Boer war, however, left Delcassé disillusioned with Germany – but no better disposed towards Britain.

This is shown clearly in his strategy for establishing a French predominance in Morocco. Direct negotiations with the sultan were accompanied by separate talks with Italy and Spain to secure their acceptance of France's ambitions. To the dismay of the French ambassador in London, Paul Cambon, Britain was to be presented with a *fait accompli*, with no concessions apart from an 'open door' commercial arrangement and the neutralization of Tangier.

It was Cambon's distaste for this underhand policy which led him in 1901–2 to make unofficial approaches to Lansdowne for a colonial settlement covering Siam, the Newfoundland fisheries and Morocco. Although Lansdowne was favourable in principle to the elimination of vexatious issues, he rejected coming to terms 'on so questionable a basis', as he put it. In other words there was little in these proposals of advantage to Britain, who preferred the *status quo* in Morocco to a French predominance, which would be harmful to British influence and possibly to its commerce.

By the spring of 1903, however, a mutually advantageous colonial settlement seemed possible. The outbreak of revolts against the sultan in December 1902 convinced Lansdowne that the *status quo* in Morocco was no longer tenable. Two months later, Delcassé reluctantly agreed to the inclusion of Egypt in the scope of the discussions. The centrepiece of an agreement had thereby been established, with good prospects for a successful outcome to the negotiations. Even so, there were numerous technically complex and contentious claims to be resolved covering Siam, west Africa, Madagascar and Newfoundland, which delayed the signing of the agreement until April 1904.

Several factors created the more cordial atmosphere in which these difficult negotiations took place and helped to sustain the momentum when they began to flag. Edward VII performed a valuable public relations exercise by making a royal visit to Paris in May 1903, which turned out to be a triumph of personality over an initially sullen or hostile reception from the pro-Boer Parisian crowds. Taken together with President Loubet's successful return visit to London in July, this exchange of courtesies seemed to show that public opinion on both sides of the Channel was receptive to the idea of an entente, after two decades of rivalry and distrust. Some organs of the press, notably the *National Review* and *La Dépêche coloniale*, advocated an agreement over Egypt and Morocco in the early summer of 1903, a policy naturally favoured by the anti-German elements in politics and the press.

Such attitudes were no more than favourable omens for an entente. The real catalysts were to be found in Egypt and Asia. The prospect of freeing the government of Egypt from the obstructive policies pursued by France in the International Debt Commission prompted Lord Cromer, the British administrator, to urge Lansdowne to make concessions to France at critical moments in the negotiations when a successful outcome seemed in doubt. For Lansdowne, however, the main objective in pursuing an entente with France may well have been the expectation that it would facilitate a *rapprochement* with Russia, which Keith Wilson regards as being 'the primary goal of British foreign policy since the late 1890s'.

Until 1904, however, the Russians saw little reason to forego their numerous opportunities to threaten British interests, from the Middle East, through central Asia, to the Far East, when Britain had little to offer in return. Although, much to Germany's disappointment, Britain had avoided a direct clash with Russia, the growing tension between Japan and Russia in the course of 1903 made a conflict seem imminent. Lansdowne's fear that the Franco-Russian alliance would operate in the Far East, thus creating the *casus foederis* of the Anglo-Japanese alliance, was a powerful incentive to proceed with the negotiations with France. Delcassé, on the other hand, was much less alarmed than Lansdowne because on the basis of misleading reassurances from the Russians he was convinced that peace would prevail. The realization that he had misread the situation induced Delcassé in early 1904 to expedite the negotiations with Britain.

The Anglo-French agreement removed French objections to British control of Egypt in return for recognition of France's aspirations to assert its influence over Morocco. In both states the principle of commercial liberty was to be upheld for a period of thirty years. Much of the text of the agreement consisted of a settlement of disputed claims across the globe: the New Hebrides; the Newfoundland fisheries, where French rights dated back to 1714; frontier delimitation in west Africa; Madagascar; and Siam. Most of these issues were technical and complex rather than important in themselves. These obscure problems do signify, however, that the basis of the entente was the desire to liquidate the friction arising from twenty years of imperial rivalry and to foster more cordial relations in the future.

There is little evidence that the Anglo-French entente was animated by a spirit of hostility towards Germany on the part of the British cabinet as a whole. Rather it reflects the Conservative government's preoccupation with imperial problems, in which France or Russia, not Germany, had been Britain's main adversary. This is not to deny that Lansdowne recognized that 'Germany might make difficulties for us all' over the entente and made provision for mutual diplomatic support against it, but he was anticipating trouble over Egypt, not Morocco. It was the German decision to provoke a major crisis with France over Morocco, first in 1905 and again in 1911, that was responsible for turning the Anglo-French entente into a quasi-alliance, directed against Germany. This development, however, was neither predictable in 1904 nor inevitable (and probably not even desirable) as far as the British government was concerned.

The same could not be said of France. Delcassé's long-term strategy, conceived in 1898, was to align Britain with the Franco-Russian alliance with the aim of creating an anti-German front in European affairs. This objective, however, would not have met with a sympathetic response from the Conservative governments that held office from 1895 to December 1905, several of whose most prominent figures were hopeful of concluding an alliance with Germany during the period 1898–1901. By 1902, however, an anti-German aspect to the prospective entente with France had begun to emerge, personified by Chamberlain who, after his rebuff by Bülow, became an ardent advocate of closer ties with France. Parts of the press, notably *The Times* and the *Spectator*, had also become outspokenly anti-German, while some of the service chiefs were more discreetly so. In addition, deep suspicion of Germany's motives was beginning to cloud the judgement of a group of increasingly influential Foreign Office officials, dubbed 'the Excitables', several of whom were later to hold important posts in Whitehall or as ambassadors in key European capitals.

The Entente Cordiale of 1904 seemed to many contemporaries to mark a further move away from the idea of 'splendid isolation' that had supposedly been the basis of British foreign policy for several decades. Lansdowne himself spoke, in November 1905, of having abandoned that idea on the grounds that 'we must do as other Powers do, who are distributed in groups.' Those who advocated the abandonment of isolation, as Chamberlain had since 1898, appeared to have a good case, as Monger has shown. Before the turn of the century Britain was already experiencing serious challenges to its former ascendancy as the leading industrial, imperial and naval power. While Germany was Britain's main industrial competitor, Russia and France were its most dangerous imperial rivals.

Control of the Mediterranean, a vital link in the shorter sea route to the east, was no longer completely assured. At the same time, Russia's continuing advance across Asia, facilitated by the construction of strategic railways such as the Orenburg-Tashkent line, created alarm over the security of India. The Trans-Siberian railway likewise seemed a potential threat to British interests in the Far East. The Franco-Russian alliance, whose scope was not precisely known, increased the vulnerability of the British empire. Not only did French capital make its ally's railway expansion possible, but the combined strength of the two fleets made retaining the Two Power Standard very burdensome. Since 1890 several new navies had come into existence. Yet for Britain, naval supremacy was deemed essential to the life blood of the nation, as an island power boasting 9 million tons of shipping and a seaborne trade of £12 million per annum. To many contemporary politicians it seemed obvious that Britain's global commitments outstripped the country's resources – 'the weary Titan', as Chamberlain put it, 'staggering under the too vast orb of his fate'.

Government expenditure had risen by about 50 per cent between 1895 and 1902, excluding the cost of the Boer war, with half of the new total of £147 million being accounted for by the army and navy estimates. When, in the wake of the Boer war, came revelations of British military inadequacies and of the extent of the hostility of public opinion on the continent towards Britain, the pessimism of some politicians in London is understandable. Balfour glumly concluded that Britain would be relegated to the rank of a third-rate power unless it secured a continental ally.

Despite the appearance that the entente with France, following only two years after the alliance with Japan, marked a clear break with Britain's traditional foreign policy, it is arguable that the treaty was not a new departure. It could well be regarded as a realization of attempts spread over the previous twenty years to resolve conflicting colonial claims. Furthermore, some historians have pointed out that more harmonious relations with France had the effect of increasing Britain's independence of its European neighbours, so that, but for the Moroccan crisis of 1905, the country could have become more 'detached' from the continent after 1904.

Ironically, Britain's earlier anxieties about maintaining its naval supremacy over France and Russia ended dramatically with Japan's defeat of the Russian Baltic fleet in May 1905. As a consequence, Taylor observes, 'the British enjoyed a naval supremacy without parallel in their history.' In similar fashion, Japan's military victories seriously impaired Russia's capacity to threaten British interests in central Asia and the Far East. In 1905, Taylor suggests, 'Isolation, far from dwindling, reached its peak.' This was the unexpected bonus for Britain of the Russo-Japanese war.

THE ORIGINS OF THE RUSSO-JAPANESE WAR

For two years before the outbreak of the Russo-Japanese war in February 1904, Russia was engaged in two sets of separate, but related, negotiations. In talks with China, the Russians were attempting to extract concessions in return for the withdrawal of their forces from Manchuria. In the negotiations with Japan, Russia's aim was to parry Japanese demands for recognition of their claim to predominance in Korea. These negotiations were characterized by endless prevarication and delay on Russia's part, to some extent as a result of the confusion and uncertainty surrounding Russian policy in the Far East. There is also evidence to suggest that the Russians were negotiating in bad faith with regard to both Manchuria and Korea.

St Petersburg's main stance in the negotiations was that Manchuria was an issue that concerned Russia and China exclusively. Other powers therefore had no right to try to influence the Chinese government to reject or amend the terms Russia offered. Although the Boxer upheavals in Manchuria had certainly involved Russia in heavy expenditure, the root of the problem was, Geyer argues, that the economic gamble implicit in Witte's policy had not paid off. Between 1897 and 1902 Russia had made an enormous outlay on constructing railways and ports, at a cost almost equivalent to the total state budget in 1903. But the revenues derived from transcontinental freight were only a tenth of the amount needed for profitability. Nor had the anticipated 'economic conquest' of northern China by Russian industries materialized. Hence Russia's determination to exclude foreign competition in defiance of the 'open door' principle. Although the opening of the Chinese Eastern Railway in July 1903 was a great boost to Russian prestige, the tangible benefits from the creation of a direct railway link from the Baltic to the Pacific were disappointingly small. The simple fact that most of the equipment for the Manchurian railways was of non-Russian origin highlights, perhaps, the fatal flaw in Witte's grand (or grandiose) design.

Russia's reluctance to abandon the dream of oriental wealth and return Manchuria to full Chinese sovereignty is therefore quite understandable. The convention signed with China in April 1902, providing for a three-stage evacuation of Manchuria over eighteen months, was little more than a tactical device. Although the first stage of the withdrawal was more or less carried out, there was little further progress.

By the summer of 1903 Russia's leaders had discussed a variety of options, ranging from the annexation of Manchuria to a complete evacuation, but they had still not defined their aims in the Far East. Divergent views abounded in St Petersburg. The tsar wavered, but hankered after incorporating Manchuria into the Russian empire; a policy encouraged by adventurers such as Bezobrazov, with an eye to profitable enterprises in Korea, and by expansionist-minded officers like Admiral Alekseyev. Those who favoured a more restrained policy, such as Lamsdorff, Witte and the war minister, Kuropatkin, had an uphill struggle in the series of conferences held in the spring of 1903. When the tsar decided in August 1903 to decentralize decision-making by creating a viceroyalty of the Far

East under Admiral Alekseyev, it not only made the confusion of responsibilities even worse but also signified the waning of the influence of the moderates. This was reinforced by Witte's removal from the Finance Ministry.

It is hardly surprising, therefore, that the other powers regarded Russian policy in the Far East as full of ambiguity and contradictions. When no reliance could be placed on the reassuring pronouncements of its foreign minister, a serious credibility gap existed in Russian diplomacy. Lamsdorff's efforts during his visit to Paris in October 1903 to secure French and British sympathy for Russia's problems in Manchuria were therefore largely unavailing, especially when Alekseyev broke off negotiations with China at this very time and reoccupied Mukden with Russian troops. Russia's real aims were becoming harder than ever to decipher. The January 1904 announcement of a guarantee of the treaty rights of other powers in Manchuria, following shortly after Alekseyev's assertion that Russia did not intend to evacuate the province, hardly constituted a major clarification of Russian policy. The purpose of the announcement in fact was probably to imply that Russia now regarded Manchuria as a matter of concern to the whole international community, in order to exclude it from the agenda of the negotiations with Japan, which had begun in 1902.

Japan's aim in initiating direct negotiations with Russia was to secure a privileged position for itself in Korea, comparable to that held by Russia in Manchuria. This aim was acceptable to Britain as in keeping with the spirit of the Anglo-Japanese alliance. It was naturally regarded as much preferable to a Russo-Japanese conflict which Britain might be drawn into, regardless of its lack of interest in Korea.

Japan's negotiating stance was fairly flexible but it concealed long-term aims which were highly expansionist. Nish maintains that until 1904 most of Japan's leaders would have settled for a deal along the lines of the 1898 *Man-Kan kokan* proposal, providing the country was not bound by a formula that obliged it to be 'disinterested' in the fate of Manchuria. If Russia would concede nothing more than Japanese predominance in the south of Korea, then Japan would insist on full recognition of its commercial interests in Manchuria and restrict Russian rights there to 'special railway interests'. Nor would Japan allow Russia to exert a political or strategic influence in north Korea through 'neutralization' of the region.

The political leadership in Japan, as in Russia, included both expansionists and conciliators in its ranks, but this did not result in the confusion of aims that bedevilled Russian policy. The crucial difference between the two states, however, lay in the existence in Japan of a war party, whose influence grew with each successive Russian refusal to offer worthwhile concessions to the moderates in Tokyo. The Russians also failed to take account of Japan's sensitivity to slights, reinforced by memories of the humiliation inflicted by Russia in 1895. The postponement of further negotiations because of the tsar's addiction to long holidays in the Crimea for most of the autumn, or for other seemingly trivial reasons, was interpreted by the Japanese as a sign that the Russians regarded them as a second-rate power.

Hence although the negotiations began quite promisingly in the summer of 1902, they failed to develop a momentum. In September Lamsdorff seemed willing to negotiate a new agreement recognizing the paramount interest of each state in Manchuria and Korea respectively, but then he suggested a postponement of the talks to December, or even until the following April. In early January, however, Witte's colleagues rejected his proposal to allow Japan a free hand in Korea and decided to wait and see what the Japanese proposed. But at the resumption of negotiations in August 1903 the Russian position seemed little different from the one adopted in 1898, denying Japan a position in Korea that mirrored Russia's position in Manchuria.

By December 1903, the lack of serious progress in the talks convinced even russophiles such as Ito that Russia was merely playing for time until its armaments programme enabled St Petersburg to dictate the fate of both Korea and Manchuria. Although the tsar insisted genuinely enough that Russia did not want war in the Far East, his ministers failed to respond to the clear signs of pressure on the government in Tokyo in favour of war. The army and navy staff had concluded early in 1903 that war with Russia was inevitable. The army chiefs, but not the navy, were pressing for war from the summer onwards and in mid-January 1904 Russia was sent a virtual ultimatum. The few concessions made by Russia were too little and too late to prevent the formal breaking off of the negotiations on 6 February, which was followed two days later by a surprise attack on Port Arthur and the invasion of Korea.

It is hard to avoid the conclusion that the Russians, who wanted peace in the Far East, at least for another year or so, played into the hands of those groups and forces in Japan which had actively campaigned for war for at least six months before its outbreak. Russia's refusal to concede anything like parity to Japanese aspirations towards Korea weakened the position of the moderates, who still favoured a cautious approach. In the broader international context, the Russians also put themselves in the wrong by their continuing occupation of Manchuria, despite their undertaking in April 1902 to withdraw their forces in stages. By failing to define their policy towards Manchuria, the Russians created widespread suspicion of their aims and destroyed the credibility of the pronouncements of their diplomats. The sheer incompetence of the tsarist regime was seemingly a major factor in the outbreak of a war that Russia could have, and should have, avoided.

The war was a long drawn-out struggle, involving fierce land fighting in Manchuria. It was not until early January 1905 that the Japanese took Port Arthur. Mukden fell to them after a long siege in March. The most dramatic event was, perhaps, the destruction of the Baltic fleet by Admiral Togo at the battle of Tsushima Straits in May 1905, which ended Russia's hopes of cutting off the Japanese armies from their homeland bases. Through the mediation of President Roosevelt, peace talks eventually bore fruit in September 1905. Korea became a Japanese sphere of influence and the Russians agreed to abandon southern Manchuria, transferring their railway rights there to Japan. The war was obviously a major disaster for Russia, but Japanese opinion was not at all satisfied with the gains made in the peace treaty.

THE ANGLO-RUSSIAN ENTENTE OF 1907

The signing of the entente with Russia in August 1907 represented, for Britain, the realization of an important aim of a decade of diplomacy. For Russia, on the other hand, the entente was more a reluctant admission that 'adventurism' in the Far East had entailed excessive risks to its reputation as a great power. In both London and Paris the Anglo-Russian entente was regarded as a natural complement to their Entente Cordiale. From the viewpoint of St Petersburg, however, the entente had involved a choice between the blandishments emanating from Berlin and the more tangible benefits obtainable from the Parisian banks.

The British desire for an agreement with Russia stemmed mainly from the vulnerability of their Indian empire and the related fear of growing Russian influence in Persia. By the 1870s the Russian advance through Turkestan had made the Russian empire and Afghanistan almost coterminous. Afghanistan thereby became a 'buffer state' between the tsarist empire and British India, providing splendid opportunities for intrigue and friction, as shown in the Afghan war of 1878–9. Further crises followed in 1885 over Pendjeh and in 1892–4 over the Pamirs. The Pendjeh crisis, following the Russian annexation of Merv in 1884, was a dangerous one, resulting from a second line of advance, facilitated by a strategic railway, from the Caspian Sea to Merv – a mere 200 miles from Herat in north-west Afghanistan. Herat's location, adjacent to the ill-defined frontier with Persia, made it accessible to a Russian move from Merv, or even from northern Persia, where Russian influence was quite strong by the 1880s.

Although all this was part of the 'Great Game', to distract attention away from the Balkans, the British government, as Geyer observes, 'reacted with nervous hostility to the spread of Russian power in Asia'. Understandably so, when even the pan-Slavist editor Katkov could wonder: 'What would England be without India?' For the Russian government, however, expansion in central Asia was a rewarding game with few risks, as revealed by a comment by one of the tsar's ministers in 1866: 'General Chernyaev has taken Tashkent and nobody knows why.' Campaigns in Turkestan and Trancaspia provided the tsarist regime with cheap glory and prestige as well as the opportunity to score off 'the mighty British Empire'. The only real risk the Russians ran was that St Petersburg might lose control over the politically ambitious 'men on the spot' or the 'Turkestanians', the adventurous military commanders (clones of the *officiers soudanais* in west Africa?), as nearly happened in 1885. This could have led to an Anglo-Russian war endangering, not strengthening, Russia's European interests.

The connection between crises in Asia and in the Balkans was quite explicit in 1878 and 1885. British ministers suspected as much, but they could not afford to take risks. Consequently the British government, and even more so the government of India, took the 'Great Game' very seriously, as shown by the doubling of British military strength (to 70,000 men) between 1884 and 1894. Britain's status as a great power was regarded as inextricably linked to the retention of its empire. In Curzon's view, 'as long as we rule India, we are the greatest power in the world', but the loss of India would reduce Britain to the rank of a third-rate power.

Since Russian intrigues in Afghanistan or Persia could not be countered by sending warships through the Khyber Pass, London faced the daunting prospect in the early 1900s that, in the event of war with Russia, a further 100,000 men (twice the number that was actually available) would be needed for the defence of India. Two

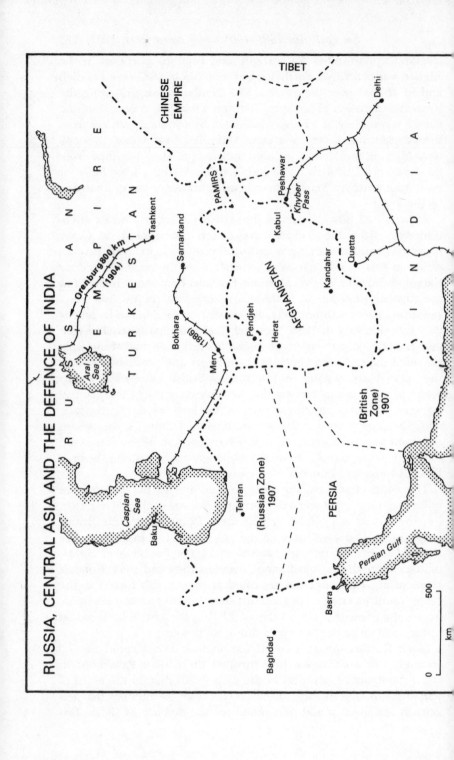

RUSSIA, CENTRAL ASIA AND THE DEFENCE OF INDIA

TIBET

CHINESE
EMPIRE

Delhi

PAMIRS

Tashkent

Peshawar

Samarkand

Khyber
Pass

Kabul

R U S S I A N   E M P I R E

Orenburg 800 km
(1904)

Kandahar

Quetta

Bokhara

T U R K E S T A N

AFGHANISTAN

(1886)

Pendjeh

Aral
Sea

Merv

Herat

I   N   D   I   A

Caspian
Sea

(British
Zone)
1907

Tehran

(Russian Zone)
1907

Baku

PERSIA

Persian Gulf

Basra

Baghdad

500

km

0

factors had made the problem more intractable by the turn of the century. First, the financial burden of rising military expenditure seemed to require raising income tax above the level then regarded as tolerable (a shilling in the pound) by the prosperous classes. Second, it was no longer possible to retaliate against Russian threats to India by sending a fleet to threaten Russia's Black Sea coast.

Denial of this traditional riposte, through the protests of the other powers at the time of the Pendjeh crisis in 1885, was followed in the 1890s by the realization that 'forcing the Straits' was no longer a viable option. Turkish hostility, reinforced by the Franco-Russian alliance, involved too many hazards for naval operations in the Black Sea. In a sense, therefore, Britain lost its most effective means of countering Russian threats in Asia at about the time when further railway development enabled its adversary to put large numbers of troops within striking distance of Kandahar or Kabul. This 'sword of Damocles hanging over Britain's head', as a British minister later called it, placed London under even more pressure from belligerent viceroys, such as Curzon, to adopt a 'forward policy' by extending British influence or control over regions adjacent to the Indian frontier, namely Afghanistan, Tibet and Persia.

Russia's growing influence in Persia, where the authority of the shah was declining (despite his bodyguard of a brigade of Cossacks) was seen as a challenge to Britain's exclusive position on the Persian Gulf, as well as yet another threat to India's borders. With the advantage of a common frontier, the Russians were able to dominate northern Persia quite easily by military means, aided by a tariff treaty and a readiness to offer loans to the shah's shaky regime. Britain's response was largely limited to preventing the southward spread of Russian influence towards India. Without government guarantees, British banks and financiers were most reluctant to provide loans which might produce political benefits but little or no return on the capital.

Although the tension generated by Russia's forward moves in Afghanistan in the 1880s and 1890s had been eased by negotiations, Russian expansion in the Far East provoked new crises in 1898 and 1901, which underlined the desirability for Britain of reaching an accord with St Petersburg. During the Port Arthur crisis Salisbury had sought an agreement with Russia in January 1898, regarding their mutual interests in the Chinese and Turkish empires. In a well-known phrase, he suggested to Muraviev: 'We aim at no partition of territory, but only a partition of preponderance.' This first British proposal for a general understanding to reduce friction with Russia met with only limited success in the form of the 1899 agreement on railway concessions.

Lansdowne's efforts for a *détente* in 1901–2 during the crisis over Manchuria also failed, despite Lamsdorff's more conciliatory attitude, because the expansionists had the ear of the tsar. His persistence with negotiations in 1903, when Japan seemed bellicose, eventually resulted in the tsar's acceptance of the principle of an entente with Britain in May 1904, but by then the war with Japan had already begun. The war soured Anglo-Russian relations because Britain was held responsible for Japan's temerity in attacking Russia. Worse still, the attack on British fishing trawlers near Dogger Bank by the Baltic fleet *en route* to the Far East in October 1904, in mistake for Japanese torpedo boats (the vodka factor?) created a serious crisis for some weeks.

When Grey became foreign secretary in the new Liberal government in December 1905 he was anxious to renew the approach to Russia, with the result that formal negotiations began in June 1906. Grey's desire for an entente with Russia is usually ascribed to his concern for the balance of power in Europe. Russia's weakness after its defeat in 1905, combined with signs of the growth of German power, created a disequilibrium. His anxiety over Germany was reflected in a comment made in February 1906 that 'an entente between Russia, France, and ourselves would be absolutely secure. If it is necessary to check Germany, it could then be done.' Hence also Grey's desire to see Russia acting again as 'a factor in European politics', since, as he said, 'it is urgently desirable that Russia's influence should be re-established in the Councils of Europe.' Nevertheless, Keith Wilson insists that 'the Anglo-Russian Agreement was devised in the interests of England's Imperial position, not for the sake of the balance of power in Europe', despite the evidence that Grey (like some of his predecessors) was at times sceptical about Russia's ability to threaten the frontiers of India. Since Grey's objectives may well have been twofold, the argument may not amount to much more than a question of emphasis.

Whereas Britain's continental and imperial interests coincided in seeking a *rapprochement* with Russia, for the tsarist government an entente with Britain meant making a choice between Russia's imperial and European interests. If Russia abandoned the French connection in favour of an alliance with Germany, it would be free to pursue expansionist policies in the Middle East and central Asia, an attractive option that would be denied by an entente with Britain. But by 1906 Russia's earlier hostility to a *détente* with London had softened, partly because Britain was no longer at odds with France in colonial matters. Above all, Russia's defeat by Japan, together with the outbreak of revolution in Russia in 1905, obliged the tsarist regime to reappraise its policies. The basic question for Russia in 1905–6, therefore, was whether the overriding need for peace and security could best be achieved by alignment with Paris and London, or by responding to the overtures from Berlin.

Before the negotiations with Britain began in June 1906, the tsar had already been tempted twice by the offer of a Russo-German alliance. Germany's first bid was made in October 1904, at the time of the Dogger Bank incident, whose peaceful outcome was a grave disappointment to Berlin. The second was made during the crisis with France over Morocco, when the tsar succumbed to the Kaiser's pressure, during their private meeting at Björkö in July 1905, to conclude an alliance. That some elements in Russia were tempted to side with Germany in an anti-British front is not surprising. Britain was regarded as having incited Japan against Russia and of having adopted an attitude far short of neutrality in the ensuing war.

Despite resentment against Britain, however, Russia was hardly in a position to coerce France into joining a tripartite alliance with Germany, as the Björkö agreement implied. Paris was more important to Russia than Berlin, if only because near bankruptcy made further French loans essential to Russian recovery. This dependence was even made explicit when France demanded Russia's diplomatic support at the international conference on Morocco in early 1906. The power of the financial weapon was also shown in April 1906, as Lieven observes, when the Russian chief of staff agreed to the French request to drop the clauses of the 1900 military agreement relating to a war against Britain, despite the army's strongly pro-German views.

In addition to the financial factor, there were a number of other reasons why Russia remained loyal to the alliance with France. The fundamental one was probably a persistent mistrust of Germany. There were fears that the German empire's military preponderance in Europe would place Russia in a subordinate position where it would experience, sooner or later, the burdensome nature of the 'German yoke'. To diplomats such as Lamsdorff, it seemed important not to abandon the European balance of power. But without an improvement in Anglo-Russian relations, the Franco-Russian alliance itself would be put under considerable strain, whereas an entente with Britain would strengthen it and encourage collaboration in European affairs.

Russian interests in Asia also worked in Britain's favour. German ambitions in the Middle East, exemplified by the Berlin-Baghdad railway project, caused Russia some alarm and suggested that Germany might become an adversary in the Middle East and Persia. Furthermore, in the Far East Russia's position was so precarious after its defeat that an entente with Japan's ally could be advantageous, by imposing some restraint on those elements in Japan which were discontented with the peace terms agreed in 1905. In a sense, the very weakness of Russia counselled against an alliance with Germany, in case Berlin exploited it, and inclined the country towards a closer relationship with Britain and France. Even so, Izvolsky, the new foreign minister in 1906, did not embark on serious negotiations with Britain until he was reassured, from his visit to Berlin in October 1906, that Germany did not object to a Russian *rapprochement* with Britain.

The terms of the entente agreed after a year of hard bargaining dealt with Afghanistan, Tibet and Persia. In accepting that Afghanistan was exclusively a British sphere of influence, Russia abandoned its earlier efforts to establish direct relations with the amir. These had caused great anxiety to the government of India, especially after the establishment of a long, common Russo-Afghan frontier in 1903. The mutual recognition of Tibet's territorial integrity meant that the Liberal government was prepared to abandon the 'forward policy', exemplified by the Younghusband expedition of 1904, adopted by the government of India under the Conservative administration. Grey was content to use Tibet as a *cordon sanitaire* against a Russian advance.

Both sides regarded Persia as the central issue of the negotiations and desired to reach an agreement before German intervention in the region caused additional complications. Persia was divided into three zones, with a neutral area separating the large Russian sphere of influence in the north from the smaller British zone in the south, adjacent to the Indian frontier. This was a tacit recognition of Russia's success in establishing its political and economic influence in northern Persia. Grey's objective in settling for a smaller British zone was based on strategic, not commercial, considerations. Even so, the viability of the agreement depended on Russian respect for both the spirit and the letter of the terms of the treaty. With regard to the Persian gulf, Grey also accepted a rather vague formula in which Russia merely recognized Britain's interest in the maintenance of the *status quo* there.

The terms of the agreement were criticized in both countries but the fact remains that, at least on paper, Russia made the most concessions. St Petersburg's acceptance of the terms was made easier by Grey's willingness to consider a review of the question of the Straits in a sense favourable to Russia, which Izvolsky deemed 'a great evolution in the relations of the two countries'. The strongest critics of the agreement in Russia were to be found in the military establishment – the counterpart, on the British side, of the government of India.

Although the entente did produce an improvement in Anglo-Russian relations after 1907, there was little of the cordiality that accompanied the entente with France. A major reason for this, apart from the obvious differences in the British perception of the French as against the Russians, was that Russia persistently failed to honour the spirit of the agreement on Persia, which became a highly contentious issue in the years prior to 1914.

The Anglo-Russian entente did not acquire the attributes of a quasi-military alliance which complicated the Anglo-French relationship by 1912 and reduced the flexibility of Britain's relations with Germany. Even so, Grey's insistence that a 'Triple Entente', as such, did not exist did not carry much credibility in Berlin, which believed that the effect of the 1907 entente was to complete the 'encirclement' of Germany.

SOURCES AND FURTHER READING

Andrew, C., *T. Delcassé and the Making of the Entente Cordiale*, London, Macmillan, 1968.

Brailey, N., 'Sir Ernest Satow, Japan and Asia', *Historical Journal* 1992, vol. 35(1): 115–50.

Fieldhouse, D. K., *Economics and Empire 1830–1914*, London, Weidenfeld & Nicolson, 1973.

Geyer, D., *Russian Imperialism 1860–1914* (transl. B. Little), Leamington Spa, Berg, 1987.

Langhorne, R., *The Collapse of the Concert of Europe 1890–1914*, London, Macmillan, 1981.

Lieven, D. C. B., *Russia and the Origins of the First World War*, London, Macmillan, 1983.

Lowe, C. J., *The Reluctant Imperialists. British Foreign Policy 1878–1902*, vol. 1, London, Routledge & Kegan Paul, 1967.

Lowe, C. J. and Dockrill, M. L., *The Mirage of Power. British Foreign Policy 1902–14*, vol. 1, London, Routledge & Kegan Paul, 1972.

Lowe, P., *Britain in the Far East*, Harlow, Longman, 1981.
Malozemoff, A., *Russian Far Eastern Policy 1881–1904*, Berkeley, Calif., University of California Press, 1958.
Monger, G. W., *The End of Isolation*, London, Nelson, 1963.
Nish, I. A., *The Anglo-Japanese Alliance*, London, Athlone Press, 1966.
Taylor, A. J. P., *The Struggle for Mastery in Europe 1848–1918*, Oxford, Clarendon Press, 1954.
Wilson, K. M., *The Policy of the Entente*, Cambridge, Cambridge University Press, 1985.
Young, L. K., *British Policy in China, 1895–1902*, Oxford, Oxford University Press, 1970.

European activities in China are well summarized in Fieldhouse. Geyer is very informative on Russian policy, which is also described in detail in Malozemoff's older work. British policy in the Far East is briefly analysed in Lowe's *Reluctant Imperialists* (which has useful documents in volume 2) and is presented more descriptively in Peter Lowe's more recent outline study. Young's is a fuller and very interesting treatment. The standard work on the Anglo-Japanese alliance is by Nish.

The origins of the entente of 1904 are convincingly explored, from the British side, by Monger. Delcassé's role is illuminated in a masterly fashion by Christopher Andrew. Lieven is not as useful on the 1907 entente as the *Mirage of Power.* Wilson gives a controversial reappraisal of British foreign policy after 1904. Langhorne offers interesting ideas on international politics after 1890. Chapters 17 and 18 of Taylor are stimulating, as usual.

5 *Weltpolitik*, the navy and Anglo-German relations, 1897–1913

The year 1897 is generally regarded as the beginning of a new era in German foreign policy. The inauguration of a 'world policy' was a conscious repudiation of Bismarck's continental policy, pursued for twenty years apart from his brief flirtation with colonies in the mid–1880s. *Weltpolitik* was also meant to give a sense of purpose to German diplomacy, which had lacked consistency since 1890. Caprivi's view of the German empire in 1890 as an essentially continental power had been challenged by a variety of pressure groups and broad sections of opinion which favoured overseas expansion. Moreover, Caprivi had also offended agrarian interests by his policy of negotiating commercial treaties to lower tariffs. Although this served to improve relations with Russia, it was not enough to undermine the Franco-Russian alliance and achieve a lasting *rapprochement* with Russia.

The Caprivi era of 1890–4 had also witnessed a marked decline in the authority of the Reich chancellorship. Wilhelm II was not the only one to take advantage of this, but his forthright declarations, combined with disagreements among ministers and the fractious behaviour of the Reichstag, weakened the prestige of the Kaiser's government. The appointment of the aged Bavarian Prince Hohenlohe to succeed Caprivi as chancellor in 1894 was unlikely, in itself, to give a sense of direction to German policy either at home or abroad.

The timing of the inauguration of a world policy, probably the only uncontroversial aspect of *Weltpolitik*, is generally related to changes of personnel in the German government. The appointment in 1897 of Admiral von Tirpitz as state secretary of the Navy Office and of Bülow as foreign minister (later chancellor), coinciding with the assertion of 'personal rule' by Wilhelm II, marked a clear break with the past. Whether it signified a clear direction for German policy in the future remained to be seen.

The Kaiser himself was enthusiastic for an expansionist foreign policy, asserting in 1898 that 'Germany had great tasks to accomplish outside the narrow boundaries of old Europe.' Precisely what these 'great tasks' were, however, remained largely undefined apart from vague assertions that Germany's future lay 'less in Europe than in the entire world'. The global manifestations of *Weltpolitik*, on the other hand, can be seen in such varied events as the occupation of Kiao-Chow, the Kaiser's visit to Damascus and the Berlin-Baghdad railway project, naval operations against Venezuela, claims to Pacific islands and negotiations for more colonial possessions in Africa.

It is hard to discern much coherence in such diverse activities except, of course, as signs of the desire to play a part on the world stage. Nevertheless, some prominent historians, especially in Germany, have attributed specific goals to *Weltpolitik*. Fischer in particular asserts that *Weltpolitik* embraced not only the construction of a powerful navy but also the determination to expand Germany's empire in central Africa (the *Mittelafrika* programme). An additional goal was to create a German-dominated customs union in central Europe (the *Mitteleuropa* programme) as a means of enlarging Germany's continental power base in order to support its pretensions to world power status.

Whether or not *Weltpolitik* contained such specific goals, there can be no doubt that embarking on a grandiose, expansionist policy would have been popular with a large section of German opinion in the 1890s. In a direct rebuttal of Bismarck's views, the editor of *Die Zukunft* asserted: 'But we are not "satiated". We need fertile land, large open areas which could buy our goods at decent prices . . . Otherwise we shall be so dwarfed that we shall become a second Belgium.' Germany's demographic and industrial growth in the late nineteenth century seemed to demand the pursuit of an ambitious overseas policy that would reflect the country's economic and military power and, once its navy had expanded, recognition of its claim to equality with the existing world empires.

Until the late 1980s, however, most historians tended to reject such an obvious explanation of the impulses behind *Weltpolitik* as being too simplistic. Instead, they followed the 'Fischer school', and to a lesser extent Wehler and others of like mind, in regarding German foreign policy from 1897 to 1914 as 'a response to the internal threat of socialism and democracy'. In other words *Weltpolitik* was a conscious attempt by the government and the ruling elites to neutralize discontent with domestic problems by seeking diplomatic successes abroad, an attitude which culminated in the decision for war in 1914. In Fischer's view the German government not only welcomed war in 1914, but also willed it in order to realize its expansionist aims, as revealed after the outbreak of war in the 'September programme' of 1914. In asserting 'the primacy of domestic policy' (*Primat der Innenpolitik*) as the key factor behind Wilhelmine foreign policy, modern German historians have turned on its head the traditional explanation of Germany's development as a nation state. Following the pioneering work of Eckart Kehr and George Hallgarten in the early 1930s, they have discounted Germany's geopolitical situation as the determining factor in the country's diplomacy (*Primat der Aussenpolitik*).

Although in a recent review of German history Herwig has stated that 'research seems to lie with Fischer', most of whose assertions (made in the 1960s) are allegedly still valid, another contributor concedes that 'a consensus about Wilhelmine Germany remains elusive.' Doubt persists particularly about the heavy, not to say exclusive, emphasis placed on domestic issues (dubbed the 'new orthodoxy') which has been challenged by two quite distinct groups of historians. Several British and American historians have disputed some of the more sweeping assertions made by protagonists of the Fischer or Wehler 'schools'. More recently still, the revival of the study of political history in West Germany in the 1980s has produced a marked swing away from many of the basic assumptions of those 'schools'.

INTERPRETATIONS OF *WELTPOLITIK*

The 'new orthodoxy' embraces the views of numerous, mainly German historians who since the 1960s have been pursuing different but related investigations into modern German history. At its fullest extent, this new orthodoxy consists of three elements. It includes the 'structural continuity thesis' of German history from 1879 to 1933. The second component, the concept of 'social imperialism', is usually regarded as relevant to the Wilhelmine period alone, although Wehler has argued for its application to the Bismarck era too. The third element, the notion of a *Sammlungspolitik* (a policy of rallying together), was initially applied only to the years 1898 to 1904, but it has been projected forwards to 1909–18 and subsequently extended backwards to 1879 as 'the key concept of an understanding of the *Kaiserreich*'.

The central domestic problem which these historians have examined from a variety of angles is the alleged peculiarity of Germany's development (or *Sonderweg*) in modern times. In essence, this consists of the view that rapid industrialization, not accompanied by political modernization, permitted the survival of influential pre-industrial elites and an authoritarian power structure. Consequently the executive power exercised by the Kaiser and his ministers, who were answerable to him rather than to parliament, was not effectively checked by the democratically elected Reichstag. Furthermore, the army, whose chiefs had direct access to the Kaiser (thus by-passing the war minister) was independent of parliamentary control. In some important respects, therefore, the appearance of constitutional government in the *Kaiserreich*, created in 1871, was little more than a façade.

It is also argued that industrialization notwithstanding, the German bourgeoisie failed to capture political power or attain social predominance. It was the *Junkers* (the old Prussian landed nobility) who continued to exercise influence at court and in politics, coopting the leaders of industry, commerce and the professions into an alliance to preserve the existing social order – a process termed the 'feudalization of the bourgeoisie'. As one historian has put it, the German empire was 'a puppet theatre with *Junkers* and industrialists pulling the strings'. The government and the ruling elites are therefore said to have had a major interest in the stabilization and preservation of the existing political system and the anachronistic social structure. They consequently devised strategies to counter threats to the *status quo*, especially those from the growing working class, which was well organized through trade unions and the Social Democratic Party, the SPD. As well as pressure for democratization of the political system, especially the notoriously unfair three-class voting system in Prussia, middle-class discontent centred on demands for making the government more accountable to the Reichstag.

The manipulative and diversionary strategies allegedly used by the regime took several forms. One of these, which Wehler calls 'social imperialism', attempted to exploit nationalist feeling as an integrating factor, particularly in the form of popular enthusiasm for an ambitious foreign policy. Widespread support for overseas expansion was utilized, according to Wehler, to block domestic progress and to defeat 'the advancing forces of parliamentarization and democratization'. Social imperialism has been summed up as a 'diversion outwards of internal tensions and forces of change to preserve the social and political *status quo*'.

Another element in the 'defensive ideology against the disruptive effects of industrialization' was the *Sammlungspolitik* inaugurated in 1897. This was allegedly an attempt to rally the 'reliable elements' in German political life behind the government through the adoption of policies which would defuse the conflict of interests between industrialists and agrarians, thereby permitting the revival of the 'alliance of iron and rye' of the Bismarckian era. The construction of a big navy would satisfy heavy industry, while the upward revision of tariffs (effected in 1902) was designed to meet the clamour of the agrarians for further protection against imported foodstuffs. Furthermore, naval policy was calculated to have a mass appeal. On the one hand, the fleet would become a symbol of German nationalism and *Kultur* in which the middle classes could take great pride, while on the other hand the working classes would be placated by the jobs made available in the busy shipyards. Hence the specific policies in *Sammlungspolitik* – 'a compromise ideology of the ruling strata of industry and agriculture' – together with the more general manipulative and diversionary strategies of social imperialism have been presented as evidence of the primacy of domestic policy in Wilhelmine Germany after 1897. Even so, the main thrust of these strategies was to exploit nationalist feeling through an expansionist overseas policy, *Weltpolitik*.

This impressive array of modern German scholarship has failed, nevertheless, to convince some historians that the evidence produced demonstrates that *Weltpolitik* was initiated for reasons of domestic policy. One critic has noted the tendency among some German historians to explain events in terms of 'abstract social forces' without ever showing how these forces influenced policy in practice. Recent research by historians (such as Eley, Blackbourn and the American D. E. Kaiser) suggests that some of the more sweeping assertions that purport to explain *Weltpolitik* (or even German policy in the July crisis of 1914) solely in terms of domestic affairs may need to be treated with caution. The critics suggest that some writers have been too vague about the real size and directness of the impact of domestic factors on German diplomacy, not to mention what effect it may actually have had.

For example, the *Sammlungspolitik*, which Stegmann has called 'the key concept' for understanding the regime from 1879 onwards, has been evaluated quite differently by Geoff Eley. He has made a powerful case that naval expansion (treated as a central plank of

Weltpolitik by Berghahn and others) was far from being an integral part of the *Sammlung* policy. Instead, the navy was an issue that divided the agrarian interest from the industrialists, as Fischer has acknowledged. The logic of Eley's argument, based on his own research, seems unanswerable. This leaves the *Sammlung* of 1897 as a not very successful attempt to create a united front for the 1898 elections out of the two Conservative parties and the National Liberals, based on a future revision of the existing commercial treaties (a euphemism for raising tariffs).

In fact the central importance attached to the tariff issue by historians of the 'new orthodoxy', as the basis for a revived 'alliance of iron and rye', is hard to discern in a recent study of Bülow as imperial chancellor. Rather than a cornerstone of Reich domestic policy, Lerman shows that tariffs were a highly divisive issue that caused such bitter feelings among the parties that no united front was possible for the 1903 elections. While the Kaiser supported the industrialists in their opposition to higher tariffs, Bülow himself even considered abandoning the tariff bill because of the difficulties it created.

The concept of the 'feudalization of the bourgeoisie' is also regarded as somewhat dubious by several British historians. In suggesting that the emphasis placed on 'feudal continuities' and 'feudal survivals' is much exaggerated, they point instead to evidence of the influence and power of the German bourgeoisie. If Eley's case that a '*de facto* parliamentary system' existed in Wilhelmine Germany is not wholly convincing, he can, none the less, draw attention to signs of vitality in parliamentary life. In addition, the important role played by the Catholic Centre Party in German politics, which has been curiously neglected by some German historians, has been well documented by Bülow's biographer. The conclusion seems inescapable that, if the support of the Centre Party was indispensable to the government's majority in the Reichstag between 1898 and 1907, then the importance of the 'alliance of iron and rye' (supposedly the basis of the *Sammlungspolitik* from 1897) has been over-stated. As against manipulation from above, there is evidence also of a 'populist challenge' from below. Taken together, much of the recent detailed research seems to suggest that the *Kaiserreich* was not such an unstable and crisis-ridden regime as it is sometimes portrayed.

In a similar vein, David Kaiser has suggested that it is a mistake to assume that the prime aim of *Weltpolitik* was to prolong indefinitely the ascendancy of the *Junker* class in German economic and political life. Rather than acting as a 'magic wand', its real function

was to be a 'patriotic umbrella'. Its initial objective in 1897 amounted to little more than securing the Reichstag parties' cooperation
with the government and raising the popularity of the Kaiser with
the public. For this purpose a few cheap foreign policy successes
would suffice. *Weltpolitik* may have been, initially at least, largely a
public relations exercise, bolstering Bülow's position as foreign minister. The creation of a powerful navy was undoubtedly popular
with a broad spectrum of German opinion. Furthermore, the 1907
elections, which Kaiser calls a 'referendum on *Weltpolitik*', demonstrated its broad appeal and therefore its usefulness as an influence
on domestic politics. Between 1909 and 1914, however, *Weltpolitik*
proved to be a diminishing asset as increasing expenditure on the
navy inhibited solutions to domestic problems and as rising expectations of more tangible achievements aboard pushed the government into more assertive policies overseas.

In his reappraisal of German foreign policy in the period
1897–1914, Kaiser emphasizes that neither Bülow nor Bethmann
Hollweg, his successor as chancellor from 1909, regarded war as a
solution to Germany's domestic problems despite their pursuit of
an overseas policy that was expansionist and, at times, aggressive.
Nor did they regard the socialists as a major threat to the regime.
Their main difficulties in domestic politics (apart from the Kaiser)
stemmed less from the SPD than from the Conservatives, who
opposed the increases in taxation on the propertied classes that
were made necessary by Tirpitz's fleet programme.

That *Weltpolitik* was largely a failure, apart from the navy issue, is
not in dispute. The disagreement among historians is whether a
world policy was adopted not for foreign policy reasons but in order
to solve domestic problems, and , if so, how fundamental those
problems were for the survival of the *Kaiserreich*.

The most sweeping critique of the 'new orthodoxy', however, has
come from the pen of German historians concerned to reassert the
study of political history in general and the role of political factors
in German foreign policy in particular. In assailing the central concept of the 'new orthodoxy' – the primacy of domestic policy – they
appear to be in a strong position, since both Geiss and Wehler
have seemingly abandoned it. The critics have also rejected the
structuralist and social-imperialist approaches. The alleged socio-
political effects of industrialism have therefore been downgraded
from the determining influence on German foreign policy they were
previously held to have exerted. This fresh approach to the problem

of interpreting Germany's development since 1871 has also revitalized the study of the Wilhelmine era.

As Schöllgen points out, a widespread, if undefined, desire for expansion was a natural outcome of Germany's growth and power by the 1890s. Furthermore, *Weltpolitik* was the logical form for this expansion to take since a European great power, anxious to pursue great power politics in this era, necessarily had to embark on a world power policy. But, in contrast to the Fischer school, Schöllgen finds little evidence of a rigorous concept or well-formulated objective behind Bülow's pursuit of *Weltpolitik* from 1897 to 1909. For Bülow, world policy seems to have meant little more than an assertion of Germany's right to 'a place in the sun' or 'the right to equality with other great nations'. *Weltpolitik* may therefore have represented a general desire to 'catch up' with the other great powers in imperialist activity, something that had been neglected by Germany's leaders for a decade after 1886.

However, the lack of planning and the divergence of views among Bülow, Holstein, Tirpitz and the Kaiser resulted in fumbling around all over the world. As a consequence, Germany's sudden intrusion into Asia, Africa or the Middle East tended to bewilder the other powers, who ascribed sinister motives to Germany's unexpected behaviour. In this sense Geiss's recent characterization of *Weltpolitik* as 'the most explosive version of modern imperialism' seems very apt.

That Germany had little choice but to expand overseas in order to demonstrate its status as a great power seems evident enough. This still left Germany's leaders with some options. Despite the complications arising from a conflict between ideology and economic interest, they could still choose between cooperation with another great power (either Russia or Britain) and the policy of the 'free hand', the policy which Bülow actually adopted, which risked alienating most of the other powers. The formation of the so-called Triple Entente in 1907, which the Germans regarded as 'encirclement', is therefore usually regarded as a sign of the failure of Bülow's diplomacy.

However, Geiss has recently put forward the interesting suggestion that the real failure of German policy lay in the inability of Germany's leaders to create a sort of European bloc which could hold its own against the existing world empires of Russia, the United States and the British empire. Obviously, it would not have been easy to persuade other states that their best interests would be served under the hegemony of Germany, as Geiss admits. But when a high degree of statecraft was called for, German diplomacy, in practice, displayed all the 'elegance of a bull in a china shop'.

WELTPOLITIK IN ACTION

By 1907 a decade of *Weltpolitik* had not produced very tangible or impressive gains for Germany. True, it had secured a foothold in China and had also acquired some islands in the Pacific. Until 1905, Germany's relations with the other great powers were quite cordial; including those with Britain, whose Conservative leaders were keen to cooperate with Germany when Anglo-Russian relations were bad. German influence in Turkey and the Middle East was also steadily increasing, partly because this was one region where Germany's leaders seem to have evolved a coherent and consistent policy.

In late autumn 1898 the Kaiser visited Constantinople and Damascus and publicly proclaimed himself the friend and protector of the sultan and the Muslim world. A more tangible sign of Germany's influence in the region was the concession granted to a German syndicate to construct a railway to the Persian Gulf. The realization of the Berlin-Baghdad railway project, however, was subject to so many delays that it was still unfinished in 1914. This was not entirely Germany's fault. Although French financiers were keen enough to provide some of the capital, Russian fears that the railway would affect its influence in Turkey and Asia Minor, together with British hostility to the extension of the line to the Gulf, impeded international cooperation. The participation of other European states in this ambitious, if potentially unprofitable, undertaking was necessary, partly because Germany lacked the capital to finance it. A further difficulty arose from the Turkish government's financial guarantee of the line, which necessitated securing the other powers' consent to the requisite fiscal changes.

A curious situation resulted. Whereas in France the government, for the sake of Russia's friendship, opposed the project (to the dismay of the financiers), in Britain the Conservative government favoured cooperating with Germany but found itself attacked by a vociferous anti-German press campaign, probably orchestrated by British commercial and financial interests who stood to lose from the construction of the railway. Subsequent attempts, for example in 1907, to secure international cooperation for the venture were blocked by the reluctance of the other powers to negotiate separately with Germany, as Berlin insisted, until Russia broke ranks in the Potsdam Agreement of 1911. Although Britain and France eventually followed suit in 1914, by that time the project amounted to little more than unfulfilled promise.

The Venezuelan affair of 1902–3 provided Germany with an opportunity to play a role on the world stage and make its influence felt overseas. The joint Anglo-German blockade of Venezuela, to put pressure on the government to settle its debts to foreign creditors, seemed to offer an opportunity for Anglo-German cooperation, in contrast to the more usual bickering between them. But not for long. The bombardment of a Venezuelan port by the Germans in January 1903 created an outcry in the United States. This in turn provoked an alarmist campaign in the British press, warning of the danger to Anglo-American relations if Britain acted as Germany's henchman in South America. The British government's reluctant withdrawal from the joint operation obliged the Germans to follow suit and submit the issue to arbitration, as the Americans, not without a hint of menace, demanded. Little prestige could be derived from this inglorious *dénouement*.

Germany's attempt to establish a claim to more territory in Africa – a step towards *Mittelafrika* – seemed to have succeeded in 1898 with the Anglo-German agreement on Portugal's African empire. A secret convention in this agreement stipulated the basis of a future partition of Portugal's colonies in the event of the country's imperial demise. Quite apart from Britain's subsequent somewhat devious guarantee of the Portuguese empire in the Windsor treaty of October 1899, the secret nature of the Anglo-German deal meant that Berlin could not even use the agreement to impress public opinion. The agreement led to an improvement in Anglo-German relations but it was not a successful public relations exercise.

In contrast, Germany's acquisition of Britain's share of Samoa in November 1899 (a sort of Boer war 'Danegeld') was primarily insisted upon for its publicity value as a patriotic and prestige victory to satisfy colonial and nationalist demands. The same concern for publicity was evident in Bülow's sycophantic congratulatory message to the Kaiser on the acquisition (by purchase) of several of Spain's Pacific islands in 1898–9. If the Kaiser and public opinion could be persuaded that acquiring Samoa and the Caroline Islands actually represented a step along 'the path which leads to world power, greatness and glory', then appearances could count for more than realities. In this sense, Bülow's pursuit of *Weltpolitik*, until the Moroccan crisis of 1905 at least, could be regarded as quite successful.

It may be necessary, therefore, as David Kaiser has suggested, to re-evaluate the apparently meagre achievements of the initial phase of *Weltpolitik*. The need to boost the popularity of the Kaiser and the government in 1897–8 seems well attested from contemporary utterances. While Holstein asserted that 'Kaiser Wilhelm's government needs some tangible successes abroad', which might result from 'a risky policy on a world scale or territorial acquisitions outside Europe', Bülow felt that 'only a successful foreign policy can help to reconcile, pacify, rally, and unite.' But if their main concern was to satisfy public opinion rather than to raise Germany's international standing as a great power, relatively minor successes, suitably magnified by the Foreign Office press bureau, no doubt sufficed.

THE 'FAILURE' OF *WELTPOLITIK*

The flaw in Bülow's direction of German foreign policy was perhaps his failure to follow up these early cheap successes with some solid achievements that actually would increase German power and influence in the world. In fact the reverse happened. The crisis of 1905 over Morocco ended in a humiliating climbdown by Germany, while the fleet programme created great tension which severely damaged Anglo-German relations. Why did German policy go so badly awry in the *Weltpolitik* era?

One factor was the chaotic nature of decision-making in the *Kaiserreich* after 1890, for which Wilhelm II himself was much to blame. The 1871 constitution narrowly confined executive authority to the Kaiser and the chancellor, at the expense of a cabinet system of government. None of Bismarck's successors exercised the power or influence of the 'Iron Chancellor', but Wilhelm II was incapable of providing the intelligent coordination needed to give coherence to government policy. As a General later lamented, there was no 'working head of state' in Germany from 1890 to 1915, despite the Kaiser's pride in being supreme military commander.

With a 'manically active, profoundly disturbed emperor' imperial Germany was, in Röhl's view, 'the best administered and worst governed country in the world'. While many historians are highly sceptical of the Kaiser's boast that 'I am the sole master of Germany's policy', few would dissent from R. J. Evans's indictment of Wilhelm II as 'the spanner in the works' rather than the moving cog at the centre of the government machine. The absence of coordination in government policy had particularly serious effects in the realm of foreign affairs. It was not unknown for the Kaiser, the chancellor, the foreign minister and senior counsellors (such as Holstein) to be pursuing objectives which were at variance or even, on occasion, incompatible with one another.

Another possible cause of the limited achievements of Bülow's *Weltpolitik* was the failure to define priorities. For example, the adoption of a tariff policy which harmed Russo-German relations was at odds with diplomatic efforts to secure a *rapprochement* with Russia. The attitude of Germany's leaders towards Britain also revealed a basic indecision as to whether a world policy should be conducted in association with Britain, or through confrontation with Britain. This was more than just a reflection of Wilhelm II's 'love-hate' sentiment towards the England of his 'grandmama'. Kennedy maintains that Bülow had in fact set his mind against an alliance with Britain but the Kaiser was seemingly not made aware of this. He in turn attempted to pull off a diplomatic coup single-handedly by negotiating privately with the tsar in 1905 for an alliance, without Bülow's knowledge. Seemingly, the question 'Who rules in Berlin?' might well have been asked before 1914. The ultimate confusion surrounding the whole concept of *Weltpolitik* was, perhaps, that many Germans (including some of the leaders) were uncertain whether Germany was pursuing a world policy as a sign that it was already a world power or because it was seeking to become one.

In retrospect, one of the major flaws in Bülow's foreign policy was that it was unduly opportunistic. Although there was a certain logic to his preference for a 'free hand', he ran the risk of leaving Germany isolated if the other major powers, irritated by Germany's clumsy diplomacy, decided to draw closer together. In the event, Bülow's reliance on profiting from other people's disasters proved unrewarding. To his dismay, the confrontation between Britain and France in Africa, and between Britain and Russia in Asia, failed to escalate into the eagerly awaited war which would have made Britain (or Russia) heavily dependent on German goodwill. This was a serious miscalculation. By 1907, Britain's rather precarious position in the 1890s as a world power had been transformed by the renewed alliance with Japan and the ententes with former colonial rivals, whereas Germany had little to show for a decade of *Weltpolitik*. Not only had Bülow's anticipated scenario of Germany enjoying a *tertius gaudens* role failed to materialize, but the over-assertiveness of German diplomacy in pursuit of ill-defined aims had led to a general distrust of Berlin's objectives.

The harmful impact of *Weltpolitik* on international relations led Germany to be regarded as an ambitious and unpredictable power which constituted a danger to the peace of Europe. The element of 'calculability' that had been a reassuring feature of German policy in the Bismarckian era was lacking in Wilhelmine diplomacy. Schöllgen suggests that a 'vicious circle' resulted from this in that Germany's pursuit of world power, an inescapable development for a European great power in such a 'boxed in' geopolitical position, created fears of hegemonial ambitions on the continent. Yet, ironically, Germany's very exposed position on the continent required a flexible balance of power to safeguard its own security. Given the fact of the Franco-Russian alliance, the continuance of Britain's uncommitted role was important to Germany's security. But as a consequence of Germany's behaviour, Britain came to regard it as a threat to the European balance of power and adopted a strategy of 'containment' accordingly.

This was not the result of *Weltpolitik* in the sense of an attempt to expand Germany's overseas empire, which was modest enough by any standards and which would not have seriously affected the balance of power in Europe. More likely it was the consequence of the brusqueness of German diplomacy. The crucial factor as far as Britain was concerned, however, was the German Navy Laws, which not only posed a direct threat to Britain's security but also created the fear of a German hegemony based on the country's combined naval and military strength.

The Navy Laws are certainly regarded by most historians as an integral part of *Weltpolitik*. Geiss, for example, has recently described the construction of the battle fleet which was designed to secure German access to the Atlantic as the 'real hard core' of *Weltpolitik*. Clearly, the expansion of its navy was essential to Germany's status as a world power in this age of 'navalism'. But a case can be made, as Schöllgen has suggested, that the specific form that naval expansion took under Tirpitz's direction was a separate issue, distinct from the vague and ill-defined objectives of *Weltpolitik* in general.

NAVAL RIVALRY

The revolution in German naval policy, effected by Tirpitz with the active encouragement of the Kaiser, led directly to the naval arms race between Britain and Germany, which became acute by 1908. By 1912 the antagonism between them had become, in the view of the Austro-Hungarian foreign minister, 'the dominant element of the international situation'. Tirpitz's objective was to create a battle fleet of sixty capital ships over a period of twenty years for use as a 'power political instrument' against England. Through the possession of this fleet Germany would attain 'world political freedom', enabling Berlin to pursue a 'great overseas policy', using the fleet as a 'lever' to extract concessions from Britain or, if need be, as a weapon of war against the British. Tirpitz may even have been secretly aiming at parity with the Royal Navy, but this was never alluded to except in his private papers.

The full scale of Tirpitz's ambitious plan was to some extent concealed by his 'step-by-step' strategy, which was intended to mislead not only the British naval authorities but German opinion as well, partly because of the enormous expenditure involved. Once it had passed the Navy Laws of 1898 and 1900, the Reichsstag was committed to a construction timetable, for which it voted the funds annually. But having agreed to a fixed establishment of ships, the new cadres were 'eternalized', as Tirpitz put it. It then remained to secure an automatic replacement of ships after twenty or twenty-five years to make the fleet totally independent of Reichstag control. Furthermore, Tirpitz exploited favourable situations, especially outbursts of anglophobia (as in 1906–7 and 1911–12), to introduce Supplementary Laws, known as *Novelle*, to secure additional funds for the fleet.

The expansion of the navy was widely popular in Germany, except with the agrarians and the military establishment, who objected to the lavish expenditure on the fleet, which benefited industrialists and workers through shipbuilding contracts and employment. In contrast to the Prussian-dominated army, the navy seemed not only 'national' but also liberal and middle-class too. The nation as a whole could therefore respond with some enthusiasm to the idea that Germany needed a powerful navy to protect its expanding overseas trade and its colonial interests, as well as to support its aspirations to world power status. Such notions were spread by the propaganda of the Flottenverein (the Navy League), which was closely linked to the Navy Office and financed by Krupp's vast industrial empire. That there was a domestic political dimension to the Tirpitz Plan seems undeniable, but Berghahn's insistence that Tirpitz conceived the fleet expansion as a 'weapon against the Social Democrats' seems unduly social-imperialist in tone. The fleet, which was certainly intended to boost the popularity of the Kaiser and the regime, actually became a hindrance in the battle against the socialists because the mounting expenditure on the navy consumed funds which were needed for social reform.

The real sleight of hand behind the Navy Laws, however, was the nature of the fleet Tirpitz wished to create. This was to be a powerful fleet of battleships, concentrated for action against Britain in the North Sea, not a navy of fast cruisers to defend colonies and commerce. Tirpitz defended the ability of Germany's numerically inferior fleet to challenge the Royal Navy with his so-called 'risk theory'. According to Tirpitz, Britain's global commitments necessitated the dispersal of its ships around the world, so that the Home Seas fleet could not engage the German navy without risking such severe losses that Britain's naval supremacy would be undermined. He acknowledged the possibility of a pre-emptive strike against his infant fleet – the 'Copenhagen complex' – but insisted that this 'danger zone' would be of relatively short duration.

The British reaction to the German naval threat was much quicker and more far-reaching than Tirpitz had anticipated. As early as 1902 the Admiralty was expressing concern at both size and the purpose of the planned German fleet. Within the next few years a series of counter-measures were implemented, concentrating more of the navy in home waters and establishing a naval base at Rosyth to cover the North Sea. The fleet was also strengthened by the Cawdor programme of December 1905, which provided for the construction of four capital ships a year. In 1905, therefore, there was no reason to lack confidence in Britain's continuing naval supremacy. With the Russian fleet all but destroyed and the German navy in its infancy, Britain seemed well able to maintain the Two Power Standard. Hence Grey could state publicly in 1906 that the new Liberal government did not regard the German fleet plans as a 'hostile act' and proposed to cut naval expenditure by reducing the Cawdor programme.

This relaxed approach to Germany's fleet expansion was shattered by the 'navy scare' of 1908–9, when the government's resistance to a press campaign to raise the naval estimates led to a panic that Britain's lead over Germany might be eliminated within a few years. Ironically it was the government's attempts to reassure Parliament and public opinion that the 1909 estimates were perfectly adequate which actually revealed how slender the British margin of superiority might be in certain circumstances.

The danger to Britain's naval supremacy, which had seemed quite secure only a few years earlier, was primarily the product of a revolution in warship technology, pioneered by Britain. The HMS *Dreadnought*, launched in 1906, combined devastating fire-power with superior speed. This new, all big-gun battleship, together with a new very powerful and even faster battle cruiser, was widely regarded as rendering existing battleships obsolete. Almost at a stroke, therefore, Britain's massive lead of three-to-one in conventional battleships over Germany became of little account. If, as was believed, such warships could be destroyed by one of the new dreadnoughts while out of range of the other's guns, the existing battleships were a sort of outmoded sea monster. As the pioneer of this warship revolution, Britain naturally had an initial advantage over Germany. In 1909, for example, it had ten dreadnoughts at sea or nearing completion before Germany had even completed one. But the announcement in 1907 of another *Novelle* to raise the German rate to four capital ships a year for the next four years created an enormous sense of alarm and insecurity in Britain. Hence the pundits could credibly claim that by 1911 the increase in the German building programme, coinciding with the reduction in the Cawdor programme, could result in Germany having thirteen dreadnoughts to Britain's twelve. The scenario for 1912 was even more alarming.

A major factor in fuelling the controversy in 1908–9 was the allegation that the Germans had accelerated their construction programme to steal a march on Britain, so that their official programme, alarming enough in itself, could no longer be taken as a reliable guide to the future size of their war fleet. German denials of any 'acceleration', in the face of reliable evidence to the contrary, only served to deepen the suspicions of their intentions. On top of this, the German shipyards were known to have reduced their completion times for ship construction. The Admiralty consequently revised its demands for new warships on the basis of Germany's shipyard capacity, not its official building programme. In fact the 'acceleration' scare was a false alarm. Tirpitz had yielded to pressure from some shipyards, without Reichstag approval, to advance the starting dates (but not completion times) on some ships to help them through a slack period, but his clumsy attempt to cover his tracks understandably gave rise to a more sinister interpretation.

To a nation accustomed to believe that Providence had decreed that Britannia should rule the waves, revelations of Britain's vulnerability, magnified by the popular press and the naval lobby, came as a rude shock. That the press had reduced a complex balance sheet to a crude numbers game of counting dreadnoughts, exemplified by the slogan 'we want eight and we won't wait', mattered little. After all, the navy scare of 1908–9 only served to heighten and crystallize fears for Britain's security that had existed since the second German Navy Law of 1900. As early as 1901 Selborne at the Admiralty had argued that, for Britain, defeat in a maritime war would be a calamity far greater than would befall any of the continental states from the destruction of their fleets. In similar vein, a newspaper editor warned in 1905 that a challenge to Britain's supremacy at sea, the life blood of the country's existence, was a threat which could not be ignored. When even the foreign secretary could assert that 'there is no halfway house between complete safety and utter ruin', it is clear that the naval issue struck deep.

One simple reason for this alarm was the proximity of the German High Seas fleet, concentrated only a few hours' sailing distance from Britain's shores, which made a 'bolt from the blue' a real possibility. Another reason was the size and efficiency of the German army. These two factors combined to give a semblance of credibility to alarmist fiction such as *The Invasion of 1910* – serialized in the popular press with publicity stunts, using men dressed up as German soldiers marching down London thoroughfares. Not that germanophobia was confined to the popular press, with its tendency to pander to the average Briton's alleged liking for a 'good hate'. Serious publications such as *The Times*, the *Spectator* and the *National Review* were markedly anti-German.

Above all, it was the pressure groups which, Kennedy suggests, 'fed off, and contributed to, the tensions generated by the Anglo-German naval rivalry'. Both the National Service League (a minuscule organization in 1905) and the Navy League, which produced 'a fanfare of alarmist cries at the time of the annual naval estimates', enjoyed a massive increase in membership from the naval race and invasion scares. Even then, their numbers came nowhere near those of their counterparts in Germany. Since the German government was also subjected to fierce criticism and propaganda broadsides from similar organizations, especially the Flottenverein and the Pan-German League, it seems clear that public awareness of the tension in Anglo-German relations was very high. Furthermore, it was pressure from these organizations which converted Tirpitz's modest demands for additional funds in 1908 into the *Novelle* that sparked off the scare of 1908–9 in Britain.

In providing for the staggering total of eight new battleships in the naval estimates in the spring of 1909, the Liberal Government seemed to be bowing, albeit reluctantly, to the passions unleashed in the press and in Parliament at the growth of the German navy. In fact the decision to build two more ships than the Admiralty had originally demanded, to say nothing of four more than the 'Economisers' in the cabinet had agreed to, (prompting Churchill's famous comment: 'we compromised on eight') was related to a new source of anxiety. Reports of dreadnought construction by Austria-Hungary and Italy, at a time when the condition of the French navy

COPYRIGHT EXPIRES.

German Tar. "'WE DON'T WANT TO FIGHT, BUT, BY JINGO, IF WE DO,
          WE'VE GOT THE SHIPS, WE'VE GOT THE MEN, WE'VE GOT THE MONEY TOO.'"
John Bull. "I SAY, THAT'S MY OLD SONG."
German Tar. "WELL, IT'S MINE NOW."

did not inspire confidence, aroused concern for the naval balance in the Mediterranean.

THE SEARCH FOR A NAVAL AGREEMENT

The enormous financial burden of the naval race, exacerbated by the additional expense of the dreadnoughts (which cost half as much again as earlier ships) gave added impetus to the campaign for a naval limitation agreement with Germany. Expenditure on the navy had risen from £27 million to £36 million between 1900 and 1904, before the announcement of the Cawdor programme. The demand for six dreadnoughts for 1909 meant adding a further £3 million to the previous year's estimates, while the subsequent programme of five capital ships a year required an expenditure of £44 million a year. When the Two Power Standard had been laid down in 1889, the naval estimates had amounted to a mere £12 million.

There was consequently a natural alliance between the 'Economisers' in the cabinet, who resented spending vast sums on battleships that reduced the scope for social reform, and the so-called 'Potsdam Party', who favoured a *rapprochement* with Germany on political grounds. Despite the rebuff of the earlier approach to Germany for a naval understanding at the Hague Conference in 1907, the foreign secretary was under constant pressure from within the cabinet and from the ranks of the Liberal Party to secure a slackening of the naval armaments race. The scare of 1908–9 naturally intensified the pressure for a further approach to Berlin.

The essence of the British proposals in 1909 was to reduce expenditure on battleships, which Grey called 'the test of whether an understanding is worth anything', by agreeing a fixed ratio of new ships to be built. Both Bülow and Bethmann Hollweg (his successor in August 1909) were eager to improve relations with Britain by defusing the tension generated by the naval rivalry. Their freedom of manoeuvre, however, was circumscribed by the unwillingness of Tirpitz and the Kaiser to permit any tampering with the fleet programme. While Tirpitz acted as a jealous guardian of his master plan, the Kaiser reacted against attempts to interfere with his fleet, which he ascribed to the 'crazy dreadnought policy backfiring'.

The German response was to offer only a relaxation of tempo in battleship construction over three years, not a reduction in the size of the fleet programme. In return for this modest concession, Berlin insisted on a political agreement which bound the signatories to neutrality if either was at war with another power. Grey was understandably unenthusiastic about the German terms, observing that 'we cannot enter into a political understanding with Germany which would separate us from Russia and France and leave us isolated.' It is not surprising that the negotiations made little progress throughout 1910, even though Grey was under pressure from the cabinet to resume talks on the basis of a German commitment not to increase their programme, as opposed to an actual reduction of it. Even then, the German chancellor insisted on a political agreement in exchange.

The tension generated by the Agadir crisis of 1911 led to further attempts to arrive at an Anglo-German understanding. The mission of Lord Haldane, the German-speaking war minister, to Berlin in February 1912 was a failure, however. A fundamental misconception existed at the outset about which side had initiated the Haldane Mission. The confusion seems to have arisen from the well-meaning attempts of two businessmen, Sir Ernest Cassel and Herr Albert Ballin, to secure an improvement in Anglo-German relations. False expectations were therefore aroused in Berlin that something of substance was on offer. The Germans also persisted in believing, despite denials, that Haldane was empowered to conclude a written agreement.

There seems little doubt that Haldane was cleverly outmanoeuvred in the course of the separate discussions he had with the chancellor and later with Tirpitz and the Kaiser. Deflected from his primary aim of securing Germany's agreement to a reduction in battleship construction, he fell into the trap of accepting the idea that the negotiation of a political agreement could take precedence over unspecified naval concessions. In the territorial discussions, Haldane also exceeded his brief in the concessions that Britain might make in Africa. But the central issue of a political agreement covering the European situation remained unresolved. Bethmann's 'sketch of a conceivable formula' not only proscribed making any 'unprovoked attack' or joining in 'any combination against the other for purposes of aggression', but also required the benevolent neutrality of one side if the other became involved in a war in which it was not the aggressor.

Bethmann's subsequent rejection, in March 1912, of the suggested formula – 'England shall neither make nor join in any unprovoked attack upon Germany' – effectively ended the possibility of an Anglo-German agreement. Significantly, it was the absence of specific reference to 'neutrality' in the British proposal that led the chancellor to dismiss it as 'worthless to our purpose'. Desultory discussions continued for some weeks, during which French alarm at what Britain might be conceding was matched by Berlin's exaggerated expectations. These false hopes had been revived by the renewed intervention of Ballin and Cassel, who misled the Kaiser into believing that an alliance was on offer. The German announcement in April of the intention to proceed with the *Novelle* signified that Tirpitz had scuppered any hopes of an agreement and that the naval race was to continue unabated. Churchill's idea of a 'naval holiday', suggested in March 1912 and repeated the next year, was rejected. The ultimate irony of the naval issue was that Anglo-German relations seemed more cordial when no further attempts were made to negotiate a naval agreement.

ANGLO-GERMAN RELATIONS

Anglo-German relations were obviously affected by other factors than the naval issue, such as economic and colonial rivalry and diplomatic problems in Europe and overseas. By about 1900 Britain's alignment with the Triple Alliance powers, formalized in the Mediterranean Agreements of 1887, had lost much of its *raison d'être*. With the Balkans relatively quiet and the Egyptian situation under control, Britain had no pressing need for Germany's diplomatic cooperation in the Near East. In the Far East, where it was earnestly desired, German support against Russia proved valueless in the Manchurian crisis of 1901.

The years 1901–2 could be regarded, Kennedy suggests, as marking a watershed in British attitudes towards Germany. The revelation of the intensity of popular hostility in Germany towards Britain during the Boer war seems to have come as a shock to British opinion. This, combined with the second Navy Law of 1900, gave rise to a feeling in some influential circles in politics, diplomacy and the armed forces that Germany now constituted a danger to Britain. By posing a threat to Britain's security, the projected expansion of the German fleet provided a focus for a variety of animosities generated earlier by commercial competition and occasional colonial disputes.

Economic rivalry was a persistent and deep-seated element in the attitude of the two nations towards each other. British opinion could hardly view with equanimity the loss to this new industrial giant on the continent of Britain's former supremacy as *the* manufacturing nation of Europe. However, competition for markets was a variable factor, which eased in periods of good trade, while commercial cooperation was, Kennedy suggests, a constant, if unspectacular, facet of business relationships, both in Europe and overseas.

Colonial rivalry, dating back to the mid–1880s, was a further source of tension between Britain and Germany. This was another area where public opinion could be inflamed by the press, colonial societies and commercial pressure groups, so that nationalism and imperialism became intertwined. A classic example of this lay behind the campaign for partitioning Morocco during the Agadir crisis of 1911, when the Pan-German League backed the dubious (if not fraudulent) claims of the Mannesmann Company to certain economic rights in Morocco. In Britain, the Conservative press displayed a markedly anti-German tone from the turn of the century onwards, at a time when most of the Conservative leaders still regarded Germany as much less of a threat to British interests than France and Russia were. In Berlin, however, Chamberlainite imperialism was a source of anxiety, particularly because of its emphasis on tariff policies that would be highly detrimental to German trade. However, colonial rivalry was an occasional irritant rather than a source of constant enmity. One reason for this was that few extra-European issues were regarded as of such importance as to be non-negotiable.

Negotiations over the Berlin-Baghdad railway, for example, had continued fitfully since the early 1900s. When the issue was raised again during the Kaiser's visit to Windsor in 1907, the British expressed two reservations: first, that control of the southern section of the line to the Persian Gulf should be in British hands; second, that the negotiations should be conducted *à quatre*, a proposal which foundered on Russian hostility to the whole scheme and Germany's desire for bilateral talks. Russia's volte-face over the issue in 1910–11 removed one obstacle. The British, however, remained adamant about the Gulf issue, while Bethmann Hollweg sought to include the Baghdad railway in a general political agreement accompanying the naval talks, delaying a solution until the summer of 1914.

Further discussions on the future of the Portuguese colonies in Africa initially seemed to hold much promise for an Anglo-German accord. On the British side there was an unusual willingness 'to study the map of Africa in a pro-German spirit' to ease some of the tension created by the Agadir crisis. This second attempt to partition Angola and Mozambique seemed justifiable because of the critical state of Portugal's finances and the accusations of maladministration of its African colonies. Although the details of the partition were settled in the course of the negotiations between May 1912 and October 1913, an unforeseen problem arose over the publication of the accord. Embarrassed by the duplicity of the Conservative government in 1898–9, Grey insisted on publication of both treaties. The Germans on the other hand were adamant that, in order to impress public opinion, only the new treaty should be made public, since they had no wish to reveal the modest nature of the gains made in 1913 compared to the 1898 treaty. Recriminations over this issue inevitably detracted from the goodwill created by reaching an accord.

Historians such as Langhorne are consequently rather sceptical whether an improvement in Anglo-German relations really took place between 1911 and 1914. Kennedy has also commented on the 'insignificance of the issues agreed upon . . . by 1914 in comparison to the more fundamental causes of disharmony'. In addition to the obvious repercussions of the naval race, the two crises over Morocco had created deep distrust of Germany's aims and objectives.

The threat of a German attack on France prompted the Anglo-French military conversations of 1906 and 1911 that led to the formation of a British Expeditionary Force for service on the continent. The danger to France naturally reinforced existing anti-German feelings within the Foreign Office and among some of the army and navy chiefs. In these circles it became axiomatic that Germany was intent on the domination of Europe. Consequently Grey was bombarded with advice to convert the ententes with France and Russia into formal alliances. But at the same time he was (as noted earlier) under continual pressure to achieve a *détente* with Germany through a naval armaments agreement.

The reasons for the failure of the attempts to reach a naval understanding are, for the most part, fairly obvious. The German demand for a neutrality agreement in return for very limited naval concessions constituted too serious a threat to Britain's delicate relations with France and Russia to be acceptable to Grey and most of the leading members of the government. Less obvious, perhaps, are the reasons for the German reluctance to secure British goodwill through more substantial concessions than a mere relaxation of tempo.

Although both the chancellors of this period expressed alarm at the intensity of the British reaction to Germany's fleet expansion and felt that German naval power had attained a sufficient level by about 1907, their pressure for a compromise was unavailing. For Tirpitz, this was partly for technical reasons. Having secured a ommitment from the Reichstag to the Navy Laws of 1898 and 1900, as well as the subsequent *Novelle*, he had all but succeeded in his aim of an *Aeternat* (sometimes called the 'Iron Budget') – an automatic replacement of warships after twenty years, making the navy free from parliamentary interference. Naturally, if his unspoken aim was parity with the Royal Navy, any diminution of the Tirpitz Plan was unacceptable to him. In the case of the Kaiser, resentment at infringement of his prerogative as supreme warlord seems to have been an important factor. Another factor was his obsessional attitude towards *his* fleet, which Langhorne has likened to the addiction of some men to model railways.

Fundamentally, Kennedy has suggested, the Anglo-German rivalry represented a clash between one power on the decline, clinging to the maritime *status quo*, confronted by the challenge of a rising power which rejected Britain's claim to 'rule the waves' for ever and anon. The fact remains that Germany's right to 'world political freedom' through the Tirpitz Plan meant that the Kaiser would command not only Europe's most efficient military machine but also its second most powerful navy.

On any objective reckoning, persisting with the Tirpitz Plan against Britain's clear determination to preserve its naval supremacy was a misguided policy. The financial cost alone (rising from 117 million marks in 1897 to 252 million by 1906) was an enormous burden which had repercussions on the German political scene. The ultimate absurdity of Tirpitz's obsession with his battle fleet was that it blinded him to the potential of the submarine, which his arch-rival, Admiral Fisher, perceived in 1912 to be 'the battleship of the future'. In the event, 1912 was Tirpitz's last victory. The decision in 1913 to give priority to strengthening the army, as the chancellor had advocated the previous year, signified an abandonment of *Weltpolitik* and naval expansion and a return to *Kontinentalpolitik.*

SOURCES AND FURTHER READING

Berghahn, V. R., *Germany and the Approach of War in 1914*, London, Macmillan, 1973.

Eley, G., *From Unification to Nazism*, London, Allen & Unwin, 1986.

Evans, R. J. (ed.), *Re-thinking German History*, London, Allen & Unwin, 1987.

Fischer, F., *Germany's Aims in the First World War*, London, Chatto & Windus, 1967.

——, *War of Illusions*, London, Chatto & Windus, 1975.

Geiss, I., *German Foreign Policy 1871–1914*, London, Routledge & Kegan Paul, 1976.

Herwig – see Martel.

Hinsley, F. H. (ed.), *British Foreign Policy under Sir Edward Grey*, Cambridge, Cambridge Unviersity Press, 1977.

Kaiser, D. E., 'Germany and the origins of the First World War', *Journal of Modern History*, vol. 55, September, 1983: 442–74.

Kennedy, P. M., *The Rise of the Anglo-German Antagonism 1860–1914*, London, Allen & Unwin, 1980.

Lambi, I. N., *The Navy and German Power Politics 1862–1914*, London, Allen & Unwin, 1984.

Langhorne, R., *The Collapse of the Concert of Europe 1890–1914*, London, Macmillan, 1981.

Lerman, K., *The Chancellor as Courtier*, Cambridge, Cambridge University Press, 1990.

Marder, A. J., *From the Dreadnought to Scapa Flow*, vol. 1: *The Road to War 1904–1914*, London, Oxford University Press, 1961.

Martel, G. (ed.), *Modern Germany Reconsidered 1870–1945*, London, Routledge, 1992.

Röhl, J. C. G. (ed.), *Kaiser Wilhelm II. New Interpretations*, Cambridge, Cambridge University Press, 1982.

Schöllgen, G. (ed.), *Escape into War? The Foreign Policy of Imperial Germany*, Oxford, Berg, 1990.

Wehler, H. U., 'Bismarck's imperialism, 1862–1890, *Past & Present*, 1970, no. 48: 119–55.

Woodward, E. L., *Great Britain and the German Navy*, Oxford, Oxford University Press, 1935; repr. London, Cass, 1964.

Fischer's views on *Weltpolitik* first appeared in English in the lengthy 'introduction' to his 1967 classic; they are elaborated and extended in his 1975 work. A recent brief restatement of his (unchanged) position can be found in Schöllgen, which also contains an example of Geiss's revised opinions. His more 'Fischerite' views are quite evident in his book on foreign policy.

The 'new orthodoxy' is discussed in Eley (chapters 1, 2, 5 and 6) and in the opening chapters of Evans. A more recent critique of German scholarship is to be found in the essays compiled by Schöllgen. Two summaries of the historiography of the period (by Retallach and Herwig) are in Martel.

A useful synthesis of German policy (on Fischerite lines but with original insights) is the work by Berghahn. Langhorne (chapters 3–5) is succinct but perceptive. A variety of aspects of the Kaiser's role are presented in the papers edited by Röhl.

The British viewpoint on the naval issue is well stated in Woodward's classic study. Marder is interesting but detailed. On the German side, chapters 2 and 3 of Berghahn (an expert on Tirpitz) are very informative. Lambi can be over-technical on naval matters but his general chapters (based on German sources) can be very illuminating on major political issues. Kennedy looks at the naval issue from both sides (chapter 20).

Kennedy is indispensable for Anglo-German relations (chapters 13 and 14). The topic is also examined by three different writers in chapters 10, 11 and 15 in Hinsley's edited work.

6 Crises and tension, 1905–1913

THE MOROCCAN CRISIS OF 1905–1906

The first Moroccan crisis began in dramatic fashion when the Kaiser, with considerable reluctance, interrupted his cruise in the Mediterranean by landing at Tangier on 31 March 1905 and made a speech in which he pointedly addressed the sultan as the ruler of an independent state. A fortnight later, the German government demanded the summoning of an international conference to determine the future of Morocco.

It was no secret that France was intent on establishing a predominant influence in Morocco. A French mission had been despatched to Fez in January 1905 to persuade the sultan to accept a programme of reforms under exclusively French supervision. The sultan's reluctance to accept France's demands had prompted the German minister at Tangier to alert Berlin to the possibilities of securing advantages for Germany through a demonstration in favour of Moroccan independence. The Tangier incident was therefore a direct challenge to France, as Bülow admitted in claiming that it 'would embarrass M. Delcassé, thwart his plans, and benefit our economic interests in Morocco'.

What was puzzling to contemporaries was that when informed of the entente, concluded almost a year earlier, Germany had disclaimed any political or territorial ambitions in Morocco, providing its economic interests were respected. Consequently the sudden German interest in the fate of Morocco, the brusque manner of the intervention and the refusal to enter into direct negotiations with France showed that Germany had every intention of making a drama out of a crisis. Tension was further increased by Berlin's insistence on the removal from office of Delcassé, the 'architect' of the Entente Cordiale and the minister responsible for France's Moroccan policy.

Delcassé's downfall in June 1905 was partly of his own making. He had given too many hostages to fortune. His major error was his refusal to open negotiations with Germany to secure its assent to the establishment of a French predominance in Morocco. Despite repeated warnings from the French ambassador in Berlin that the Germans regarded their exclusion from discussions over Morocco as an affront to their self-esteem, he persisted in his obduracy which even his admirers regarded as 'the height of imprudence'. Their fears were well founded. According to Williamson, Bülow had persisted in the view that a mere hint from Germany 'would cause France to apply to her for sanction of the French penetration of Morocco'. After the Tangier incident Delcassé offered no real concessions to the Germans and abandoned even these tentative approaches to them after their demand in mid-April for an international conference.

Delcassé was convinced that the Germans were bluffing in their war threats because he was, mistakenly, completely confident of British support in the event of a German attack on France. His ministerial colleagues, however, especially Rouvier, the prime minister, felt otherwise. In a state of near panic on receipt of a disturbing report on the unpreparedness of the French army for war, Rouvier secretly made contact with the German embassy in Paris in late April, with an offer to remove Delcassé in order to placate Berlin. Under renewed pressure a month later, Rouvier finally yielded and secured Delcassé's resignation on 6 June 1905. To his dismay, however, this did not open the way to a negotiated settlement with Berlin; in early July he was obliged to accept Germany's demand for an international conference on Morocco.

As a sign of the Kaiser's delight at Delcassé's downfall, Bülow was created a prince. The French foreign minister, who had been in office since 1898, had come to be regarded in Berlin as the evil genius of French diplomacy, thwarting German ambitions worldwide. Not only had Delcassé negotiated the entente with Britain, he had also averted a serious clash between Britain and Russia over the Dogger Bank affair of October 1904. The crucial factor in 1905, however, was the fear in Berlin that Delcassé would succeed in his attempt to mediate between Russia and Japan, an achievement which would strengthen the Franco-Russian alliance and might lead to a triple entente with Britain. That such fears were prevalent in Berlin is shown by Bülow's admission in mid-May that Germany's interests in Morocco were 'minimal as compared with those which would be at stake at the conclusion of peace between Russia and

Japan', if achieved under French auspices. Berlin's virtual ultimatum to Rouvier to secure Delcassé's removal in early June can therefore be related directly to the prospects of peace in the Far East, which greatly increased after the Russian naval defeat at Tsushima on 27 May 1905.

If, following Delcassé's fall, the German government had opened bilateral negotiations with France it could have ended the crisis over Morocco with prestige and profit. Rouvier was willing to make two major concessions: French financial participation in the Baghdad railway and territorial compensation in the Congo. Both of these concessions would have contributed towards the realization of two of the more specific aims of German policy – expansion into the Middle East and *Mittelafrika*. Furthermore, Franco-German cooperation, which Rouvier favoured in principle, might then have developed along amicable lines in such a way as to pre-empt Germany's later obsession with 'encirclement'. Instead, the German leaders decided to persist with the demand for an international conference which subsequently resulted in Germany's humiliating climbdown at Algeciras in March 1906.

Germany's motives in provoking the crisis over Morocco are readily understandable. Less intelligible are the reasons why Berlin mishandled the situation after its considerable triumph in securing Delcassé's downfall and obtaining offers of compensation from Rouvier in return for a settlement of the issue. One explanation is that the crisis highlights the flaws in the conduct of *Weltpolitik* in the Bülow era.

In the first place, Germany's perfectly legitimate demand to be consulted about the fate of Morocco was asserted in an unduly provocative and menacing manner. Second, Germany's objectives were far from clear, so that contemporary statesmen became alarmed and suspicious about Berlin's true motives. Since the underlying German aim (to split the entente) could only be achieved by a threatening posture, tension had to be kept up and this itself raised the spectre of war. Third, the absence of agreed aims within the German leadership made a consistent policy towards France virtually impossible to achieve. One aspect of this was that the Germans 'boxed themselves in' by their initial demands, which subsequently made it difficult to extricate themselves with honour or profit. Finally, the resultant blow to German prestige and the absence of tangible gains meant that Germany's intervention in Morocco had resulted in the opposite of what had been intended – hardly an accolade for Bülow's statesmanship or *Weltpolitik*.

The abrasive nature of German diplomacy in the *Weltpolitik* era, and the suspicion of sinister intent which frequently arose from it, tends to obscure the fact that Germany sometimes had legitimate grounds for objecting to the actions of the other powers. With regard to Morocco, for instance, the 1880 Treaty of Madrid entitled Germany to be consulted about proposed changes to the status of that country. Germany was correct in the assumption that Morocco would become in time 'another Tunisia' and Berlin was therefore entitled to assurances of equality of opportunity for German commercial, financial and industrial interests. Moreover, despite the demands of the newly founded German Morokkan Association, the German government was being realistic, as well as showing restraint, in its assessment that a German sphere of influence in Morocco was not practical politics. Delcassé's imprudence in excluding Germany from any say in Morocco's future, when he had negotiated with Italy, Spain and Britain over it, therefore justified Holstein's complaint that 'if we allow our feet to be stepped on in Morocco without a protest, we simply encourage others to do the same somewhere else.' Berlin could feel doubly offended. Not only was Germany one of the leading great powers, it was also an industrial giant with a growing appetite for overseas markets and sources of raw materials, such as Morocco's iron ore.

The Kaiser's dramatic landing at Tangier in March 1905 therefore seemed to be a clear, if bellicose, warning to France that Germany was concerned at the fate of Morocco. In a sense, of course, it was, but the real objective was quite different. German policy was operating on at least two levels. The open espousal of the sultan's independence was really a cover for the underlying aim of disrupting the Anglo-French entente. There may have been an even more sinister motive as well.

Whether Germany sought to provoke a preventive war against France in 1905 has long been a matter of contention. Russia's defeat in the Far East and the subsequent revolution in 1905 obviously presented the German military with a very tempting opportunity to settle accounts with France. Since Russian military power in Europe was regarded as negligible after March 1905, the likelihood is that Schlieffen, chief of the general staff, gave serious consideration to the idea of war against France. Holstein, who was the prime instigator of Germany's Moroccan policy, was in frequent contact with him during the crisis. Holstein and Bülow could well have been tempted to take advantage of the situation to gain security for the Reich's continental power base, which had been impaired by the

ON TOUR.

(Tangier, March 31.)

Kaiser Wilhelm *(as the Moor of Potsdam) sings:—*

"'UNTER DEN LINDEN'—ALWAYS AT HOME,
'UNDER THE LIME-LIGHT' WHEREVER I ROAM!"

Anglo-French entente, providing the odds were in favour of British neutrality in a war. This was an important proviso, given that in the period October 1904-April 1906 Germany's leaders lived in fear of a British naval attack.

However, the evidence of intent to launch a preventive war in 1905 is rather fragmentary. On the other hand, Bülow subsequently claimed that 'I did not hesitate to confront France with the possibility of war' as a means of putting pressure on France to comply with Germany's demands. Holstein, who consistently pursued a firm line during the crisis, regarded war as preferable to backing down, if faced with French intransigence. On balance, however, the evidence suggests that German policy was not aiming at war but was directed towards achieving France's isolation and the break-up of the Entente Cordiale.

In Kennedy's view there is no doubt about the dismay felt in Berlin at the news of the signing of the entente in April 1904. In the Wilhelmstrasse it was regarded as 'one of the worst defeats for German policy since the Dual Alliance' of 1894, while Holstein complained that 'no overseas policy is possible against England and France'. The premises on which Bülow's policy of the 'free hand' had been based were revealed as false. Two decades of imperial rivalry had ended in a *rapprochement* between Britain and France, an outcome which Bülow had believed was either impossible or was bound to result in the disruption of the Franco-Russian alliance.

The Moroccan crisis was therefore designed to reverse this failure of German diplomacy by securing the break-up of the entente. This was to be achieved by demonstrating to France that 'perfidious Albion' was an unreliable ally in a crisis and that henceforth France should appreciate that the realization of its colonial ambitions depended upon Germany's goodwill. Hence the policy of maintaining a level of tension which would break the French government's nerve and make it amenable to Germany's demands.

One of the flaws in this strategy was the emphasis publicly placed on protecting the sultan's independence and the insistence on an international conference. Consequently Berlin was not able to take advantage of the chance to obtain worthwhile compensation through negotiations with Rouvier after Delcassé's fall in early June. Everything then depended on the outcome of the conference at Algeciras, which did not meet until January 1906. Holstein's hard-line strategy, based on the premise that France would be defeated and humiliated at the conference, was unduly optimistic and made no allowances for a change of heart on the part of either Bülow or the Kaiser.

However, shortly after France had been forced to agree to a conference on Morocco, the Kaiser was embarking on a policy of his own. At a private meeting with the tsar on the island of Björkö in late July 1905, Wilhelm persuaded the impressionable Nicholas II to sign a Russo-German defensive alliance. But the Kaiser's success with Russia necessitated adopting a conciliatory attitude towards France, so as to facilitate French participation in the projected Continental League. This new twist to German diplomacy frustrated Holstein's strategy of defining the programme of the conference in advance in such a way as to ensure France's defeat. Instead, the agreed programme, accepted in late September, meant that the future of Morocco would be determined by the conference itself. Bülow, in order to placate the Kaiser, had abandoned Holstein's firm stance, saying 'all that matters is to get out of this muddle over Morocco' with as much prestige as possible.

Consequently the Germans were left with few cards to play at Algeciras, despite Bülow's assertion that 'we could not tolerate a diplomatic triumph for France' and that he 'would rather let things come to a conflict'. But having let France off the hook in September, the Germans discovered to their chagrin in October and November that the net cast around the tsar at Björkö was full of holes, through which Nicholas proceeded to escape. By then peace had been concluded with Japan, thereby reducing Russia's need for German goodwill, while the French government left St Petersburg in no doubt that further loans from Paris were conditional upon Russian support at Algeciras. Furthermore, by the time the conference assembled a new government had come to power in Britain which was determined to give France its full diplomatic support. Far from destroying the Entente Cordiale, German diplomacy had greatly strengthened it.

The initial British reaction to the Kaiser's visit to Tangier was one of astonishment rather than alarm. The German demand for an international conference did little to dispel the foreign secretary's confusion and uncertainty about Germany's motives, since Berlin had previously disclaimed any territorial or political interests in Morocco. Lansdowne was therefore content to offer France the diplomatic support which the 1904 agreement required but, in general, he did not take the German challenge to the entente very seriously. His strongest reaction was to rumours of German designs on a port in Morocco. In late April he pledged full British support for France to resist such demands, but he made no promises of British aid in the event of a Franco-German war, which he regarded as unlikely. The French therefore had to make do with an assurance of Britain's willingness to concert with them on the measures to be taken if the situation deteriorated.

Unknown to the French, Lansdowne's main concern even in May 1905 was to offer only as much support as he judged necessary to ensure that France did not do a deal with Germany that might be harmful to British interests. On the other hand, influential individuals in the Admiralty, War Office and Foreign Office, as well as the British ambassador in Paris, were strongly in favour of a much more positive British commitment to France. It was largely the indiscreet talk of such individuals, combined with Edward VII's contact with French leaders during his Mediterranean cruise in April, which enabled Delcassé to assert that 'the British will back us to the hilt' in a conflict with Germany. Significantly, when in late June Lansdowne eventually judged it politic to warn the German ambassador of Britain's reaction to a possible attack on France, he explained the government's inability to remain neutral on the grounds that 'it could not be foreseen how far public opinion in England would drive the government to support France.'

The equivocations evident in the attitude of the Conservative government towards the crisis over Morocco ended when Sir Edward Grey became foreign secretary in the new Liberal government formed in 1905–6. In Grey's view, the rights and wrongs of the Moroccan question were secondary to the real issue at stake – the European balance of power, which was seemingly threatened by an ambitious and restless Germany. Britain's policy must therefore be to support France and strengthen the entente. Accordingly, he gave his approval to the continuance of the military conversations which had taken place on an unofficial basis between the British and French army staffs. On two occasions in early 1906 he also repeated the warnings to the German ambassador about the reaction to a German attack on France in more explicit terms than those used by the cautious Lansdowne, and he informed the French of his actions. Above all, he insisted on complete support for France at the Algeciras Conference, even when the French rejected reasonable compromises.

The Algeciras Conference, which lasted from mid-January to late March 1906, was a disaster for Germany, albeit a boon for the Spanish delegate, who owned the largest hotel. Deadlock ensued when the French sought control over the Moroccan bank and the police against Germany's insistence on Morocco's independence. At the outset of the crisis the Germans had believed it was inconceivable that the other powers and signatories of the 1880 convention would be willing to hand Morocco on a plate to France. They had placed great hopes, in particular, on the United States as a champion of the 'open door' principle but, according to Anderson, Roosevelt suspected the Germans were aiming to bring about the division of Morocco into sectors by 'big bully' methods, which nearly wrecked the conference. The blustering tactics of the German delegate, Count Tattenbach, also alienated the other delegates, who realized that the German counter-proposals were patently unworkable. This resulted in Germany's isolation at the conference table. On a crucial vote of the thirteen delegates, only Austria-Hungary and Morocco supported Germany. Financial considerations alone ensured Russia's loyalty to France, while Britain, Spain and Italy had already conceded the principle of French predominance in Morocco. France therefore secured its objectives in Morocco, with Spain as a junior partner, while Germany had to be content with guarantees of commercial freedom, which could have been secured without a crisis.

Bülow's press propaganda tried to claim that the outcome of the conference was a triumph for German diplomacy, but all that Germany had achieved was to limit French rights in Morocco by the Act of Algeciras. More telling is the fact that Holstein was subsequently dismissed and that Bülow had a heart attack while defending his Moroccan policy in the Reichstag. But the main damage done by the first Moroccan crisis was to create prolonged international tension and to raise the spectre of a Franco-German war. It was therefore, in A. J. P. Taylor's view, 'a true "crisis" ', a turning point in European history which 'shattered the long Bismarckian peace'. As a consequence, Britain had, for the first time in forty years, contemplated sending a military force to the continent – marking the beginning of what Michael Howard has called the 'Continental Commitment'. Grey himself concluded in late February 1906: 'An entente between Russia, France, and ourselves would be absolutely secure. If it is necessary to check Germany it could be done.'

THE AGADIR CRISIS OF 1911

Between the signing of the Act of Algeciras in March 1906 and the outbreak of the Agadir crisis in the spring of 1911, the French and German governments made some attempts to reach a *modus vivendi* over Morocco. True, an acute, but short-lived, crisis had erupted in 1908, when the German consul at Casablanca proved reluctant to hand over some deserters of Germanic origin from the Foreign Legion, who had sought refuge at the consulate. The Casablanca incident inflamed opinion on both sides of the Rhine but it was not a contentious issue for long. The real issue was resolved by the Franco-German agreement of February 1909, by which Germany recognized France's special political interests in Morocco in return for a stake in the economic exploitation of the country. France's failure to honour the spirit or the letter of this agreement, however, was a source of ill-feeling even before the onset of the crisis in 1911.

The deterioration in Franco-German relations in late 1910 that was caused by this issue, aggravated by the lack of progress in other schemes for joint ventures in Africa and the Near East, was nothing like as serious as the effect of the naval rivalry on Anglo-German relations from 1908 onwards. Furthermore, tension among all the great powers had been greatly increased by a revival of Balkan problems, in the form of an Austro-Russian duel over Bosnia in 1908–9. In view of the rise in international tension after 1905, provoking another crisis over Morocco was not a statesmanlike action, but this was precisely what Kiderlen-Wächter, the German foreign minister, proceeded to do by despatching a warship to the Moroccan port of Agadir in July 1911.

The absurdity of the second Moroccan crisis was that Kiderlen was alone in wanting to create tension in order to achieve an objective that was probably obtainable without a crisis. Neither the Kaiser nor the chancellor, Bethmann Hollweg, were in a belligerent mood, while Caillaux, the French premier from late June, was pacific. Ironically, like Rouvier in 1905, he was an advocate of a Franco-German *rapprochement*, as was Jules Cambon, the ambassador in Berlin since 1907. In Britain, Grey was under pressure from the radical wing of his party to reach a *détente* with Germany and had no objection to France's 'buying off' Germany with territorial compensation in central Africa. Kiderlen therefore had an opportunity to pull off a considerable diplomatic success and bring about a Franco-German reconciliation. Instead he overplayed his hand, thereby provoking a crisis which seemed, at times, to bring Europe within sight of war.

The despatch of French troops to Fez in mid-April 1911, following the outbreak of revolts against the sultan, was widely regarded as an excuse for tightening France's grip on Morocco. The action itself was of questionable legality, despite French assertions that assistance had been requested by the sultan (which was untrue) and that it was necessary for the protection of foreign nationals. Moreover, the occupation of Fez on 21 May, which put central Morocco under French control, was followed by an advance into the interior. This made the assurances of a prompt withdrawal of French troops increasingly hollow, despite German warnings against prolonging military action.

Recent research suggests that French policy in Morocco was more provocative than earlier treatments of the crisis have allowed. According to Keiger, a succession of weak foreign ministers after the fall of Delcassé enabled a clique of nationalist and germanophobic officials at the Quai d'Orsay to exercise a growing influence over both the formulation and execution of French foreign policy, especially on colonial issues. The 'diplomacy of adventure', as it has been called, began in earnest when Cruppi, who was both weak and totally inexperienced in diplomacy, became foreign minister in March 1911. Under pressure from 'the bureaux', Cruppi reneged on agreements made under his predecessor for Franco-German cooperation in Morocco with regard to railways, mining and loans. In addition, the decision to send troops to Fez was taken under suspicious circumstances in that the foreign minister gave the orders for their despatch when the rest of the cabinet had dispersed for the Easter holidays. It was with some justice, therefore, that Caillaux, who inherited this situation when he became premier in late June, and the ambassador, Jules Cambon, both blamed the ensuing crisis on the 'intransigent nationalist officials' at the Quai d'Orsay.

Germany was not alone in its opposition to France's thinly veiled attempt to use the unrest in Morocco to create a *de facto* protectorate. The Spanish government reacted by occupying two districts to which Spain had a claim, while the British government expressed irritation at the prolongation of the French occupation of Fez, fearing it might lead to a tripartite division of Morocco, which would be detrimental to British interests.

Such fears seemed well founded with the dramatic appearance on 1 July of a German warship at the Atlantic port of Agadir – the '*Panther*'s leap to Agadir', as it came to be known. Kiderlen's objective, however, was not the partition of Morocco but substantial compensation in central Africa, for which the *Panther*'s presence at Agadir was intended to act as a pledge. His strategy in the crisis, however, was so maladroit that he failed to extract much of substance from a very favourable situation. Germany, after all, had a good case. It was entitled to compensation if Morocco became a French protectorate in contravention of the agreements of 1906 and 1909. Furthermore, the French government, certainly when Caillaux became premier in late June, was willing to negotiate on the basis of colonial concessions.

The *Panther*'s arrival at Agadir was badly mistimed. It was also a serious miscalculation of how to exploit the situation to Germany's advantage. Since Caillaux, regardless of the views of his foreign minister, de Selves, was anxious for a Franco-German reconciliation, the situation required an amicable atmosphere if the negotiations were to succeed. But Kiderlen had decided to 'thump the table', even though the purpose of this was 'to make the French negotiate'. The German Foreign Office seemingly discounted the possibility of generous offers of compensation, on two grounds: first, that Britain would oppose it, which was untrue; second, that the French press would attack concessions to Germany, which was probably correct, given the tendency of the anti-German bureaux officials to leak information to the press in order to sabotage any improvement in Franco-German relations.

The simplest answer to the riddle of the *Panther*'s leap lies, of course, in Kiderlen's insistence that, by way of compensation, 'we must obtain the entire French Congo.' Even such an ardent advocate of a Franco-German *détente* as Jules Cambon was aghast at the scale of the German demands, which made an amicable settlement almost impossible. Kiderlen's solution to French reluctance was dangerously simple: 'they must feel that we are prepared to go to the extreme.' Although Kiderlen seems to have calculated that the threat of war would make it easier for Caillaux to overcome the reluctance of his colleagues to agree to Germany's demands, there may also have been a more sinister motive. By forcing France into a settlement of the Moroccan issue on Germany's terms, Kiderlen hoped to weaken, if not destroy, France's entente with Britain, just as Berlin had tried to do in 1905 – a tactic that Schöllgen calls 'Flucht nach vorn' (an escape forward).

The success of Kiderlen's brinkmanship, which involved screwing up the tension on France, depended on Britain staying out of the crisis. This additional miscalculation was made despite two warnings to the German ambassador that Britain would be obliged to support France over Morocco. Not that the British government, as opposed to the Foreign Office, felt any enthusiasm for becoming involved in a quarrel which, it was felt, the French had largely provoked, especially at a time when attempts were being made to improve Anglo-German relations.

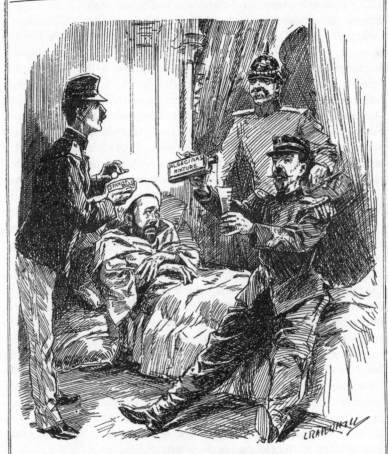

PROFESSIONAL ETIQUETTE.

Sultan of Morocco. "HALLO! ANOTHER DOCTOR! HADN'T YOU BETTER HOLD A CONSULTATION?"

German Surgeon. "WELL, TO TELL THE TRUTH, I HADN'T THOUGHT OF CONSULTING THESE OTHER GENTLEMEN. I RATHER MEANT TO OPERATE ON MY OWN ACCOUNT. STILL, IF THERE'S A GENERAL FEELING IN FAVOUR OF A CONVERSAZIONE——"

Grey was in a difficult position. He had no objection to Germany's securing compensation in the Congo but he felt it necessary to sustain the entente against German pressure, though hoping to avoid having to take too determined a stand. When faced with the breakdown of Franco-German negotiations after Kiderlen's full demands had been made known in mid-July, the British government was at a loss to know what to do. The German ambassador, who was also kept in the dark as to Berlin's intentions, could offer no convincing explanation of Germany's objectives. Since the normal diplomatic channels were of no use, resort was made to a less conventional method for issuing a timely reminder to Berlin that Britain could not be treated as of no account 'where her interests were vitally affected'. This warning shot, delivered in the course of Lloyd George's speech at the Mansion House on 21 July, had all the more impact because the chancellor of the exchequer was well known for his pro-German sympathies.

It is hard to avoid the conclusion, however, that this British salvo misfired on at least two counts. First, it encouraged the French foreign minister to offer only minimal concessions to Germany, thereby prolonging the negotiations, even though Kiderlen had modified his demands in late July. Second, the hostility that the speech aroused in Berlin and in the German press created considerable tension in Anglo-German relations to which, in turn, some leading figures in the British government overreacted. One of the strangest paradoxes of the Agadir crisis, as A. J. P. Taylor has pointed out, was the fact that whereas war between France and Germany was never in sight, 'war between Britain and Germany stood clear on the horizon' in 1911. Plans for military support to France were finalized at a meeting of the Committee of Imperial Defence in late August. In September the fleet was put on alert as a precaution against a sudden attack by Germany.

These measures demonstrate the degree of tension generated by suspicion of Germany's motives, but neither the Kaiser nor the chancellor were prepared to back a strategy of brinkmanship once Britain became involved in the crisis. Kiderlen had perforce to resume negotiations with France but in much less favourable conditions, despite Caillaux's secret contacts with Berlin behind the back of his more inflexible foreign minister. Kiderlen's task was further complicated by the belligerence of German public opinion, whose expectations of major colonial gains for Germany, possibly including a foothold in Morocco, were now a major embarrassment to the government. For this he had only himself to blame, since he had encouraged German commercial interests to mount a campaign over Morocco earlier in the year. Hence the comment from Aehrenthal, the Austro-Hungarian foreign minister, on Germany's Moroccan policy, which he was at a loss to understand, as 'just Krupp and Mannesmann'.

By late September the Agadir crisis was more or less over but it was not until early November that the Franco-German accord was finally signed. Germany conceded France's claim to a protectorate over Morocco, but with a guarantee of equal opportunities for German firms, in return for a very modest slice of the French Congo. This territory was absorbed into the existing German colony of the Kameruns, providing access to the River Congo, but its size was a mere 275,000 square kilometres with 1 million inhabitants. *Mittelafrika* remained a distant prospect.

The outcome of the crisis was regarded in Germany as a national humiliation, for which the government was fiercely attacked in the press and in the Reichstag, especially by the parties of the Right. German nationalists not surprisingly identified Britain as the main obstacle to Germany's overseas expansion, while enthusiasts for the fleet conceded that Agadir was 'very useful to naval propaganda'. Tirpitz was quick to exploit 'the growing irritation at home' to secure approval for a new navy bill.

In France, the government could naturally claim the credit for extending French control over Morocco, but Caillaux himself was soon forced to resign after revelations of his secret contacts with the Germans. Even this was no consolation to Berlin, since it brought to power Raymond Poincaré, the champion of the 'national revival', at a time when Franco-German relations had become embittered by Kiderlen's clumsy diplomacy. The resurgence of French nationalism with a powerful anti-German motif also led to closer ties with Russia, at a time when some restraint was needed on Russia's attitude towards Balkan problems.

The effect of the crisis on British politics was also significant because it converted two of the 'Potsdam Party', Lloyd George and Churchill, into ardent protagonists of the entente with France. During the crisis Grey had been unable to give the French the positive assurances of British support that they sought because of the determined opposition of many of the cabinet to British involvement in what one of them called 'a purely French quarrel'. In fact the Agadir crisis highlighted the ambivalence of Britain's relationship with France by raising again, as in 1905, the issue of whether 'diplomatic support' was sufficient to deal with all contingencies.

After the crisis Grey conceded that 'diplomatic support implied, if it was to be of any value, the possibility of military support.'

Difficulties arose in 1911, however, because the military conversations of 1905–6 had never been revealed to the full cabinet. The resumption of these talks, to finalize the technical details of British military cooperation with the French army, was therefore arranged in some secrecy by the War Office. When the defence committee (CID) was convened on 23 August to appraise plans for aiding France, several of the cabinet noted for their aversion to a continental commitment were mysteriously not informed of the meeting. Angered by this ruse, which occurred only a month after Lloyd George's unauthorized warning to the Germans in the Mansion House speech, the radicals retaliated. In November they secured (by a majority of fifteen to five) two resolutions that proscribed staff talks implying a British commitment to intervention in a continental war without the prior approval of the cabinet.

In 1911 Grey persisted in the view expressed in 1906, 'that the Government was quite free, but . . . that the military people knew what to do if the word was given'. This sort of view was hardly reassuring to the French government in the middle of a crisis and it naturally attempted to obtain a more positive commitment from its entente partner. Hence Grey's observation to the cabinet on 1 November that the could not 'conduct negotiations with France if he was not to be able to assume our landing forces to help France, if Germany invaded her'.

The view expressed by L. C. F. Turner that the entente had become 'virtually a military alliance' as a result of Agadir and the *Novelle* of 1912 has some validity but technically is incorrect. Both the War Office and the Foreign Office certainly wanted closer ties with France, but the Liberal government was deeply divided on the issue. It remained so down to 1914, even after the defection of Lloyd George and Churchill from the 'pro-German' group, which considerably strengthened the position of the Liberal Imperialists such as Grey, Haldane and Asquith. Their pre-eminence within the cabinet, and Churchill's promotion to the Admiralty, even made possible an extension of the entente with France in the form of naval conversations in 1912.

The Admiralty's desire for a naval understanding with France stemmed from concern at the implications of the *Novelle* which Tirpitz had secured with relative ease, thanks to the outcry in Germany against Britain's intervention in the Agadir crisis. The effect of the *Novelle* was not only to augment Germany's active fleet by the creation of a third squadron, but also to increase the striking power of the naval forces which Germany could, in theory at least, launch against England at a moment's notice. The problem the Admiralty faced was how to strengthen the home fleet to meet the threat posed by the fact that by 1913 the German active battle fleet would consist of 25 battleships, instead of 17, plus 8 battle cruisers, instead of 4.

The Admiralty's response to the threat, announced by Churchill as first lord in 1912, was to concentrate its modern battleships in the North Sea at the expense of the battle fleet based in Malta which was eight days' sailing time from home waters. To meet the challenge from Triple Alliance dreadnoughts in the Mediterranean, which rendered Britain's pre-dreadnought battleships vulnerable, Churchill proposed a naval agreement with France by which the French would, in effect, guard the Mediterranean by concentrating their modern warships at Toulon. This seemingly efficient disposition of the entente's naval resources all but foundered on the rocks. Scylla and Charybdis paled into insignificance compared to the difficulties Churchill's proposals encountered.

The French were quick to grasp the opportunity to obtain a clearer definition of British aid to France in the event of war with Germany as the price for the withdrawal of their fleet from Brest, which left the northern coast exposed to a German naval attack. This demand stood no chance of acceptance by the Liberal government, many of whose members were uneasy about Britain's existing commitments to France. Equally, they would not agree to further increases in the naval estimates to provide the new dreadnoughts needed to safeguard the Mediterranean.

Churchill's plan was also opposed by the Foreign Office on the grounds that it would weaken British influence in a strategically important area, endangering imperial communications and the security of Egypt. Although the Admiralty yielded to pressure and agreed to base a battle squadron at Gibraltar, in July the defence committee insisted on the need to observe a One Power Standard (equivalent to eight dreadnoughts) based on a Mediterranean port, even though this could not be achieved before 1915.

Churchill therefore persisted in his search for a defensive naval arrangement with France that would only be operative if both countries were at war. In November 1912 the French agreed to an exchange of notes, which merely required the two powers to consult together if war threatened. This was followed in February 1913 by an agreement on naval cooperation, to become effective if the two powers were allies in a war against Germany and/or the Triple Alliance. It was the omission from this agreement of a preamble, affirming the autonomous nature of the dispositions of the two navies, that enabled the French ambassador to claim in 1914 that Britain had a moral obligation to defend the northern coasts of France. His claim was based on the view that the French fleet had been withdrawn from Brest at Britain's request in 1912–13, when in fact this decision had already been taken in principle in 1907.

Nevertheless, the *Novelle* of 1911–12, itself the outcome of Agadir, had the effect of adding to Britain's commitment to defend France against a German attack. In addition, by 1912 Balfour, the Conservative leader, had come to the conclusion that a formal alliance with France was preferable to the uncertainties of an entente. This was not an option, however, for the dissension-ridden Liberal administration, even though some of its members felt that 'we have all the obligations of an alliance without its advantages.' The negotiations with France to safeguard the Mediterranean made it more difficult to resist Russian pressure for an agreement about the Baltic, in which the British government showed very little interest. The only significance of the Anglo-Russian naval talks, to which the British agreed with reluctance in May 1914, was that Grey made a serious error of judgement in denying their existence in June, when they had not yet commenced. Since the German chancellor knew of the talks through a spy in the Russian embassy in London, Grey destroyed his credibility in Berlin at a moment when Anglo-German trust was important if war was to be avoided following this latest crisis in the Balkans.

THE BOSNIAN CRISIS OF 1908–1909

Although the Moroccan crises of 1905 and 1911 contributed significantly to the growth of international tension before 1914, their effect on the relations between the great powers as a whole was limited, if only because both Russia and Austria-Hungary displayed almost complete indifference to Morocco. On the other hand Balkan problems, which inevitably revived old tensions in Austro-Russian relations, had wider repercussions. Following the entente of 1907, Russia looked to London as well as Paris for sympathy and support for its interests in the Balkans. In Berlin, an Austro-Russian confrontation could not be ignored, especially when Britain could no longer be expected, as in Bismarck's day, to play a prominent role in resisting Russian pretensions in the Balkans. Germany could therefore hardly allow its only reliable ally to suffer a major setback at the hands of Russia and the Slavs, however reluctant it might be to become involved in Vienna's squabbles in the Balkans. Moreover, Germany now had important interests of its own in the Near East, which had not been the case during the Bismarck era.

A clash of interests in the Balkans could easily result in a highly explosive situation in which Austria-Hungary stood ranged against Russia and its Slav protégés. The danger to the peace of Europe was further increased by the probability that the alliance systems would come into play if a crisis became serious. Until about 1912, however, both Berlin and Paris were on occasion equivocal about giving their respective allies strong support in Balkan disputes, while Britain's looser entente ties left it some scope to adopt a mediating role, if London so wished. What made Balkan issues so dangerous was the growth of Slav nationalism. If Russia's patronage of the Balkan states was an essential attribute of its prestige as a Slavic great power, for Austria-Hungary unchecked Slav nationalism was a threat to its very survival as a multi-national empire. Given that Austrian and Russian interests in the Balkans were fundamentally irreconcilable, the added dimension of ethnic claims to areas still under Turkish rule, coupled with rivalries among the Balkan states themselves, made it a highly unstable region.

Amid the complexity of Balkan politics, one factor stood out as a source of potential disaster in the 1900s; namely, the triangular relationship between Austria-Hungary, Serbia and Russia. Austro-Serb antagonism was a new factor. Until the overthrow of the Obrenovich 'dynasty' in a bloody palace revolution in 1903, Serbia had behaved, albeit with some reluctance, as an Austrian client state. A few years later, the new Serbian regime turned to Russia for protection and contemplated plans for the creation of a Greater Serbia. Vienna's unsuccessful attempts to bring Serbia to heel through economic pressure, including a ban on Serb livestock imports – the so-called 'Pig War' of 1906 – only deepened the antagonism. Serbia was only a small state but its geographical proximity to Austria-Hungary meant that Serb hostility could not be ignored, especially as the country was allegedly, according to Aehrenthal's predecessor, 'intriguing incessantly against the Monarchy . . . , stirring up the Serbo-Croat population and agitating against Austria-Hungary in Bosnia and the Herzegovina'.

The formal annexation of these two provinces, administered by Austria-Hungary since 1878, was part of Aehrenthal's plan, when he became foreign minister in late 1906, to boost the prestige of the

Dual Monarchy by way of a vigorous foreign policy. Most of Aehren-thal's schemes seem to have suffered from a lack of regard for the sensitivities of others. His Sanjak railway project was a commercially viable scheme for a direct rail link through Macedonia to Constant-inople, but it aroused resentment in Russia because of the boost it would give to Austrian political influence in the Balkans. Similarly, in secretly encouraging the assertion of Bulgaria's *de jure* indepen-dence from Turkey in October 1908, he antagonized Britain because of the blow this dealt to the prestige of the new regime in Constant-inople. Aehrenthal also seriously underestimated the strength of Ottoman nationalism after the Young Turk revolution in July 1908. He too readily assumed that the withdrawal of the Austrian garrison from the Sanjak of Novibazar and its return to full Turkish sover-eignty would placate the Turks for the loss of Bosnia and Herzegov-ina. Their annexation by Austria-Hungary in October 1908 was deemed necessary in order to forestall a possible move by the Young Turks to reassert sovereignty over them and to enable the emperor to grant the provinces a formal constitution within the Dual Monarchy.

Aehrenthal's major miscalculation was his belief that Turkey and the great powers would recognize that the annexation was not a forward thrust, but an essentially conservative move demonstrating the finality of Austrian territorial claims on the Ottoman empire, as the evacuation of the Sanjak 'proved'. His successor, Berchtold, accurately diagnosed the flaw in Aehrenthal's diplomacy as his 'frightful characteristic of overlooking facts that do not fit into his complicated political house of cards'. Not that his Russian counterpart, Izvolsky, was immune to this weakness. Between them they created the Bosnian crisis of 1908–9, which increased Serbian hostility towards the Dual Monarchy and also destroyed the Austro-Russian *détente* in the Balkans, which dated back to 1897.

This was a curious twist of fate since, according to F. R. Bridge, Aehrenthal believed he had secured Russian acceptance of the annexation of Bosnia, as part of an agreement designed to put new life into the flagging Balkan entente. In the course of general discussions in 1908 between St Petersburg and Vienna about the nature and purpose of the 1897 understanding, the Russian foreign minister had proposed a deal. In return for Vienna's support for the opening of the Straits to Russian warships, Russia would not object to the annexation of Bosnia and Herzegovina. At a private meeting at Buchlau in September 1908, the basis of the deal was seemingly agreed, but the absence of a formal record of the talks led to subsequent confusion and recriminations.

The premature announcement of the annexation in early October took Izvolsky by surprise and destroyed any chance of the deal proceeding as planned. But Aehrenthal seems only to have advanced the date by a few days. The fact remained, none the less, that Izvolsky still had much ground to prepare, since the response to his soundings about the Straits in Paris and London was rather disappointing. Worse still, he had yet to secure the full approval of the tsar and the other ministers to the scheme, let alone prepare public opinion in Russia for what might well be regarded as a betrayal of the Slav cause in the Balkans.

Izvolsky's reaction to the premature announcement of the annexation was to demand an international conference on the issues of Bosnia and the Straits, as well as insisting on compensation for Serbia and Montenegro. While the Buchlau agreement apparently included a reference to some sort of conference, possibly as a formal ratification of a *fait accompli*, compensation for Serbia had been specifically excluded from the deal. It looks as though Aehrenthal unwittingly put Izvolsky in a hopeless position, but for the most part Izvolsky had only himself to blame. The Buchlau deal was an enormous gamble, involving great risks to Russia's prestige as the protector of the Slavs, for the sake of a personal diplomatic success.

The crisis over Bosnia dragged on until March 1909, because no acceptable compromise could be reached. For several months the entente powers backed Izvolsky's demand for a conference empowered to decide the validity of the annexation and the nature of the compensation due to the injured parties. Aehrenthal, however, would not agree to a conference whose deliberations or decisions might impair the dignity of the Dual Monarchy. His decision in December 1908 to publish extracts of the negotiations, showing Izvolsky's acceptance of the annexation, reduced Austro-Russian relations to a nadir.

Meanwhile the Turks, for their part, had begun a boycott of trade with Austria-Hungary, whose depleted treasury made financial compensation for Turkey unlikely. After the danger of an Austro-Turkish war had passed, a settlement including cash compensation was eventually reached in early 1909, leading to better relations. With Serbia and Montenegro, however, no settlement was possible. Encouraged by British support, which may have been misguided, the Serbs made clamorous demands for territorial compensation, backed by military preparations. Of more lasting significance was the founding of a new patriotic propaganda society, the Narodna Odbrana, which spread into Bosnia itself. Aehrenthal's offer of generous commercial concessions, including a railway link to a Dalmatian port, were brusquely rejected. Despite this, he held out against the high command's demand to settle accounts with the Serbs by military action.

Aehrenthal's insistence on a diplomatic solution to the crisis owed little to fear of Russia. By late January 1909 he was assured of full military support from Germany if Russia mobilized: an unlikely event since the latter was in no condition to wage a major war until it had recovered from its defeat in 1905. In addition, Izvolsky lived in constant fear that Aehrenthal would reveal that he had agreed not to support Serbian pretensions towards Bosnia at the Buchlau meeting. His advice to Serbia in late February to abandon its claim for compensation was of no avail. Hence, faced with the threat of an Austrian attack on Serbia, Izvolsky turned in desperation to Berlin to get him off the hook. With a remarkable lack of finesse for an experienced diplomat, Kiderlen responded by sending a peremptory request to St Petersburg to recognize the annexation of Bosnia, otherwise Germany would not restrain its ally from invading Serbia. Izvolsky happily complied with the German 'ultimatum' and on 31 March the Serbs finally promised 'to live in future on terms of friendly and neighbourly relations' with Austria-Hungary.

The crisis ended with the recognition by all the powers of the Austrian annexation of Bosnia. This was regarded as a resounding diplomatic defeat for the Triple Entente, whose initial solidarity had weakened as the crisis dragged on. French support had been lukewarm from the outset, partly because France looked to Vienna for help in resolving the Casablanca dispute with Germany. British backing for Russia was confined to purely diplomatic efforts but Grey's interventions, especially those on Serbia's behalf, do not seem to have been very helpful in resolving the crisis. His support for Turkey's claims was more successful, but the new regime in Constantinople expected even more than this from Britain.

The long-term results of the crisis suggest that Austria-Hungary paid a high price for its success in annexing Bosnia and Herzegovina without a war. Serbian propaganda and terrorist activities directed against the Dual Monarchy intensified, making the south Slav problem more intractable than ever. Conciliation of the Bosnian Serbs and Croats though social reforms continued to be hampered by the opposition of the government in Budapest to any measures or expenditures deemed contrary to Hungarian interests. The Bosnian crisis also cost Austria-Hungary some of its best markets in Turkey and the Balkan states, mainly to the advantage of Germany.

In diplomatic terms, the Bosnian affair did enormous damage to Austria's relations with the great powers and other states, who were not easily persuaded that Vienna cherished no further expansionist designs. The Russians in particular were convinced that the Bosnian annexation was just the first step of an Austrian march on Salonika. This quite unfounded suspicion not only deepened Russian hostility towards the Dual Monarchy but also led the new foreign minister, Sazonov, to encourage the formation of a Balkan League to block the alleged 'ambitious designs of Austria-Hungary'. The crisis may have demonstrated the greater coherence of the Austro-German alliance compared to the Franco-Russian alliance and the Triple Entente, but it had the effect of making Vienna far more dependent on Berlin than it had been for over a decade.

THE BALKAN WARS, 1912–1913

Between the loss of Bosnia and Herzegovina in 1909 and the outbreak of the Balkan wars in 1912, the Ottoman empire suffered another blow to its prestige with the Italian annexation of Tripoli in September 1911. When the Italian military expedition sent to conquer Tripoli encountered unexpectedly stiff resistance from the Turkish forces in this outlying province of the Ottoman empire, Italy resorted to naval operations near the Dardanelles and in the Aegean Sea, capturing numerous islands. The Turks responded to this extension of the war into the heartland of their empire by closing the Dardanelles to all shipping, to the consternation of the great powers, especially Russia. Ominously, the Balkan states took a keen interest in the fortunes of the Tripoli war, which dragged on until October 1912.

The war was an embarrassment to the great powers, even though Italian designs on Tripoli were no secret. Neither Austria-Hungary nor France were in a position to censure the Italians in view of their conduct in Bosnia and Morocco. But even the British, who deplored any further weakening of Turkey, were anxious not to alienate Italy and drive it back into the arms of its alliance partners through an outright condemnation of Italian aggression. The Russian response to the Italo-Turkish war was even more cynical. Their ambassador in Constantinople, Charykov, offered a Russian guarantee of Constantinople and the Straits in return for the opening of the Straits to Russian warships. When the 'Charykov Kite' (as it was called) was rejected, Russia sought to secure peace terms favourable to Italy, in the hope of enlisting Italian support against Austria in the Balkans. The European Concert did not make an impressive showing in this dispute, where the merits of the case were subordinated to other considerations, especially the effect on the alliance system. Furthermore, although all the great powers accepted the principle of five-power mediation, none was willing to risk offending either of the belligerents by proposing specific terms for ending the war.

Before the Italo-Turkish war was over a far more serious threat to the survival of the Ottoman empire had arisen in the shape of the Balkan League. The objectives of the league also represented a major challenge to Austria-Hungary, to whom any further diminution of Turkish power in Europe was most unwelcome. Despite this, neither Aehrenthal nor Berchtold, his successor in February 1912, fully recognized the gravity of the threat to Austrian interests and influence in the Balkans posed by the league, even though its chief instigator was Serbia.

The resurgence of nationalist rivalries and animosities in eastern Europe in the 1990s makes it easier to comprehend now the aggressive passions behind Balkan politics in the years before 1914. What might be termed 'the unacceptable face of nationalism', revealed by the Serbian attack on Croatia and Bosnia in 1991–2 and particularly by the policy of 'ethnic cleansing', serves to demonstrate both the nature and the destabilising effect of Serb ambitions for the creation of a Greater Serbia prior to 1914. Another dangerous aspect of the era was that the expansionist goals of the Balkan states became intertwined with the policies and interests of two of the great powers.

Negotiations for a Serb-Bulgar alliance, which Russia had encouraged for several years, were brought to a successful conclusion in March 1912 with the assistance of the Russian ministers in Belgrade and Sofia. Hartwig, a rabid austrophobe and pan-Slavist, revelled in Balkan intrigues largely unchecked by St Petersburg, encouraging Serbia's expansionist schemes directed against both the Turks and the Austrians. What Sazonov failed to grasp fully was that the Balkan League was plotting the seizure and partition of the remaining provinces of Turkey-in-Europe. An agreement on the division of Macedonia was the indispensable basis of a Serb-Bulgar treaty, given the bitter ethnic rivalries of the region. A defensive arrangement in March 1912, seemingly designed to exclude 'outside' intervention in Balkan affairs by states such as Austria-Hungary or Italy, was followed in May by a military convention for an offensive against Turkey. Later in the year Greece and Montenegro joined the league.

Until the autumn of 1912 the great powers assumed too readily that the Balkan states were only making provision against the inevitable disintegration of the Turkish empire, which seemed imminent in the summer of 1912. Hence Sazonov's glib comment that the league represented '500,000 bayonets to guard the Balkans' against the spread of Austrian influence. The Austrians, who had more to lose, unwisely persisted in regarding unity among the Balkan states as a chimera. Nevertheless, the powers could not ignore the evidence of Turkey's serious difficulties – an unfinished war with Italy, a revolt in Albania and confusion in Constantinople where a new government was attempting to weaken the Young Turks, thereby disorganizing the army.

In August and September 1912 alarm bells began to ring belatedly in the chancelleries of Europe. In Vienna, Berchtold contemplated limited military intervention to discourage the Balkan states from starting an offensive, but he received no support for an active policy from either Berlin or Rome. The only viable alternative was to define the Dual Monarchy's priorities – an independent Albania and denial of access to the Adriatic for Serbia – while awaiting the outcome of events. At the eleventh hour Austria-Hungary and Russia, pushed into acting as spokesmen for the great powers, attempted to warn off the Balkan states from attacking Turkey by proclaiming that they would not permit changes in the territorial *status quo*, but to no avail.

The war, which began in October 1912, was a series of disasters for the Turks. By December, when they sued for peace, they had lost most of Albania and Macedonia to the forces of the Balkan League. Since the territorial *status quo* had vanished beyond recall, the main problem for the great powers was to secure a peace settlement acceptable both to them and to the belligerents. The powers' acceptance of Grey's invitation to hold a conference of ambassadors in London, alongside the peace conference of the belligerent states, enabled the great powers to act as the Concert of Europe in resolving disputed issues. The successful outcome of the conference owed much to the willingness of Grey and the German ambassador to work together to mediate between Russia and Austria-Hungary, whose mutual hostility threatened to wreck the proceedings of the conference.

The situation in the Balkans created persistent tension between St Petersburg and Vienna from November 1912 to the following

THE BOILING POINT.

March. In both countries the army command was pressing for military action. Russia's trial mobilization in September was followed by large troop concentrations on the borders with Galicia and calls for a showdown with the Austrians in November. In Galicia and Bosnia-Herzegovina the Austrian forces were strongly reinforced and the military continually pressed for war against Serbia. Grey therefore had good cause to fear that disputes over remote towns in Albania might well precipitate an Austro-Russian war that would embroil the other powers.

The root of the problem was that Austria's determination to limit Serbia's gains to a minimum conflicted with Russia's desire or obligation to support the claims of its protégé. The Austrians resisted Serbian demands for a port on the Adriatic and insisted on the creation of an independent Albania which, as a Catholic, non-Slav state, could become a useful ally in the Balkans. The early sessions of the conference went quite smoothly when Russia persuaded the Serbs to abandon their demand for a port and agreed to the creation, in principle, of an independent Albanian state.

The delimitation of its boundaries, however, caused endless recriminations. The fate of Scutari, in particular, a well-defended mountain fortress still held by the Turks, caused a series of crises. The Austrians had insisted at the outset on its inclusion in Albania on ethnic grounds alone, but it was not until March 1913 that Sazonov yielded to pressure from Grey to grant Scutari to Albania in return for concessions to Montenegro and Serbia in north-east Albania. However, although the Serbs agreed to call off their besieging forces the Turkish commander of Scutari subsequently surrendered it to the Montenegrins in a mysterious transaction involving a suitcase full of bank notes. Consequently the fate of Scutari was seemingly being decided by a tiny Balkan state in defiance of a decision of the great powers, and moreover one that had been laboriously arrived at. Once more, the Concert of Europe did not make an impressive showing. A naval demonstration by the European powers, agreed after considerable delay, failed to overawe the recalcitrant Montenegrins. An Austrian ultimatum had more effect, but possibly not as much as the 2 million francs paid to the devious King Nikita, in securing Montenegro's eventual agreement to evacuate Scutari on 5 May.

Difficulties also arose over the fate of Adrianople, to which the Bulgarians laid claim at the London conference, despite their failure to capture it from Turkey by December 1912. Britain was reluctant to agree to coercion of the Turks, who naturally resisted pressure from the powers to cede the city, until its eventual capture by the Bulgarians in March 1913 after the renewal of hostilities. In the event, it was retaken by the Turks in late July in the course of the second Balkan war.

The second Balkan war began in late June 1913, when Bulgaria fought alone against its former allies and Roumania. Serbian demands for compensation for the loss of Albanian territory originally designated to Serbia were rejected by the Bulgars, who had already ceded the town of Silistria to Roumania as a reward for its neutrality in the first Balkan war. A secret Serbo-Greek agreement to reallocate parts of Macedonia at Bulgaria's expense was strengthened by the support of Roumania, which had developed a taste for Bulgarian territory. The Bulgars placed too much reliance on Russia's goodwill in their dispute with Serbia, and after Sazonov's mediation efforts failed they attacked Serb and Greek positions in Macedonia. The Bulgar offensive turned into a total defeat for its forces, with the result that Bulgaria forfeited its former gains to Serbia and Greece. In addition, it had to surrender to Roumania the whole region of Silistria, while the Turks managed to recover Adrianople.

Austria's concern at the defeat of Bulgaria was mitigated by the confident assumption that the terms of the Treaty of Bucharest (August 1913) were subject to revision by the great powers. However, this belief was confounded by the Kaiser's unexpected intervention. He decided to send congratulatory telegrams to the peacemakers, which gave an air of finality to the treaty ending the second Balkan war – a war which Berchtold viewed with even greater dismay than the first one.

As a result of the first Balkan war Serbia had doubled in size, while Turkey had ceased to be a viable bulwark against Balkan nationalism. Furthermore, Russia had backed Serbian demands and adopted a threatening posture, especially on the Galician frontier. On the other hand, patient diplomacy had secured the Dual Monarchy's minimum demands regarding Albania, including Scutari, and had denied Serbia a port. In addition, Britain and, to a lesser extent, France had played a moderating role, but German support had been equivocal at times. This suggested that Berlin still had not fully grasped just how dangerous the south Slav issue was to Austria-Hungary. The dominant influence in the Balkans which Austria had enjoyed after the Bosnian affair had gone forever after the first Balkan war. Instead Russia, whose pan-Slav agents had helped to

THE BALKAN WARS, 1912 – 1913

Vienna

Budapest

AUSTRIA – HUNGARY

RUSSIA

BOSNIA (1908)

Sarajevo

HERZEGOVINA

MONTENEGRO

Scutari

Belgrade

S E R B I A

Novibazar

ROUMANIA

Bucharest

River Danube

Silistria

DOBRUJA

BULGARIA

Sofia

Black Sea

ALBANIA

MACEDONIA

Salonica

Adrianople

Constantinople

Straits

GREECE

Mediterranean Sea

CRETE

Territory lost by Turkey in 1912 – 1913

Turkey in Europe after the Balkan Wars

0   200
km

precipitate the conflict, reaped the benefit of the successes of the Balkan League.

The second Balkan war was an unmitigated disaster for Vienna. Bulgaria, regarded as a potential ally against both Serbia and Russia, was gravely weakened. The aggrandizement of Serbia, on the other hand, had grown apace. Nor had the Austrians found much comfort from the behaviour of their German ally. The vagaries of the Kaiser's attitudes, especially his dynastic predilection for Greece and hostility towards the Bulgarian king, worked at cross-purposes to Austro-Hungarian diplomacy.

The greatest casualty of the Balkan wars was, in some ways, the Concert of Europe. Enjoying a brief resurgence under Grey's skilful chairmanship of the conference of ambassadors, assisted by Germany, the Concert nevertheless proved to be, in Berchtold's view at least, incapable of effectively coercing recalcitrant states. Consequently Berchtold drew the conclusion from the experience of the Balkan wars that military threats were much more productive of results than patient diplomacy. This belief was reinforced by a further crisis in the autumn of 1913 when Serbia continued its intrusion into Albanian territory, in defiance of earlier warnings from the great powers. When the Serbs ignored further warnings by the Austrians, Vienna despatched an ultimatum to Belgrade, demanding the evacuation of Serbian forces from all Albanian territory within eight days.

The bitterness created in Serbian political and military circles by this forceful diplomacy, however, gave the *coup de grâce* to some rather tentative steps towards an Austro-Serb *détente*, which had taken place in the summer of 1913. Furthermore, as Williamson points out, Berchtold's diplomatic successes in 1912 and 1913 had turned each issue between Austria-Hungary and Serbia into a matter of prestige, which the Dual Monarchy had to win. This was a dangerous situation for a great power whose very existence was an affront to ardent Slav nationalists. It was an even more dangerous situation for Europe that a third Balkan war would not find Austria-Hungary very receptive to the counsels of peace.

THE 'GERMAN PROBLEM' ON THE EVE OF THE 1914 WAR

The 'German Question', as Geiss calls it, was 'the most complex and most explosive of all European national questions in the nineteenth century'. In the twentieth century, the problem relates to Germany's role in causing two world wars and the degree of continuity that allegedly existed in German policy from 1879 or 1897 to 1939. In broad historical terms the crux of the problem was what use the new German empire would make of the latent hegemonial position it had recently acquired, following the defeat of France in 1871.

This fundamental issue had become more acute several decades later for two distinct reasons. First, the imbalance between Germany and the other European powers had arguably increased after 1871, so that by 1914, Kennedy suggests, Germany's 'national power . . . was well ahead of either France or Russia and had probably overtaken Britain as well'. Second, by 1900 it was abundantly clear that Germany's leaders, with much public support, had abandoned the self-imposed restraint implicit in Bismarck's *Kontinentalpolitik* in favour of an expansionist policy.

The outlets for German economic drive and political ambition, however, were dangerously limited by about 1900. Surrounded by the other great powers because of its location in the centre of Europe, the only obvious outlet for Germany's pent-up energies was overseas. But by this time the Germans discovered that they were also hemmed in on a global level by what Geiss calls the 'economic and imperialist giants of the immediate future'. A possible solution to the German dilemma was to create a hegemonial position for itself on the continent, by demonstrating through self-restraint and persuasiveness that 'the overall interest of Europe would coincide with the enlightened self-interest of Germany', as Geiss puts it. But, given that Germany under Wilhelm II lacked the diplomatic skill and subtlety to pull off such a challenging and sophisticated policy, the alternative was *Weltpolitik*, in its familiar erratic form, eschewing even a partnership with either Britain or Russia.

The German Problem became more evident in the decade before 1914 largely because Europe was once again the focal point of great power diplomacy, in a way that it had not been, except for the Bulgarian crisis, since the early 1880s. Langhorne rightly emphasizes the significance of the fact that the centre of gravity of international affairs had shifted away from Africa and Asia by 1905. If there had been a 'German Problem' during the heyday of the age of imperial expansion, it was not the main preoccupation of the foreign or colonial ministers of the other great powers, especially Britain, for whom Germany was an irritant rather than a threat in the way that France and Russia were. But just as Fashoda marked the ending of Anglo-French rivalry over Egypt and Africa, the battles of Mukden and Tsushima Straits signified the end of Russia's expansionist drive in the Far East. The ending, or at least softening, of these imperial rivalries, however, did not usher in a period of relative calm and tranquility in the European states system. Instead, the decade following the Russo-Japanese war witnessed a sharp increase in international tension which led, directly or indirectly, to the outbreak of war in 1914.

A key question, therefore, is how far Germany can be held responsible for the growth of tension among the great powers in this period. A useful starting point is provided by what might be called the 'Hinsley thesis'; namely, that the responsibility of the German government for the outbreak of war in 1914 lay far more in the actions it took between 1904 and 1913 than in the decisions it made in the July crisis itself.

That Germany bears a large measure of blame for the growth of international tension after 1905 seems unquestionable. In specific crises, its culpability was much greater than that of any other power. As noted earlier, Germany not only deliberately provoked a crisis over Morocco in 1905, it also prolonged the tension until the French agreed to an international conference. Taking advantage of Russia's military incapacity in 1905, Germany's leaders used the threat of war to secure Delcassé's downfall. The Tangier affair also revealed a dangerous flaw in German diplomacy – the failure to provide an honourable means of escape from a crisis. The same mistake was made again in 1911, when excessive demands were made which could only be achieved by 'thumping the table'. This miscalculation resulted in the Agadir crisis becoming an Anglo-German confrontation, in which expectations of war were once again raised. Kennedy's comment that 'Wilhelmine Germany never enjoyed the luxury of a coherent strategy' seems apt enough. Tempting as it may be to blame the ineptitude of German policy over Morocco on the Kaiser, who combined insanity with intellectual brilliance in unpredictable proportions, the record shows quite clearly that his role in these crises was relatively minor.

The same could not be said, of course, about his role in the expansion of the German navy, which developed into a pointless and ruinously expensive naval arms race with Britain. Although the harmful effect of the naval rivalry on Anglo-German relations was obvious enough by 1909, as recognized by both Bülow and Bethmann Hollweg, the Kaiser and Tirpitz remained obdurate in their resistance to a reduction in the shipbuilding programme. The opportunity for a *détente* with Britain that might have led to a significant relaxation of tension in Europe was thereby missed.

The anxiety felt by other states at the erratic course of German diplomacy was naturally compounded by awareness of the disparity in power between Germany and its neighbours. The sheer speed and extent of Germany's growth in economic and military/naval terms between 1890 and 1913 was awesome. The strength of the German economy on the eve of 1914 seems undeniable. For example, Ruth Henig's claim that Germany 'dominated continental Europe economically by 1914' is paralleled by Kennedy's assertion that Germany 'had become the economic powerhouse of Europe'. Although way behind Russia in demographic growth, Germany's population increase from 49 million in 1890 to 66 million in 1913 exceeded that of all the other states. In industrial terms, the country achieved a tripling of coal production, an output of steel greater than that of the Triple Entente states combined, and a dominant position in the new technologies of electrics, optics and chemicals. Germany also boasted the second largest merchant fleet for its rapidly increasing export trade, while the navy rose from sixth to second rank in the world between 1898 and 1914. The relative neglect of the German army in financial terms ended after Agadir, with the doubling of the army budget between 1910 and 1914. With well-trained reservists to reinforce its peacetime army, Germany possessed a formidable military force that qualitatively outclassed the peasant armies of the tsar.

Germany also stood out from the other powers, but especially from Russia, as 'the best educated and best organized state in the world', as Geiss modestly observes. The country's capacity to maximize the full potential of its human and other resources naturally stands out in stark contrast to the incompetence of the tsarist regime. The remarkable efficiency of the Prussian military machine, run by an unusually competent general staff which had no equal in Europe, made it feasible to plan the rapid movement of 2 million troops and half a million horses, plus supplies, by exploiting the full potential of railway networks. To contemporary observers the combined might of the foremost army on the continent with the second largest navy, both commanded by a totally unpredictable supreme warlord, constituted the essence of the German Problem. Hence the desire for some means of containing a power whose standards of international behaviour left much to be desired.

The Reich's situation was not seen in the same light, however, by Germany's political and military leaders. In a recent review of new works on aspects of German policy before 1914, Niall Ferguson has come to the startling conclusion that 'For all her economic strength, Germany in 1914 was a power in military decline.' In terms of manpower, of course, it was obvious enough that Germany was no match for Russia. Even when combined with its ally, Austria-Hungary, there was a population deficit of about 50 million in relation to the Russians. Hence the frequently expressed fears of the 'Slav hordes' that threatened to engulf Germany.

In military terms, Germany's war strength of 2.2 million faced a Russian force of between 3 and 4 million. The raising of the peace-time strength of the German army in 1912–13 to 760,000 which, combined with the Austro-Hungarian army, resulted in a total of 1.3 million troops in 1914, still left the German powers at a severe disadvantage to the Franco-Russian alliance, whose peacetime forces totalled 2.5 million. The discrepancy in the size of the forces of the two alliance blocs is partly attributable to the adoption of the Three-Year Service Law in France in 1913. But the main factor was Russia's army reform programme, due for completion in 1916–17, comple-mented by the construction of more strategic railways.

From the perspective of Berlin the problem overshadowing Europe was not the 'latent hegemony' of a Germany 'bursting with every conceivable expression of strength' but how Germany itself could ensure its supremacy, or even its survival, in the face of Russia's demographic strength and growing economic power. One answer, Ferguson suggests, was to strengthen the defence capability, for which task Germany appeared to have adequate economic and financial resources. In one respect, that of the navy, Germany's defence capability had obviously been greatly increased by 1914, but this would not be of much help in a land war with Russia. If the army was denied additional funds after 1900 because priority was given to the Tirpitz Plan, its objections were seemingly muted because of Prussian fears of conscripting 'unreliable' elements (such as socialists) into the ranks and of diluting the officer corps with non-aristocrats. Not that the latter objection made much sense, given that only 30 per cent of army officers were of noble origin by 1912.

The main point is why Ludendorff's proposal of December 1912 to raise the call-up rate from 50 per cent to 80 per cent, in line with the French rate, was not adopted as the obvious solution to German fears of the Slav hordes. Moltke's answer would have been that 'our enemies are arming more vigorously than we, because we are strapped for cash', as he noted at the time. It seems strange that a state as strong as Germany could have been short of funds for something as vital as defence. But curiously enough Germany's defence expenditure, when measured as a percentage of its GNP, had only risen from 3.3 per cent in 1891 to 3.8 per cent in 1913. This was less than that of France (3.9 per cent) or Russia (4.6 per cent), justifying Trebilcock's observation that 'quantification of Germany's military effort serves only to stress its modest dimensions.'

The reason why the Germans did not spend more on defence to ease the Kaiser's alarm at the Russian armaments programme was, in Ferguson's view, because the size of the German army was determined by domestic politics. The major obstacles to higher military expenditure seem to have stemmed from the complex financial structure of the Reich and the government's difficulties in securing majorities in the Reichstag for unpopular fiscal measures. As a result of the German government's inability either to borrow as much as its counterparts in France or Russia did, or to raise as much in direct taxes as Britain did, 'the Reich could not win the arms races it engaged in with its rivals.' Hence the paradox that for all Germany's much vaunted economic strength, this 'super great-power of the continent', as Geiss and Kennedy call her, had grounds to fear for its security on the eve of 1914.

SOURCES AND FURTHER READING

Anderson, E. N., *The First Moroccan Crisis 1904–1906*, Chicago, Chicago University Press, 1930; repr. Hamden, Conn., Archon Books, 1966.

Andrew, C., *T. Delcassé and the Making of the Entente Cordiale*, London, Macmillan, 1968.

Bridge, F. R., *From Sadowa to Sarajevo. The Foreign Policy of Austria-Hungary 1866–1914*, London, Routledge & Kegan Paul, 1972.

Bridge, F. R. and Bullen, R., *The Great Powers and the European States System 1815–1914*, Harlow, Longman, 1980.

Ferguson, N., 'Germany and the origins of the First World War: new perspectives', *Historical Journal*, 1992, vol. 35(3): 725–52.

Geiss – see Schöllgen.

Hinsley, F. H., *Power and the Pursuit of Peace*, Cambridge, Cambridge University Press, 1963.

—— (ed.), *British Policy under Sir Edward Grey*, Cambridge, Cambridge University Press, 1977.

Howard, M., *The Continental Commitment*, Harmondsworth, Penguin, 1974.

Keiger, J. F. V., *France and the Origins of the First World War*, London, Macmillan, 1983.

Kennedy, P., *The Rise of the Anglo-German Antagonism 1860–1914*, London, Allen & Unwin, 1980.

——, *The Rise and Fall of the Great Powers*, London, Fontana 1989.

Lambi, I. N., *The Navy and German Power Politics 1862–1914*, London, Allen & Unwin, 1984.

Langhorne, R., *The Collapse of the Concert of Europe 1890–1914*, London, Macmillan, 1981.

Lieven, D. C. B., *Russia and the Origins of the First World War*, London, Macmillan, 1983.

Lowe, C. J. and Dockrill, M. L., *The Mirage of Power. British Foreign Policy 1902–14*, vol. 1, London, Routledge & Kegan Paul, 1972.

Schöllgen, G. (ed.), *Escape into War? The Foreign Policy of Imperial Germany*, Oxford, Berg, 1990.

Taylor, A. J. P.. The Struggle for Mastery in Europe 1848–1918, Oxford, Clarendon Press, 1954.

Turner, L. C. F., *Origins of the First World War*, London, Arnold, 1970.

Williamson, S. R. Jr, *The Politics of Grand Strategy 1904–14*, Cambridge, Mass., Harvard University Press, 1969.

—— *Austria-Hungary and the Origins of the First World War*, London, Macmillan, 1991.

Wilson, K. M., *The Policy of the Entente*, Cambridge, Cambridge University Press, 1985.

For the Tangier affair and the Algeciras Conference, Anderson's classic is still useful. Delcassé's role in the 1905 crisis is closely examined by Christopher Andrew, while Keiger contains some important information on French responsibility for Agadir in 1911. Williamson's *Grand Strategy* needs some revision, perhaps, but provides full coverage of both Moroccan crises. Lambi also has interesting material on German aims in 1905 and 1911. Grey's policy is examined in chapters 5 and 14 of Hinsley's edited work. Wilson's revisionist views are of relevance.

Austria-Hungary's role in the Balkan crises is explained in detail in Bridge (pp. 288–309 and chapter 7) and also in Williamson's invaluable new work. Russian policy is treated briefly in Lieven. British policy is examined by Lowe and Dockrill. The general works, Langhorne and Bridge and Bullen, offer valuable insights. Taylor (chapters 19–21) is well worth consulting, as usual.

On the 'German Question', Geiss's essay in Schöllgen has some interesting ideas. Hinsley examines several aspects of the German problem before 1914 in chapter 13 of his book. Chapter 5 of Kennedy's general book is useful.

7 The great powers and the July crisis, 1914

INTRODUCTION

The 'July crisis' began with the assassination of Franz Ferdinand in Sarajevo, the capital of Bosnia, on 28 June and ended with the outbreak of war in the first days of August 1914. The conspirators who carried out the murder of the heir to the Austro-Hungarian throne were young Bosnian Serbs, aided by members of a Serbian secret society, operating from Belgrade. In the shadows of the conspiracy lurked the chief of Serbian military intelligence, known as 'Apis'. His involvement in a plot, but not the details of it, was suspected by the Serbian prime minister and the minister of the interior.

After the initial shock of the assassination had passed, a deceptive lull fell over the chancelleries of Europe for several weeks. State visits and royal cruises went ahead as planned. Senior military personnel took their summer leave. The semblance of normality ended abruptly on 23 July when an Austrian ultimatum was delivered to Belgrade, with a time limit for reply of only forty-eight hours. The Serbian reply belied its conciliatory appearance by its refusal of the key demand for the participation of Austrian officials in an investigation into the assassination plot. At the time much was made of respect for Serbia's sovereignty, but the evidence now suggests that the key factor behind its rejection was almost certainly the fear of what Austrian officials would uncover about the complicity of the Serbian authorities.

The government in Vienna rejected the Serb reply and broke off diplomatic relations with Belgrade on 25 July. Three days later Austria-Hungary formally declared war on Serbia, though very few shots were fired for the next two weeks. London's belated attempts at mediation between 23 and 27 July foundered because of Germany's reluctance to restrain its ally and Austria's determination to press on with the chastisement of Serbia, come what may. By 26 July serious military preparations were under way in Russia, culminating in full mobilization on the 30th. Although discussions had at last begun between Vienna and St Petersburg, time had almost run out for a diplomatic solution to the crisis.

Russia's mobilization impelled the German high command to follow suit the next day and, because of the exigencies of the Schlieffen Plan, to proceed from mobilization to a declaration of war against Russia on 1 August and against France two days later. Germany's refusal to respect Belgian neutrality enabled the hesitant and divided Liberal government in Britain to agree on an ultimatum to Berlin, which brought Britain into the war on 4 August. The prime mover in the crisis, Austria-Hungary, eventually got round to declaring war on Russia on 6 August.

THE AUSTRO-SERB CONFLICT

The confrontation between Austria-Hungary and Serbia not only initiated the July crisis, it may also have played a major role in causing the outbreak of a general European war in August 1914. Two aspects of Austrian policy seem worthy of particular notice. First, why was Berchtold so determined to provoke a 'third Balkan war' in 1914, when he had strenuously avoided a military solution to the Serbian problem in 1912–13? Second, given his commitment to the use of force, why did he fail to launch a rapid riposte against Belgrade in early July 1914?

That Berchtold was not contemplating war against Serbia before the Sarajevo outrage is shown by the Matscheko Memorandum, completed in June 1914. In this wide-ranging appraisal of the Dual Monarchy's predicament in the Balkans after the wars of 1912–13, a resort to force was not one of the recommended options, despite the gloomy prospects for the future that it outlined. To remedy Austria-Hungary's ills – enumerated as the aggrandizement of Serbia; Roumanian unreliability; instability in Albania; a possible Serb-Montenegrin union, and a new Balkan League – the memorandum placed reliance on forceful diplomacy alone. One obvious diplomatic option – a *détente* with St Petersburg, which was favoured by Franz Ferdinand – was ruled out on the grounds that Russia's newly assertive foreign policy, which now had French backing and funds, left no hope for a compromise in the Balkans. The Dual Monarchy's best hope was deemed to be an aggressive foreign policy with firm backing from Berlin, directed towards isolating Serbia from the other Balkan states. If Austro-German pressure on Roumania failed to secure from the latter's Hohenzollern king an open commitment to his long-standing secret alliance with Austria-Hungary, then Vienna should seek to win over Bulgaria and Turkey to the Triple Alliance camp. The recommendations of the Matscheko Memorandum provide clear evidence therefore that Berchtold was not intending war against Serbia before Sarajevo, despite the disastrous outcome of the Balkan wars.

The assassination of Franz Ferdinand on 28 June, however, changed all that. Although widespread misgivings had existed about the archduke's suitability as the heir to the Habsburg throne, the brutal murder in Sarajevo was regarded as deliberate provocation by Serbia. Within five days of the crime the Austrian authorities had obtained evidence that linked the assassins with Belgrade. The complicity of some elements of the Serbian military was undoubted, but the Austrians could not prove it, nor could they determine just how far the conspiracy extended into the ranks of the civilian leadership. Nevertheless, by early July there was evidence enough that the conspiracy was hatched in Belgrade with the connivance, if not complicity, of Serbian officials.

The government in Vienna reacted to the assassination with a determination to settle accounts with Serbia, but divergent views were expressed as to how this should be done. The army's chief of staff, Conrad, and the more belligerent ministers were all for a surprise attack on Serbia. Berchtold, once convinced that the Serbian government was implicated in the conspiracy, favoured a diplomatic confrontation that would probably result in war. The stumbling block was Tisza. The Hungarian prime minister, whose constitutional position was such that notice had to be taken of his views, refused to countenance anything more than diplomatic pressure on Belgrade. His persistence in this attitude until mid-July nullified the consensus of the other ministers at the common ministerial council meeting on 7 July in favour of a strong ultimatum to Serbia, followed by a localized war.

This was the major reason for the fateful delay in Austria-Hungary's retaliation against Serbia. By the time Tisza's opposition had been overcome two other complications had arisen to prevent rapid action. The first – a curious one in view of Conrad's preference for a quick strike – was that troops could not be recalled from 'harvest leave' without arousing suspicion. The second was the state visit of the French president to Russia, from 21 to 23 July. Berchtold assumed that Poincaré's presence in St Petersburg would facilitate a vigorous, concerted response to the ultimatum by the Franco-Russian alliance, but the president could hardly have been more bellicose than the ambassador to Russia, Paléologue. Vienna decided to delay the despatch of the ultimatum to Belgrade until 23 July, more than three weeks after the incident at Sarajevo, despite pressure from Berlin to take prompt action against Serbia.

The delay owed nothing to uncertainty about the reliability of Austria-Hungary's German ally in the event of Russian intervention. Germany's unconditional support was promised during the visit of the hawkish emissary, Count Hoyos, to Berlin on 5–6 July. But the so-called 'blank cheque' was accompanied by an exhortation to 'act quickly'. Although there were strong hopes in Vienna that Germany's backing would deter Russia, the Austrians were prepared to face the risk of war. Curiously, they neglected to consider possible approaches to St Petersburg that might have persuaded the tsar to stand aside from an Austro-Serb conflict.

The laboriously prepared ultimatum, cataloguing Serbian misdeeds since 1908, was designed to provide the Dual Monarchy with a formal justification for declaring war on Serbia. By itself, the demand that Austrian officials should participate in the investigation of the conspiracy more or less guaranteed its rejection. The conciliatory appearance of the reply belied the fact that the Serbian government committed itself to nothing.

Once the forty-eight hour time limit had expired, the Austrians began a headlong rush into war, in marked contrast to their dilatory conduct before 23 July. Diplomatic relations with Serbia were broken off on the 25th, followed only three days later by partial mobilization and the declaration of war. From a military point of view this was quite pointless, since Conrad announced, somewhat surprisingly, that the army would not be ready to begin the invasion of Serbia for another two weeks. The declaration of war was in fact made at Berchtold's insistence, with some prompting from Berlin, for fear that Vienna would be subjected to intense pressure to accept some sort of worthless diplomatic formula that would leave the Serbian menace unresolved. Hence his rejection of the subsequent 'halt in Belgrade' proposal from Berlin on 28 July, when the German chancellor made a desperate appeal to Vienna to allow time for last-minute diplomatic negotiations to produce results. Despite news of Russia's mobilization on 30 July, the common ministerial council at its meeting the next day reaffirmed its decision for war against Serbia.

In fact, Conrad was so determined to have his war with Serbia that he committed the ultimate folly of despatching divisions to the Balkan front that should have been deployed against the Russians in Galicia. Their subsequent redirection northwards deprived the Austrians of the chance of victory over the Serbs, while their belated arrival in Galicia ensured that the offensive against the Russians would end in disaster for the Austro-Hungarian army.

In assessing Austria-Hungary's responsibility for the outbreak of war in 1914, historians generally give some consideration to the influence of domestic factors on Vienna's foreign policy and the extent to which that policy was 'made in Berlin'. A case of sorts can be made that Austria-Hungary's leaders, despairing of the insoluble nature of the country's domestic problems, opted for war in 1914.

Evidence of political strife in both Vienna and Budapest certainly abounds. The renewal of Czech-German clashes led to the prorogation of the Reichsrat in Vienna in March 1914. At about the same time, the Hungarian prime minister was battling against Magyar assaults over concessions to the Roumanian minorities, which turned out to be too limited to satisfy their nationalist party. However, in the opinion of two recent authorities on the Habsburg Monarchy, there was nothing unusual about seemingly intractable political problems in Austria-Hungary – this had become a way of life, summed up in the laconic observation: 'the situation is hopeless, but not serious.'

Domestic chaos was not, by itself, a powerful enough reason for war in 1914. The real challenge to the survival of the Dual Monarchy at this moment was external, particularly the Serbian threat. But it would be unrealistic to ignore the interplay of foreign and domestic factors in an era of growing Slav nationalism. The right conclusion is perhaps that failure to act decisively in a major diplomatic crisis increased the chances of disintegration from within, which was a sort of 'occupational hazard' of a multinational empire in the early twentieth century.

Notwithstanding the evidence of Germany's 'war guilt', there is a plausible case that 'Austro-Hungarian policy was not made in Berlin', as Bridge asserts. In similar vein, Williamson contends that 'the steps that pushed Europe toward war were taken in Vienna.' The war that the Austrians wanted was, of course, a strictly localized war against Serbia. Full mobilization of the Austro-Hungarian army, to prepare for war against Russia, did not take place until 4 August, a week after the partial mobilization against Serbia on 28 July. The fact that this move was not taken until a whole month had elapsed since the Sarajevo crime might suggest that it was even more a case of the steps that Vienna did not take which made a European war unavoidable. Albertini's comment that 'Berlin could encourage and spur on to attack, but the initiative was taken by Austria' may credit the Germans with more influence over their dilatory ally than they actually had. If Austrian troops had occupied Belgrade within a week of Sarajevo, thereby presenting the Triple Entente powers with a *fait accompli*, there was a good chance that this action would have been tolerated even by Russia, given the shock aroused by the assassination of the heir to the Habsburg throne. After all, as late as the last week of July it still seemed possible that St Petersburg might accept that some 'chastisement' of Serbia was permissible.

Berchtold's determination to press on with preparations for war against Serbia, despite clear signs of Russia's intent to intervene, suggests that a sense of fatalism had taken hold in Vienna that was not present before Sarajevo. In seeking an explanation for this change of front, historians have suggested a number of possible factors. For Conrad and the 'war party' in Vienna, of course, Sarajevo provided the perfect excuse for a war that they had wanted for some years, which in Conrad's case meant as far back as 1908. For Berchtold and the emperor, on the other hand, the decision to risk all in a conflict that might well draw in Russia represented an abandonment of the caution and prudence that had been such striking features of Vienna's 'crisis management' during the Balkan wars of 1912–13.

The simplest explanation, of course, is that Sarajevo was merely the 'last straw' in a series of provocations extending over the past decade. But there was more to it than that. As Bridge points out, Sarajevo struck at the heart of the Dual Monarchy – its prestige and standing as a great power – presenting the foreign minister with a stark choice. Action meant the risk of destruction in war. Inaction could result in the disintegration of the empire under the growing clamour of south Slav nationalism, encouraged by Serbia. The assassination of the heir to the throne seemed to demonstrate that Belgrade's defiance of Vienna knew no bounds, given the evidence of links between the conspirators and the Serbian military, possibly extending to the government itself. Unless checked, pan-Serbism would make the Dual Monarchy's position in Bosnia-Herzegovina untenable and encourage Roumanian nationalism in Transylvania. This was seemingly the decisive factor in Tisza's belated change of front over the use of force against Belgrade.

Ironically, in assassinating Franz Ferdinand the conspirators had

THE POWER BEHIND.

Austria (*at the ultimatum stage*). "I DON'T QUITE LIKE HIS ATTITUDE. SOMEBODY MUST BE BACKING HIM."

eliminated an influential force for peace in the Balkans and a champion of some measure of autonomy for the south Slavs within the Dual Monarchy. The archduke had also been virtually a lone advocate of *détente* with Russia.

The Russian threat is regarded by Williamson as an important factor in the reactions of both the Germans and the Austrians to Sarajevo. Serbia's overt hostility to Austria was made possible by Russian patronage of its most reliable client state in the Balkans. More than that, the Russian minister at Belgrade had been actively fomenting anti-Austrian attitudes for years. So great was Hartwig's influence that he was said to have kept the Pašić government in power in its struggle with the Serbian military, one of whose leaders was the head of a secret society which was involved in the assassination. The conclusion of an arms deal on very favourable terms for the Serbs suggests, in Williamson's view, that 'the client had indeed become the manipulator and the initiator.' According to a British diplomat, Serbia had become virtually a Russian outpost by 1913. The Austrians certainly believed that Russia was intent on challenging them in the Balkans at a time when their own influence in the region was already on the decline.

The Russian threat was not even confined to the Balkans. Vienna was also alarmed by reports that Russia was arousing pan-Slav feeling in Galicia and Bukovina, even though the Dual Monarchy refrained from exploiting opportunities to retaliate in Russian Poland. Although the relationship between pan-Slavism and official circles in St Petersburg was mostly fairly tenuous, there is no doubt that Vienna regarded the Russian government as responsible for the spread of doctrines that jeopardized the survival of Austria-Hungary.

Another important factor in Berchtold's pessimistic outlook during the July crisis was, Langhorne suggests, his lack of confidence in the fair-mindedness of the Concert of Europe. Disillusioned by the way the great powers had behaved during the conference on the Balkan wars, at which 'horse trading' prevailed over decisions based on the merits of the case, Berchtold refused to allow the latest manifestation of the Austro-Serb conflict to be determined by an international conference or by mediation by the 'disinterested powers'. Consequently he and the other decision-makers in Vienna were resolved on military action against Serbia in 1914. Remak's conclusion that both Austria-Hungary and Serbia displayed great recklessness in 1914 is hard to fault. In the sense that the critical decisions were taken by Berchtold and Pašić, rather than Bethmann and Sazonov, it was their brinkmanship with a vengeance that caused the 'third Balkan war' in 1914, from which Russia was unlikely to stand aside.

RUSSIA AND THE BALKANS

The Austrian ultimatum to Serbia presented the Russian government with a dilemma. If it reacted strongly, the outcome might well be a European war for which Russia was not well prepared. On the other hand, if its response was regarded as weak Russia would suffer a major diplomatic defeat which would damage its prestige as the champion of the Slavs and as a great power. It would also arouse the wrath of public opinion and the press, already highly critical of the alleged weakness of the regime's foreign policy in recent years. In deciding how to respond to the Austrian threat to Serbia's independence, the Russian government was naturally very concerned about its influence in the Balkans. Less obvious is the degree to which anti-German sentiment coloured the attitude of Russia's leaders in the July crisis.

Russo-German relations had periodically been subject to serious strains since Bismarck's time. In the six years before 1914, however, a note of bitterness developed in Russian attitudes towards Germany. The so-called 'ultimatum' of 1909 during the Bosnian crisis was naturally regarded as a humiliating blow to Russian pride. Subsequently, in the settlement of the Balkan wars Sazonov complained that Germany had not been even-handed in the concessions demanded of Russia and Austria-Hungary. Finally, in late 1913 Germany and Russia became locked in a major diplomatic crisis over the appointment of a German general, Limon von Sanders, to reorganize the Turkish army and to command the garrison at Constantinople.

The possibility that Germany might dominate Constantinople and the Straits created serious alarm in St Petersburg, which the Kaiser did nothing to ease by his typically tactless remark that 'the German flag will soon fly over the fortifications of the Bosphorus.' As Sazonov objected, a hostile power in control of the Straits (through which passed nearly two fifths of Russia's exports and three quarters of its grain shipments between 1903 and 1912) meant the 'complete subordination of the economic development of the whole of Southern Russia'.

Sazonov's determination to face up to Germany over the Limon von Sanders affair was not weakened by British and French coolness towards the issue. Once Grey was assured that Limon von Sanders's powers were nothing like as extensive as originally reported, he was reluctant to damage the friendly relations recently restored between London and Berlin by pressing his original protest. Besides, the Foreign Office was embarrassed by the discovery that a British admiral actually commanded the Turkish fleet in peacetime. In addition, a British firm had just acquired a monopoly of dockyard and naval arsenal work for the Turkish navy, which had recently purchased two British dreadnoughts. Britain was hardly in a position, therefore, to complain about a German general being appointed to command a military mission to reorganize the Turkish army in 1913, when a British naval mission had been directing the Turkish fleet since 1909.

Although Germany had been foolish not to negotiate with Russia about the appointment of General von Sanders, Sazonov's overreaction to the affair and talk of an ultimatum to Berlin illustrate Russian sensitivity to what was regarded as Germany's high-handed behaviour. The crisis was eventually resolved by a compromise in which von Sanders was promoted to the post of inspector-general of the Turkish army, which removed him from a direct connection with Constantinople or the Straits. The unspoken objection of St Petersburg to German military influence at the Turkish capital was, of course, that it might impede a Russian seizure of the Straits if the Ottoman empire collapsed. In the spring of 1914 Sazonov learned that Germany had similar designs on the Straits, which created further hostility towards Berlin.

Russo-German relations were also adversely affected by the growth of German economic influence in Turkey, Asia Minor and Persia, since the Russians were well aware that their trade in these regions would suffer from German competition. German penetration of the Russian domestic market, especially the growth of German exports to Russia from 1905 to 1913, also caused resentment and led to talk of Russia becoming an economic 'colony' of its industrialized neighbour. Given that roughly 45 per cent of both Russia's imports and exports were linked to Germany, some unease at this dependence on trade with the Germans was understandable.

Russia's well-founded sense of inferiority to Germany in the economic sphere was compounded by the display of German arrogance towards the Slavs as a race. This affronted the dignity of the Russian people, who regarded themselves as one of the leading nations of Europe. By 1914, therefore, anti-German sentiments were quite widespread among the educated classes and landowners in Russia. The traditional germanophile views were by this time confined to a very narrow group. Furthermore, the emotional slavophilism of Russian nationalists led to vigorous criticism in both the press and the Duma of Sazonov's allegedly 'ineffective diplomacy' during the Balkan wars. The fact that these attacks were often based on ignorance and unrealistic expectations was little consolation to the tsarist regime. As a consequence, the foreign minister and his colleagues were unlikely to retreat when confronted by German threats in July 1914. Their determination to stand firm was reinforced by the belief that the Russian army was stronger than it had been in previous crises. Another factor was their confidence of complete French support in the event of war with Germany, following Poincaré's visit to St Petersburg in late July.

Sazonov reacted to the news of the Austrian ultimatum by declaring in his excitable way, 'C'est une guerre européenne.' He assumed, correctly, that the Austrians intended to attack Serbia, buttressed by an assurance of German support if the conflict did not remain confined to the Balkans. Taken aback by the severity and unexpectedness of the ultimatum, Sazonov does not seem to have initiated rigorous enquiries into the possible involvement of the Serbian authorities in the conspiracy. He was too easily satisfied by a report which implied that Austrian allegations against Belgrade were groundless. Indeed, Sazonov's assertion that 'pan-Serb agitation in Austria was an internal growth' reveals an alarming lack of judgement and knowledge of the activities of organizations such as the Narodna Odbrana and the Black Hand, not to mention Hartwig's anti-Austrian antics in Belgrade. In the July crisis Sazonov seems to have shown little awareness of the danger to Austria-Hungary's survival from the 'ferment of nationalities' within the Dual Monarchy, as a more prescient colleague termed it, especially when aggravated by Serb and Roumanian irredentism.

At the meeting of the council of ministers on 24 July Sazonov asserted that abandonment of Russia's historic mission as protector of the Slavs would reduce it to the rank of a second-rate power. Convinced of Germany's intent to extend its power in central Europe and the Near East, he argued that Russia's conciliatory stance in earlier crises had been interpreted in Berlin as a sign of weakness. This time Russia must stand firm, even at the risk of war. Most of the other ministers expressed similar views, believing that vital Russian interests were at stake. Some also argued, on slender grounds, that a firm and energetic response was the best way to discourage the German powers from persisting in an aggressive policy. In similar vein, the service ministers argued for firmness even though Russia's rearmament was not complete. In private, however, the war minister admitted that the army was not prepared for war – an important factor that might have influenced the decisions being taken if it had been more widely known.

The consensus of the council of ministers was clearly that Russia should stand by Serbia and trust to firm diplomacy to maintain peace, failing which sacrifices were necessary to preserve Russia's honour. Accordingly, Serbia was to be urged to adopt a conciliatory stance consistent with safeguarding its independence, while Vienna would be asked to extend the forty-eight hour deadline to allow more time for negotiation. As a warning to Austria-Hungary, however, the ministers decided to mobilize the southern military districts if the tsar gave his assent.

The council of ministers seems to have made two miscalculations, one diplomatic and one military. First, it assumed that Russian support for Serbia would make Belgrade adopt a more conciliatory approach towards the Austrian demands. In fact, it seems to have encouraged equivocation. Second, the decision on partial mobilization was taken in ignorance of the complications it might cause later, while the notion that it would do no more than serve as a warning to Vienna took little account of the realities of the alliance obligations or military planning of the German powers. The tsar's approval of the council's decisions permitted the declaration on 26th July of the 'Period Preparatory to War' which, while greatly facilitating the subsequent mobilization of the Russian army, caused considerable alarm in Berlin. By this time, the more competent elements within the Russian army command had informed the government that partial mobilization could severely hamper a subsequent switch to general mobilization if war with Germany threatened.

Following Austria-Hungary's reckless declaration of war on Serbia on 28 July and the bombardment of Belgrade, despite Serbia's seemingly conciliatory reply to the ultimatum, Sazonov despaired of a peaceful outcome to the Austro-Serb conflict. Berlin seemed either unwilling or unable to restrain its ally from precipitating war. Instead, Russia was sent a warning that Germany would mobilize unless Russian military preparations ceased.

The burden of decision rested with the tsar. Reluctant to unleash a European war, especially if more time might permit negotiations to succeed, Nicholas II was none the less highly sensitive to the need to uphold Russia's honour. Partial mobilization, to which he had consented on 28 July, was regarded as a necessary response to

Vienna's belligerent stance. General mobilization, signifying war with Germany, was a quite different matter. Hence his wavering on 29 July, cancelling the decree issued earlier in the day for full mobilization. But Sazonov and other ministers, as well as the military leaders, insisted that war with Germany was inevitable and that delaying general mobilization would put Russia at a serious disadvantage, given Germany's ability to deploy its forces much more rapidly. At this point the argument that chaos would result from attempting to implement general mobilization if partial mobilization was already under way became crucial. Finally, on 30 July, the tsar yielded to pressure from Sazonov, with the result that the French prime minister's advice to avoid provoking German mobilization arrived too late. Having issued a final severe warning to St Petersburg on 31 July, Germany declared war on Russia on 1 August.

Russian policy during the July crisis was largely a reaction to decisions taken by the Austrians and the Serbs. Discussion of Russia's responsibility for the outbreak of war usually focuses therefore on two policy decisions taken after the Austrian ultimatum to Belgrade; namely, the decision taken on 24 July to back Serbia and the decree for general mobilization on 30 July. Two additional questions, however, need to be considered: first, whether Russia's Balkan policy was irresponsible; second, whether the Russian government opted for war in 1914 in order to divert domestic discontent with the tsarist regime. The latter can be dismissed fairly readily as a major factor in the decisions taken in July 1914. Most of the evidence suggests that the government opted for war despite, not because of, fears of domestic unrest and that the tsar's ministers were surprised by the patriotic upsurge which greeted the news that Russia was at war. The question marks surrounding Russian policy in the Balkans can conveniently be considered in relation to the decisions of the council of ministers on 24 July.

The decision to stand firm against the German powers and to support Serbia was taken in the knowledge that this would probably result in a European war. Could Russia, as the protector of the Slavs, have done otherwise? One possibility perhaps is that Sazonov might have investigated more fully the Austrian assertion of Serbian involvement in the assassination conspiracy. Instead, the promise of Russian support for Belgrade seems to have stiffened the Serbian response to the ultimatum. Telegrams despatched between 23 and 31 July by the Serbian ambassador in St Petersburg, reporting conversations with Sazonov, may have played a crucial role in the attitude of the Serb government. This provided the Austrians with the excuse they wanted to reject the Serb reply. On the other hand, Lieven argues that total compliance by the Serbian government with the terms of the ultimatum would not have guaranteed peace, since Serbian opinion and especially the army would have refused to accept the infringement of Serbian independence implied by Austria's demands. Be that as it may, the Austro-Serb conflict would have been postponed, thereby giving diplomacy more time to find a solution.

Although Russia's prestige as a great power and its influence in the Balkans were on trial in 1914, as Lieven rightly observes, the stakes were even higher for Austria-Hungary, since its survival as a multi-national empire was threatened by pan-Slavism and, more directly, by pan-Serbism. If in the 1920s it was easy to dismiss Austria-Hungary as an anachronism and to regard 'self-determination' as a progressive policy, seventy years later the equation of national statehood with peace and progress is less clear.

The tsar and his ministers undeniably faced some hard choices in 1914, but even Lieven wonders whether, in purely rational terms, the issues at stake 'justified running the appalling risks Russia faced in entering a European war'. The promulgation of general mobilization on 30 July was certainly a fateful step, provoking Germany to follow suit within forty-eight hours. Turner is highly critical of this decision, on the grounds that there was no military necessity for it, since the preparations begun on 26 July had given Russia several days' advantage over Germany. Furthermore, he argues, the more the Austrians concentrated their forces for an attack on Serbia, the more vulnerable they became to a Russian offensive in Galicia. The technicalities involved in achieving a smooth transition from partial to general mobilization are harder to pass judgement on, but Lieven makes a case for the complexity of Russia's military organization involving the calling up of reservists.

Russia's main responsibility for the catastrophe in 1914 may lie less in its conduct during the July crisis itself than in the policies pursued in the Balkans in the years immediately prior to the war. Encouragement of the Balkan states' desire to end Turkish rule over Macedonia was a legitimate policy for a Slav great power to pursue, but Russia's inability to exercise much control over Serbia, whose expansionist ambitions were a threat to another great power, was fraught with danger for the peace of Europe.

Sazonov's unfounded obsession that Austria-Hungary was pursuing an expansionist policy in the Balkans clouded his judgement. The reality was that Russia was the expansionist power, but the

Balkan situation was slipping out of its control, as the Balkan wars demonstrated. St Petersburg seemed to exercise little control over its own minister in Belgrade, even though Serbia was virtually 'a Russian province' by 1913. In the spring of 1914 it was far from clear that the Serbian government had much control over its own army, let alone the patriotic organizations and secret societies which engaged in anti-Habsburg propaganda and subversive activities. Consequently the Serbian prime minister, Pašić, failed to react effectively to well-founded suspicions that the head of military intelligence, who was also the leader of the Black Hand, had encouraged a somewhat amateurish conspiracy to assassinate the Austrian archduke.

Although shocked by the unexpected murder of Franz Ferdinand, many of Russia's leaders, including the tsar, had been eagerly awaiting the demise of the aged Franz Joseph, which, they assumed, would lead to the disintegration of the Habsburg empire. In allowing their hostility to Austria-Hungary to colour their judgement, they failed to heed the warning of Prince Trubetskoy that 'the existence of an independent Austria is as much a necessity for Russia as for Europe.'

GERMANY AND THE POLICY OF 'CALCULATED RISK'

If Germany's leaders were intent on war in 1914, as Fischer maintains, Sarajevo provided them with an almost ideal opportunity. In contrast to the earlier crises over Morocco, to which Berlin's ally had been indifferent, a confrontation with Serbia necessarily involved Austria-Hungary's vital interests. On the basis of these assumptions, German policy in the July crisis becomes relatively easy to explain.

Three main features of German policy can be identified in this scenario: first, pressure on Vienna to retaliate against Serbia; second, Bethmann Hollweg's rejection of mediation proposals; third, military pressure on the government to ensure that the declaration of war followed shortly after mobilization. In early July Germany's leaders were certainly not urging restraint on Vienna. The Kaiser's reaction to the news of Sarajevo was to exclaim: 'We must finish with the Serbs.' On 5 July Count Hoyos was assured of Germany's full support, even if Russia intervened. A few days later the Austrians were informed that 'Berlin expected the Monarchy to act against Serbia and would not understand it if they missed the chance.' One obvious reason for German pressure to act was Moltke's view that 'a moment so favourable from the military point of view might never occur again.'

Fischer's view that Germany willed the war also casts a different light on Bethmann Hollweg's role in the crisis. Instead of the leader of the 'doves' against the 'hawks' in Berlin, the chancellor is portrayed as craftily manoeuvring to secure British neutrality and to cast Russia as the aggressor, so that public opinion would believe that Germany was engaged in a defensive war. In late July, therefore, when he had rejected most of Britain's mediation proposals, Bethmann Hollweg's aim was not to avoid a major war but to clear Germany of responsibility for it.

That the Fischer thesis commanded widespread acceptance for almost two decades is a testimony perhaps to Fischer's archival research and to his persuasiveness. The great strength of his interpretation was possibly its coherence, linking together the failures of German diplomacy in the era of *Weltpolitik* with the policy pursued during the July crisis. Paradoxically, the more the inconsistencies in Wilhelmine policy came to be revealed, the less convincing the Fischer thesis appeared to be.

Discussion of Germany's responsibility for the war has more recently sought to explain German policy during the July crisis in terms of the 'calculated risk' of achieving changes in the European power balance to Germany's advantage, without a major war. Consequently this approach emphasizes the factors which influenced the attitudes of the leading political figures and which, from the outset, limited their freedom of manoeuvre.

According to Jarausch and others, Bethmann Hollweg's key objective in July was the localization of the Austro-Serb conflict, thus enabling Austria-Hungary to rebuild its influence in the Balkans and to restore its prestige as a great power. The policy of the calculated risk was based on the premise that by presenting Europe with a *fait accompli* while the shock of the assassination was still fresh, war could be avoided. A rapid Austrian strike against Serbia, justified as a chastisement for Belgrade's complicity in the conspiracy, would be followed by the opening of negotiations with the entente powers for a peaceful settlement of outstanding issues, especially in the Balkans. If all went well the crisis would be over in about three weeks, that is by the end of July.

The 'blank cheque' to Austria-Hungary on 5 July was obviously a gamble. If there was a fair chance that Britain's cooperation could be obtained to act as a restraining influence on its entente partners to keep the conflict localized, the chances that Russia would stand aside, because it was unprepared for war, and agree to some sort of *rapprochement* with Germany were not so good. If Russia did decide to support Serbia, was there a fair chance that France might back away from war, thereby splitting the entente? But if the odds were not all that favourable for success, the alternative of abandoning the Dual Monarchy to its fate seemed worse. Germany would be left without a reliable ally against the Triple Entente and exposed to future 'blackmail' from the Franco-Russian alliance with no guarantee of British support in such a situation. The German chancellor undoubtedly feared that without a promise of support, the Austrians would 'throw themselves into the open arms of the Western powers and we lose our last important ally'.

The German military agreed to give the chancellor's strategy a chance, while secretly making preparations for war against Russia. But a time limit was set for a diplomatic solution to the crisis, giving Bethmann Hollweg until 23 July (later extended to the 26th) before the army command would seek to impose a military solution.

To have any chance of success the policy of the calculated risk required that the entente powers did not suspect Austrian action against Serbia and, above all, that the military action was accomplished as quickly as possible. By inviting British cooperation to keep the conflict localized, albeit with some vagueness as to the meaning of 'localization', Bethmann Hollweg was able to reduce the risk of intervention by the other powers. He failed completely, however, in the vital task of pressing the Austrians to heed Berlin's promptings to act quickly, commenting despairingly that 'they seem to need an eternity to mobilize'. Oddly enough, there was little communication between Vienna and Berlin for about ten days in mid-July because Berchtold, aware of indiscretions by German diplomats, revealed little of his plans to Berlin until 22 July.

Vienna's decision not to launch a surprise attack and the delay in despatching the ultimatum to Belgrade until 23 July undermined Bethmann Hollweg's reliance on a *fait accompli* to avoid Russia's intervention. Somewhat surprisingly, there seem to have been no plans to meet such a contingency, with the inevitable result that the policy of calculated risks moved relentlessly into a new phase in which the risks were vastly greater than they had seemed in the first week of July.

In late July Russian intervention seemed almost unavoidable. French participation in a European conflict seemed likely. Yet the chancellor largely ignored British mediation proposals, made on 23–7 July, because he could not accept the idea of a 'tribunal' sitting in judgement on Austria-Hungary. The remarkable speed shown by Vienna in its dealings with Serbia between 25 and 29 July virtually pre-empted any last-minute diplomatic initiatives. So too did pressure from the German high command.

By 27 July the prospects of successful Anglo-German cooperation to localize the conflict were small, especially after Berlin's rejection of Grey's proposal for a conference of ambassadors. Thereafter, decisions were increasingly subject to military needs. Moreover, in Berlin the chancellor was giving priority to rallying the nation to face the prospect of war with Russia and to securing British neutrality by the clumsy device of a guarantee of French and Belgian territorial integrity at the end of the war. In London Grey's main efforts were by this time directed towards winning cabinet approval for assurances to France of British military support in the event of a German attack.

Nevertheless, attempts continued to be made to localize the conflict. The Kaiser urged the Austrians to 'halt in Belgrade' and negotiate with Russia on the basis of Serbian territorial integrity. However, this belated attempt by the Kaiser and the chancellor to restrain the Austrians coincided with Moltke's pressure on Conrad to mobilize against Russia, prompting Berchtold's famous question: 'Who rules in Berlin?' In fact, Moltke was desperate to divert Conrad from his obsession with preparing for war against Serbia when danger loomed on Germany's exposed frontier, where only thirteen divisions faced the Russians. Even so, on 29 July Moltke supported the chancellor in opposing the war minister's demand for the proclamation of the preparatory stage before mobilization, insisting on its delay until Russia had incurred the odium of mobilizing first. Curiously enough, Trumpener's enquiry into the activities of German military intelligence in July 1914 suggests that the Prussian general staff was not convinced of the inevitability of war until 29 July, when the implications of Russia's preparations were fully appreciated.

When Berlin's formal warning to Russia on 31 July to cease all military preparations had no effect, mobilization was proclaimed in Germany. This meant not only that war must begin very soon, because of the exigencies of the timetable of the Schlieffen Plan, but also that the war would begin with a massive offensive against France. As the Kaiser discovered on 1 August when he suggested that the German armies should be directed against Russia, the high command had no plans prepared for an eastern offensive in 1914. It was the Schlieffen Plan or nothing. Germany declared war on

Russia on 1 August and demanded passage of its armies through Belgium the next day, declaring war on France on 3 August.

Recent trends in historical opinion suggest that Germany's responsibility for the outbreak of war in 1914 may have been considerably less than the Fischer school has maintained. A consensus, however, remains elusive. An unrepentant Fischer has recently reasserted that 'The determination to act came from the German side.' While the government in Vienna was hesitant and divided in the week immediately after Sarajevo, Berlin was exerting pressure, Fischer maintains, 'menacingly urging the Austrians to use the propitious moment for action against Serbia'. Although Geiss has modified some of his earlier views on the impact of domestic factors on *Weltpolitik*, his previous assertion that 'Germany was the aggressor . . . deliberately provoking Russia' is echoed in his recent conclusion that 'it was the Germans themselves who created the decisive conflict which escalated into the world war.'

Those historians who reject the Fischerite interpretation concede that even if Germany did not will the war, its actions could not be described as purely defensive. The war was not an 'accident'. It was the outcome of a 'series of gambles that did not work out', Remak suggests, because Germany's leaders took too many risks and failed to make a single constructive move during the crisis.

The view that Germany was the prime mover throughout the crisis, pushing a reluctant ally into a confrontation with Russia, no longer seems tenable. In 1914 Bethmann Hollweg faced what Jarausch calls the 'old dilemma' of Austrian policy in the Balkans: 'If we encourage them, they say we pushed them into it. If we discourage them, say we left them in the lurch.' The decision to act against Belgrade and to proceed to a declaration of war with Serbia on 28 July, despite the fact that military operations could not begin for another two weeks, was taken in principle by Berchtold, even if prompted by Berlin to advance the timing of the declaration by twenty-four hours.

In early July, Bethmann Hollweg's hopes of presenting the entente powers with a *fait accompli* were not wholly unrealistic and offered the central powers the prospect of a significant improvement in their situation. Once the premises were shown to be invalid, however, the chancellor seemingly had no alternative strategy for a diplomatic solution and acted too late and too ineffectually to rein in Germany's incompetent ally, which was clearly hell-bent on war with Serbia, regardless of the international consequences. By late

July Bethmann had, as Berghahn says, 'bluffed himself into an impasse" from which he could not easily extricate himself.

One avenue of escape was, of course, the solution pressed by the army command shortly after Sarajevo, but held in abeyance for the sake of the chancellor's policy of the calculated risk. That war would follow only days after mobilization was the result of Moltke's latest revision of the Schlieffen Plan, in which the surprise capture of Liège was crucial. Neither the Kaiser nor the chancellor were made aware of this fact until the last day of July. Faced with the argument that victory depended on strict observance of military timetables once mobilization had been declared, the politicians and diplomats had little room for manoeuvre. By eliminating the possibility of eleventh-hour diplomatic moves, Germany's high command ensured that the July crisis would be followed by the guns of August.

BRITAIN AND THE FAILURE OF MEDIATION

The crisis that perturbed the majority of British ministers for most of July was the threat of civil war in Ulster, arising from the Liberals' Irish Home Rule Bill. It was not until 24 July (after the ultimatum to Serbia) that the cabinet considered the Austro-Serb dispute, and this was the first time foreign affairs had been discussed for a month. Clearly the Liberal government was not exactly preoccupied with the European situation after Sarajevo. Consequently the foreign secretary and the Foreign Office had a free hand to explore possible solutions to the Austro-Serb dispute.

The surprising feature of Grey's policy for most of July was that he sought a diplomatic solution to the crisis through cooperation with Germany, rather than by showing solidarity with Britain's entente partners. Several reasons have been suggested for this rather odd policy, reflecting a change in the foreign secretary's assessment of the European situation since 1912.

The success of Anglo-German cooperation in the Balkan wars undoubtedly exercised a powerful influence on Grey's approach to the latest crisis in the Balkans. A second factor was his desire to preserve the recent *détente* with Germany. A few days before Sarajevo he revealed his coolness to the Triple Entente as an anti-German bloc when he asserted: 'we are on good terms with Germany now and desire to avoid a revival of friction with her', adding, significantly, that he wanted 'to discourage France from provoking Germany'. Third, Grey was anxious about Germany's response to the growth of Russian military power, which Ekstein calls 'the major development in international relations in the year or two before the outbreak of war', and felt it politic to offer Germany some reassurance on this count. Fourth, in Grey's view Russian policy was fickle and unprincipled, while French diplomacy had become more truculent since the *réveil national* of 1911–12. As a result, Grey now regarded the Triple Entente as something of a liability, in that Britain's partners might well lead the country into unwanted difficulties with Germany.

Nevertheless, despite his disenchantment with the entente, Grey was aware of Britain's dependence on Russian goodwill for the safety of its interests overseas, especially India. Ironically, it was the need to avoid alienating the tsarist government that led to his agreeing to naval talks with Russia in the spring of 1914, and these talks in turn made Bethmann Hollweg sceptical of Grey's integrity in pursuing a policy of non-alignment during most of July.

If Grey had any illusions about the gravity of the Austro-Serb dispute they were quickly dispelled by an interview with the German ambassador on 6 July. Lichnowsky warned Grey of the 'anxiety and pessimism' prevailing in Berlin, especially over Russia's military strength. Grey seems to have concluded from this conversation that Germany could be persuaded to restrain the Austrians if Berlin was offered some reassurance about Russia's intentions. Hence the request to his entente partners to ease German apprehensions and his decision not to put pressure on Berlin for some weeks. In the belief that a battle was being waged between 'doves' and 'hawks' in Berlin, Grey decided to give the doves a chance to achieve their aim of keeping the conflict localized.

Historians have naturally questioned how realistic this policy of cooperation with Germany was. For one thing, 'localization' of the conflict was an imprecise term open to various interpretations. Second, if Austria-Hungary's position in the Balkans was to be bolstered by diplomatic means, would the requisite changes in the alignment of the Balkan states be acceptable to Britain and its entente partners? An even more fundamental question was whether Grey was not putting too much trust in Bethmann Hollweg's good faith and in his capacity to deliver. Grey's advisers certainly thought so. Most Foreign Office officials and senior diplomats had for years been deeply suspicious of German policy, which led them to emphasize the need for a display of Triple Entente solidarity.

By mid-July the foreign secretary was becoming uneasy at the deceptive calm in Vienna and Berlin. A week later his fears that Germany was not acting as a peacemaker were confirmed by a report from Berlin on 22 July that Jagow, the foreign minister, admitted Germany was not urging restraint on Vienna. What was to be done? Grey's attempt to urge the Russians to engage in direct talks with the Austrians provoked the testy response from Sazonov that a coordinated warning to Vienna by the Triple Entente powers would be more appropriate.

The severity of the Austrian ultimatum shocked Grey and led to a series of mediation proposals between 24 and 27 July, for which he hoped to secure Berlin's active cooperation. But the initial proposal, that the four 'uninvolved' powers should offer their good offices to facilitate an Austro-Russian solution, was not passed on to Vienna. The second, for a conference of ambassadors in London, was rejected by Berlin as tantamount to a tribunal sitting in judgement on Austria-Hungary. The flaw in such proposals was, as noted earlier, that once Russia began military preparations, the military option would no longer be viable for the German powers if the outcome of the deliberations was unacceptable to the Austrians. Fearing that mediation might fail, Grey changed course. He now accepted that resistance to Germany's *Drohpolitik* (policy of threats) required the full weight of the Triple Entente.

The Austrian declaration of war on Serbia on 28 July, which led to the collapse of the Austro-Russian talks in St Petersburg, convinced Grey that he had been duped by Germany. But, unable to pursue a bold line because of the divisions within the British government, he took the remarkable step of giving a private warning to the German ambassador on 29 July that Britain's neutrality could not be counted on. Lichnowsky's report of this is said to have had a shattering effect in Berlin. Bethmann Hollweg, seemingly resigned to the prospect of a continental war by late July, was still hopeful that Britain would stand aside, at least in the early stages of such a war. Hence his frantic appeal to the Austrians to accept the 'halt in Belgrade' idea and his assurances to London of his efforts to secure a diplomatic solution to the crisis. Berlin's sudden change of front encouraged Grey to press St Petersburg to accept the 'stop at Belgrade' formula and to revive mediation efforts by the four powers in support of the new Austro-Russian talks, which had begun in Vienna. Although military moves prejudiced the success of such last-minute diplomatic efforts, they persisted until 1 August with George V's appeal to the tsar to delay Russian mobilization, in response to the Kaiser's offer the previous day to restrain Austria-Hungary.

There is general agreement that British policy was dangerously indecisive during the July crisis. Britain neither participated in a display of entente solidarity that might have deterred the central powers, nor gave Germany an official warning not to rely on British neutrality in the event of a general war. Foreign Office officials, especially Nicolson the permanent under-secretary, became increasingly restive, fearing the loss of Russia's friendship at a time when Germany was supposedly aiming at 'a political dictatorship in Europe'. At the same time, the director of military operations, Sir Henry Wilson, who was responsible for organizing the despatch of the British Expeditionary Force (BEF) to the continent, was becoming frantic at the shilly-shallying of his political masters.

The problem was not simply Grey's reliance on German goodwill and cooperation, which was waning fast by the last week of July. The main obstacle to a resolute policy as the crisis deepened was the aversion of the majority of the Liberal cabinet to involvement in war. At a series of cabinet meetings from 27 July onwards no agreement could be reached on guaranteeing support for France if it was attacked by Germany. It was hoped that the 'doves' in Berlin might yet save the day. Grey was only authorized to inform the French and German ambassadors that the British government was unable to pledge itself either to stand aside or to go to war. As late as 31 July procrastination was deemed preferable to a cabinet split. Not that hostility to war was confined to the ministers. The City was in turmoil, while the Liberal press and many Liberal MPs, especially those belonging to the influential foreign affairs committee, clung to the belief that British interests did not require the country to participate in a European war. Appeals from President Poincaré were of no avail. Cambon was told that the desperate plight France found itself in was the result of its alliance with Russia, not the Entente Cordiale.

The deadlock was broken on 2 August. The prospect of a coalition government influenced the waverers in the cabinet to back Grey when the Unionist leaders promised Asquith their full support for a policy of aid to France, so as to avoid 'disgrace and lasting danger and insecurity'. Belgium's neutrality was also a powerful influence on the waverers. It was agreed that although a partial infringement of Belgian neutrality might be tolerated, a substantial violation of its territory, as implied by the German demand on 2 August for free passage of its troops through Belgium was a threat to British security. The sudden realization that Britain had a moral obligation to defend France's Channel coast from a German naval attack also had an effect. Finally, Grey's persuasive case for British intervention, delivered in the House of Commons on 3 August, won general parliamentary approval for a policy of standing by France and Belgium, just when Bank Holiday crowds in London were demonstrating support for this policy. With Parliament and public opinion seemingly reconciled to the prospect of war, the cabinet was able to agree (with only two dissentients) to an ultimatum to Germany to cease its violation of Belgian neutrality, an ultimatum which expired before midnight on 4 August.

Britain's responsibility for the outbreak of war in 1914 was largely limited to its failure to make its position clear to Germany in good time. This issue apart, Britain bore little direct responsibility for the war. The country was in no sense a prime mover in the crisis. It had no firm alliance commitments, unlike the French, obliging it to mobilize its armed forces. Military schedules were so far from determining policy, even in the hectic last days of July, that the decision to send the BEF to France was not taken until two days after war with Germany began. Even if Britain's leaders were guilty of sins of omission, the fact remains that the foreign secretary made several mediation efforts, albeit somewhat belatedly. The main questions about British policy during the July crisis, therefore, are why the British government decided to go to war at all and why it took so long for the decision to be reached.

Grey later explained Britain's entry into the war on the grounds that 'if we did not stand by France and stand up for Belgium against this aggression, we should be isolated, discredited and hated.' More prosaically, Zara Steiner suggests that the decision was taken because Britain 'feared a German victory in western Europe which would threaten her safety and her empire.'

Despite this, as shown above, the majority of the Liberal cabinet was averse to being drawn into a European quarrel unless Britain itself was attacked. The pacifism of Grey's colleagues seems to have encouraged his own illusions about the viability of a policy of cooperation with Germany to resolve the Austro-Serb dispute. As a result, he allegedly 'lacked a capacity for decisive action in the July crisis' and 'followed the wrong course'. Clearly, the severity of the ultimatum to Serbia made his self-appointed task of restraining Russia very difficult. In addition, seeking German cooperation was liable to be misinterpreted as a desire to remain neutral. Since a world war which included Britain went beyond the policy of calculated risk, a blunt warning to Berlin on 26 July that Britain would not remain neutral would possibly have stopped Bethmann Hollweg from prompting Berchtold into a premature declaration of war on Serbia that was, from a military point of view, unnecessary. Whether

a display of Triple Entente solidarity from the outset would necessarily have deterred Berlin from backing Austria's proposed punitive
action against Serbis is uncertain. Arguably, it could have increased
Germany's sense of desperation to break the ring of 'encirclement'.

It is possible that in the years before the outbreak of war Britain
could have done more to lessen German fears of encirclement,
which the Anglo-Russian entente of 1907 fostered. K. M. Wilson has
even suggested that the Foreign Office invented the 'bogey' of
German hegemony to bolster Britain's role as the arbiter of Europe
in order to conceal its decline as a great power. But the need to
'contain' Germany, following the first crisis over Morocco and the
development of the naval rivalry, seemed justified at the time. The
subsequent 'naval scare' and the Agadir crisis postponed an Anglo-
German *rapprochement* until the outbreak of the Balkan wars. By
1912–13 Grey, but not the Foreign Office, was showing an awareness
of German anxieties towards Russia and an impatience with the
assertiveness of both the Russians and the French, but the scope
for a *détente* with Germany was rather limited by 1914.

A persistent difficulty in negotiating with Germany was, as Steiner
and other historians point out, that 'the German riddle was hard
to read'. Contemporaries were very conscious of this. In 1904 the
diplomat Spring-Rice anticipated Eyre Crowe's musings on Germany's aims and world policy when he observed: 'Germany is a
mystery. Does she simply want the destruction of England, pure and
simple . . . or does she want definite things which England can help
her to get?' If the Germans themselves were unsure of their
country's rightful place in Europe and where its ambitions would
find their proper outlets, it was almost impossible for others to
negotiate successfully with them.

In 1914, by contrast, the issue was clear enough to those who had
thought through the implications of a German victory in the west.
The Conservative MP, Leo Amery, showed a better grasp of realities
than many of Grey's colleagues in urging that 'If we wish to . . .
preserve our supremacy on the sea, it is on the land that we must
meet her (Germany). . . . The entente is not a mere convenience,
it is a matter of existence.' Grey's fears of the rise of 'a supremacy
in Europe' left him in no doubt that Britain could not stand aside
when German armies were about to invade France.

FRANCE AND THE ABSENCE OF RESTRAINT

France's role in the outbreak of war was essentially a negative one, reacting, rather tardily perhaps, to situations created by others. As Keiger, a recent apologist for French policy, points out, France's leaders had less opportunity to influence events than did their counterparts in other states. With both the president and prime minister literally at sea during the crucial period of 23–9 July and victims of the vagaries of unreliable radio communications, French policy was necessarily muted and uncertain.

The older critiques of France's role in the origins of the war which charged France with belligerence towards Germany, stemming from revanchism and a determination to recover Alsace-Lorraine, carry little credibility. More recent critics, such as Turner, have accused France of giving Russia *carte blanche* to pursue an expansionist policy in the Balkans from 1912, while tightening the bonds of the Franco-Russian alliance. The evidence for this, however, is not very clear-cut. What does seem incontrovertible is that French diplomacy was over-assertive in St Petersburg during the July crisis and unduly temporizing in Paris and Berlin.

For most French people, politicians and public alike, the 'crisis' in July 1914 centred around the trial of Madame Caillaux, which dominated the pages of the French press. That the wife of the minister of finance had shot dead a newspaper editor who had published her love letters was quite a juicy scandal in itself. The crucial aspect of the trial, however, was the danger of revelations of diplomatic intercepts, which could have had serious political and international repercussions. It was not simply that, in terms of its newsworthiness, the assassination of a not very popular archduke (a not uncommon event) was comparatively speaking pretty small beer, but that the Sarajevo incident had no obvious bearing on French interests. Before the middle of July, therefore, there seemed no occasion for alarm in Paris and no reason to cancel the state visit to St Petersburg of the president and prime minister. Consequently, from 15 to 29 July Poincaré and Viviani were largely out of touch with developments. What they discussed with Sazonov in the course of their visit to Russia on 21–3 July remains conjecture, since no official record of the talks was made. Meanwhile, the group of inexperienced 'second-raters' left in charge of French diplomacy in Paris gave the German and Austrian ambassadors to understand that France would not object to retaliatory action against Serbia.

In response to the news of the ultimatum to Serbia, the French suggested an extension of the time limit to respond to it and proposed that the enquiry into the assassination be conducted by an international commission, not just an Austro-Serb one. A few days later France's loyalty to its ally was demonstrated in a previously prepared telegram stating that France 'is ready in the interests of the general peace wholeheartedly to second the action of the Imperial Government'. Was this expression of blanket support for Russia altogether wise in the circumstances? Poincaré later seemed to have doubts. Keiger explains it as a reassurance to Sazonov, whose position was not strong, and as a discouragement to the pro-German faction at the court and in the army. However, this reading of the political situation in St Petersburg does not seem well founded. The only clear appeal to Russia to exercise restraint was made on 30 July, when it was urged to avoid measures which could provide Germany with a pretext for mobilization. Even then, this advice arrived too late to have any influence.

One factor which has led some historians to apportion substantial responsibility for the outbreak of war to France is the conduct of Paléologue, the French ambassador in St Petersburg during the July crisis. Paléologue's impulsiveness seems to have misled the Russians about the French government's attitude to the crisis, while his failure to supply Paris with adequate and timely information made it difficult for the French government to caution restraint. If France was bound by its alliance to aid Russia there was no need for Paléologue to rush in with offers of unreserved French support on 24 July, without authority from Paris. Moreover, his boasting about his friendship with Poincaré invested his personal opinions with a quasi-official air. To compound this error, he failed to alert Paris to the decision of the council of ministers on 24 July in favour of partial mobilization and delayed sending news of Russia's general mobilization until late on 30 July and the 31st. Consequently, even after Poincaré's arrival in France on the 29th, the president was not being kept up to date with developments in St Petersburg. French mobilization on 1 August was followed two days later by Germany's declaration of war on France.

French policy between 1912 and 1914 may have had some influence on the course of events in the summer of 1914. Some writers allege that France gave Russia a free hand in the Balkans in 1912, but this notion, possibly fostered by Izvolsky as ambassador in Paris, conflicts with the evidence of French pressure to maintain the *status quo* in a region where French and Russian interests were at variance. Keiger argues that Poincaré's aim was certainly to increase the cohesion of the French-Russian alliance, a quality that had been lacking in 1908 and 1911, but also to exercise more restraint over Russia.

The French participants in the Franco-Russian military talks in 1912–13, on the other hand, pressed for an early Russian offensive in the event of war with Germany and agreed to the allocation of more funds for improving strategic railways. The assertiveness of the French high command was demonstrated in 1914 when it pressed the Russian general staff to demand general, not partial, mobilization, and when on 27 July it requested preparations for an offensive according to the terms of the military convention.

The conclusion would seem to be that France's leaders had little opportunity to influence events in late July 1914, but that such influence as was exerted through diplomatic and military channels was not designed to restrain Russia from responding in a forceful manner to the Austro-German challenge.

MILITARY PLANNING, MOBILIZATION AND THE CULT OF THE OFFENSIVE

Conrad's ironic comment, 'Who rules in Berlin, Bethmann or Moltke?', highlights the danger that, as the July crisis reached an acute stage, decision-making was passing from the civilian leaders to the military chiefs. 'The military', Gustav Schmidt points out, 'launched into a diplomacy of their own', regardless of the danger of escalating a political crisis into war. They insisted that success depended on 'the timely execution of the mobilization schedules' worked out in previous staff talks. In both Germany and France the general staffs regarded their ally's preference for partial mobilization as potentially disastrous. The German high command, in particular, staked all on a rapid offensive, which had to begin within days of general mobilization.

It is obvious enough that the widespread addiction of the general staffs of the great powers to an offensive strategy had a major influence on the nature and course of the First World War. However, some historians go further in maintaining that the war planning and mobilization schedules of the high command of the continental powers had an important influence on the development of the July crisis itself. Snyder, for example, argues that the offensive military strategies adopted by the continental powers 'increased the likelihood of war', while van Evera makes a larger claim in asserting that the cult of the offensive was 'a principal cause of the First World

War', creating or magnifying many of the dangers inherent in the crisis.

A major reason for this cult was the belief that an offensive could achieve a rapid and decisive victory over an opponent, whereas a defensive strategy would lead to a long drawn-out conflict, ending in a compromise diplomatic settlement. Offensive strategies also made possible a pre-emptive strike against an opponent when favourable circumstances provided 'windows of opportunity'. It was the cult of the offensive, van Evera suggests, 'that made the "window logic" which governed German and Austrian conduct ... so persuasive.'

The absurdity of the addiction to an offensive strategy was that improvements in fire-power had given an overwhelming advantage to the defence. This had been demonstrated in Ivan Bloch's work, *Is War Now Impossible?*, accessible to European readers in 1899. The lessons were clear to see in both the Russo-Japanese war and the Boer war, but military strategists chose to disregard such unpalatable truths and invented reasons why the evidence was inappropriate to warfare in continental Europe. The cavalry was thereby able to survive, at least until the shooting began, even though supplying fodder for the horses was a logistic nightmare for all the armies in Europe. However, it seems almost indisputable that a defensive strategy would have been much more appropriate to the security of the three leading continental powers in 1914 – Germany, Russia and France.

The basic assumption on which the Schlieffen Plan was based was that Germany would have to fight a war on two fronts against a numerically superior enemy. The slowness of Russian mobilization however, meant that its forces could not be fully deployed for four to six weeks, providing the Germans with a 'window of opportunity' which could be exploited by a lightning offensive. This could yield a rapid victory without heavy losses in manpower and with a minimum disruption of economic activity. The revisions to the plan made by the younger Moltke, Schlieffen's successor as chief of staff after 1905, did not eliminate the weaknesses in timing and logistics of the original. In fact, Moltke's last revision in 1913 created a new imperative – the need to seize Liège on the third day in order to facilitate the rapid movement of troops through Belgium.

Paradoxically, the substantial violation of Belgian territory demanded by the Schlieffen Plan virtually ensured Britain's participation in the war, even though it was the fear of a British blockade of Germany which, in part, made a rapid victory in the west necessary. At the same time, reliance on the strategy of defeating France within four to six weeks, regardless of the circumstances in which the war broke out, guaranteed that Germany would have to fight a war on two fronts. Hence Snyder's conclusion that 'the Schlieffen Plan prepared for the worst case (a two front war and British intervention) in a way that ensured that the worst case would occur.'

The alternative, favoured by the elder Moltke in the 1880s, was for a limited offensive in the east combined with an initial defensive posture against France. Although improvements in Russia's strategic position in Poland made such an option less appealing well before 1914, the acceleration of Russia's mobilization schedule by this date also made the western strategy much less viable.

The persistent bias of the German general staff towards the offensive suggests that a 'dogmatization of doctrine' had set in. The numerous drawbacks of the Schlieffen Plan were largely ignored. Difficulties simply had to be overcome by superhuman efforts. The possible advantages of an alternative strategy were never fully explored. What the general staff offered the German government was the attractive possibility of a quick and decisive victory. What it did not provide was a strategy flexible enough to take account of different situations. Yet Bethmann Hollweg's policy of calculated risks required a flexible military response to the diplomatic situation, not an immediate riposte to Russia's mobilization which ruled out last-minute negotiations. For Germany mobilization meant war. More than that, it meant war against France. This is why the Kaiser's suggested change of tactics in 1914, to switch the offensive to the east and thereby avoid the violation of Belgian neutrality, met with an immediate rebuff. Hence also Moltke's desperate appeal to Conrad for general mobilization against Russia on 30 July to relieve the pressure on the mere thirteen divisions in East Prussia, facing a Russian force over twice its size.

The military plans of both Russia and France show that belief in the merits of an offensive strategy was not actually a well-established cult in 1914. In both cases, an earlier defensive strategy was only abandoned in about 1912 in favour of offensives which proved well-nigh disastrous when war began. In 1912 the Russian general staff rightly believed that in the opening stage of a war Germany would throw the bulk of its forces against France. Some Russian generals favoured an offensive against Germany on two counts. First, it would relieve pressure on France, whose early defeat would leave Russia on its own against the German army. Second, the weakness of Germany's forces in East Prussia made it very vulnerable to a Russian attack. Despite this, for many Russian commanders the attractions of an offensive against Austria-Hungary were too great to be ignored. The result was a compromise, achieved by reducing the size of the forces available on each front. To compound the error, the Russians yielded to strong French pressure to plan to launch an attack on the fifteenth day, by which time only half the forces designated for the German theatre would be ready for action. Hence the disaster at Tannenberg in late August 1914, when 100,000 Russians were taken prisoner.

Danilov's pessimism about France's chances of survival against Germany, combined with pressure from the French for an early Russian offensive, contributed to the decision to begin preparatory measures for war on 26 July and to opt for full mobilization on the 30th. The latter decision was, in Turner's view, militarily unnecessary, as has been shown earlier.

The adoption of an offensive strategy by the French was probably the most absurd military plan of any of the continental powers. Joffre's glorification of the offensive, which helped to protect the professional army against those politicians who pressed for full use of reservists, placed great reliance on the mystical, if not mythical, *élan* of the French infantry. Not that Joffre was alone in this. Foch asserted: 'Faire la guerre, c'est attaquer.' The disastrous Plan XVII, adopted in 1911–12, committed large numbers of troops to a useless offensive in Lorraine (at a cost of 50,000 casualties within days) – troops who were desperately needed to counter the German advance through Belgium. This left the BEF outnumbered by two to one by the German right wing. The availability of railways to the defender to switch troops from one front to another, as demonstrated by France before the battle of the Marne and by the Germans in the defence of East Prussia, was one of the many advantages of defence over attack, largely ignored by the general staffs before the war. In 1914, Snyder suggests, 'the war might never have occurred had the advantages of the defender been better appreciated.' Ironically, the offensive strategies adopted decreased the chances of victory.

THE ORIGINS OF THE FIRST WORLD WAR

Germany's responsibility for the outbreak of war in 1914 has been a matter of controversy ever since the victorious powers saddled the country with 'war guilt' in the Treaty of Versailles. Even though the outbreak of the Second World War in 1939 cast doubts on the 'relativist' interpretation of the inter-war years, which shared the responsibility among all the powers, the post-war period saw a surprising revival of this approach, with its stress on the accidental nature of the war that began in 1914. A consensus began to emerge that divided the blame between 'impersonal forces' (such as nationalism and imperialism) and the 'international anarchy' of the European states system. All the great powers were held to be responsible, in part, for the outbreak of the First World War, even if some of them, especially Germany, were more responsible than others. This sort of interpretation, although rejected by a number of dissenting voices, naturally had a strong appeal to 'good Europeans', eager for a Franco-German reconciliation. It also suited the political climate of the cold war, when Stalinist Russia constituted the major threat to peace and security in western Europe. It was therefore comforting to be able to dismiss the Nazi era as an aberration in Germany's development and to get away from the time-worn cliché of 'war guilt', which could only embarrass the liberal democratic West German regime.

Hence, in part, the storm provoked in the 1960s by Fritz Fischer's reassertion of Germany's responsibility for the outbreak of war in 1914 and the subsequent emergence of the theme of continuity in German history from Bismarck to Hitler. Fischer's thesis, that Germany willed the war in 1914 in order to realize expansionist ambitions in Europe and overseas as part of its bid for world power, was partly based on the evidence of the September Programme. This statement of war aims, which showed the German government's desire to expand its European power base at the expense of its neighbours, was in Fischer's view merely an elaboration of the pre-war *Mitteleuropa* programme. Fischer also claimed subsequently that the decision for war was taken in December 1912 by Germany's leaders, who had come to see a preventive war as an answer to the inevitable conflict between Teutons and Slavs in which time was against Germany. Furthermore, war was seized upon as a way out of the insoluble domestic crisis, a theme elaborated and emphasized by other German historians.

Fischer's assertions naturally generated a wide-ranging debate. The controversy over his interpretation of the origins of the war and Germany's responsibility for it was sometimes bitter and partisan. Some historians reacted by examining anew the culpability of the other great powers in 1914, especially Russia, which produced some valuable insights, but the investigation of the influence of domestic factors on the decisions of these powers during the July crisis has proved a rather negative line of enquiry.

In a rather different analysis, the German military establishment was identified by Pogge von Strandmann as the main culprit for causing the war in 1914 on the grounds that the general staff wanted war for expansionist reasons. The fear of Russia's future military superiority he dismisses as a 'pretext' for action in 1914, asserting that 'the German position in 1917 could not have been worse than in 1914. On the contrary, it could have improved.' While this might have been true of the diplomatic situation, it is difficult to see its validity in military terms. The combination of sheer numbers and strategic railways was widely regarded by civilian and military leaders in Berlin as a nightmare scenario that implied, as Bethmann observed, 'The future belongs to Russia.' The 'sustained lobbying campaign' by the general staff in favour of a preventive strike against Russia seems to have been based on a genuine assessment of the relative decline in Germany's future military capability *vis-à-vis* Russia.

Geiss, on the other hand, identifies Germany's *Weltpolitik* as the factor 'which plunged Europe into the world war', even though he recognizes that the immediate cause of the conflict was Berlin's backing for a punitive strike against Belgrade. The problem that this sort of approach creates, as Ferguson has recently pointed out, is finding a direct connection between German *Weltpolitik*, inaugurated in 1897–8, and the decision to support Austria's retaliation against Serbia in 1914. Explanations which present Serbia as blocking alleged Austro-German expansionist drives into the Balkans seem less than convincing.

The difficulty in establishing a link between *Weltpolitik* and the July crisis illustrates the broader problem historians encounter when attempting to evaluate the role of general or long-term factors in the origins of the war. For example, Balkan problems not only contributed to the growth of international tension both before and after 1900, but they also played a more specific part in the crisis of 1914. Much the same could be said of the alliance system and the armaments race. On the other hand, the role of impersonal forces such as capitalism, imperialism and nationalism in the origins of the war is less obvious and more indirect. In such a situation, Joll's concept of 'concentric circles' of factors operating at varying levels that both influenced and circumscribed the decisions taken by Europe's political leaders in 1914 has much to commend it.

Balkan crises reflected the recurrent conflict of interests between Austria-Hungary and Russia which was a source of tension in European affairs for almost forty years before 1914, except for a phase between 1897 and 1907. What made the situation in the Balkans so dangerous in the 1900s was the interaction of the nationalist ambitions and ethnic conflicts of the Balkan states with great power rivalries in the region. The Bosnian crisis and the Balkan wars reactivated the Austro-Russian antagonism in a heightened form, while the very fact that Britain no longer played a leading role in opposing Russian designs on Constantinople or the Straits tended to highlight the clash between the Austrians and the Russians. Furthermore, the replacement of Bulgaria by Serbia as Russia's main Balkan protégé shifted the focus of tension from the eastern Balkans westwards to the very frontier of the Dual Monarchy.

The Serbian challenge to Austria-Hungary was double-edged. As a protégé of Russia, Serbian hostility and desires for aggrandizement were a perpetual irritant to Austria-Hungary as a great power, whose last remaining zone of influence and prestige lay in the Balkans. As an outpost of pan-Slavism, and the instigator of pan-Serb propaganda directed at the increasingly disaffected south Slavs within the Dual Monarchy, Serbia constituted a challenge to the very survival of the multi-national Habsburg empire. The outcome of the Balkan wars of 1912–13, from which Serbia benefited greatly, was a severe blow to Austria-Hungary. The brinkmanship displayed by both sides in the July crisis led to what some historians have called the 'third Balkan war' in 1914, but whether the crisis in the Balkans was the occasion, rather than the cause, of the First World War remains a matter of continuing debate.

The Balkan situation, by itself, does not explain how an Austro-Serb conflict became a European or world war. This was the effect of the alliance system which, also taken by itself, cannot answer the question why war broke out in 1914 and not at some other time. As part of Joll's pattern of concentric circles, the alliance system also illustrates how the options available in 1914 were restricted by previous decisions.

At first sight, German support for Austria-Hungary and French support for Russia in 1914 were simply the inevitable outcome of their alliances. In each case, however, an offensive direction had been superimposed on the original defensive nature of the alliance, which therefore failed to act as a restraining influence. Germany's 'blank cheque' to the Austrians in early July 1914 was paralleled by France's commitment in 1912 to support the Russians under any circumstances, including over Balkan issues.

That alliances reduced the flexibility of response in 1914 is obvious enough. On the other hand, it can be argued that regardless of alliance commitments France could no more afford to see Russia overwhelmed than Germany could allow Austria-Hungary to be destroyed. Furthermore Italy, despite its alliance obligations, stayed out of the war until 1915 (when it joined the Allied side), while Britain, which had not concluded any formal alliances, entered the war at the outset. Nor were the alliances quite as rigid as is sometimes supposed. Between 1908 and 1913 both the Austrians and the Russians complained of the lukewarm support offered by their allies, while the Germans failed to observe, or draw appropriate conclusions from, the signs of tension within the Triple Entente before 1914. In fact, German doubts about the reliability of its ally in a crisis that did not bear directly on Austrian interests may well have provided a powerful impulse to act in 1914 over a Balkan issue. The crucial factor in 1914, perhaps, was less the alliance system itself than the Prussian general staff's reaction to the Franco-Russian alliance; namely, the Schlieffen Plan, which deprived German policy of much needed flexibility in a major crisis, especially one originating in the east.

The existence of alliances was a reflection of the feelings of insecurity prevalent in the late nineteenth century, but one power's desire for security led to another power's insecurity. For example, French fear of Germany made Russia seem a desirable ally, but the Franco-Russian alliance caused Germany great anxiety. Similarly, Grey regarded the Triple Entente as a way of containing Germany, but the Germans regarded it as 'encirclement'.

The secret negotiations that lay behind the alliance system were widely regarded in the 1920s as a baleful aspect of the 'international anarchy' prevailing before 1914. Hence the belief after 1918 that 'open covenants openly arrived at' would lessen the risk of war in the future. Critics of old-style 'cabinet diplomacy' argued that an international system based on sovereign states pursuing their national interests in competition with each other was bound to lead to war sooner or later. The explanatory power of this approach to the origins of the war, however, is very limited, as it fails to explain why war broke out in 1914 and not earlier, even though 'international anarchy' had been a fact of life for over forty years since 1871.

The crucial question to be asked, perhaps, is why the alliance system, supposedly an aspect of the balance of power, failed to act as a restraining influence in 1914. One answer might be that at least one state believed that the previous balance was being tilted against it and that time was not on its side. The decline of the

Concert of Europe aggravated such fears, as Langhorne has suggested, especially in the case of Austria-Hungary, which would have no truck with 'worthless face-saving formulas'. Similarly, Bethmann Hollweg explicitly ruled out a possible solution to the crisis through the mechanism of the Concert in late July, on the grounds that Germany 'could not bring Austria-Hungary's dealings before a European tribunal'. A plausible justification for Germany's attitude to the Concert is suggested by Bridge and Bullen on the grounds that Russia's mobilization eliminated the military option if the Austrians were eventually faced with a humiliating diplomatic defeat at the hands of Russia and France. The Concert of Europe could not operate successfully in 1914 because at least one of the great powers was unwilling to run the risk of damage to its power or prestige, which a compromise solution implied.

The arms race, like the alliance system, was both a cause and an effect of international tension. Russia's army reforms, which aimed to expand its peacetime strength to 2 million men by 1916–17, caused great alarm in Germany, whose army had been static for over a decade. Between 1912 and 1914 the Germans, as well as the Austrians and the French, increased the size of their army. The governments of the continental powers were clearly reacting to the military preparations of their neighbours and, in the case of Germany, the army command took a pessimistic view of the chances of military success against Russia beyond 1914–15. In May 1914 Moltke commented: 'To wait any longer meant a diminishing of our chances'; in late July he insisted, 'we shall never again strike as well as we do now.'

By contrast, the heat had gone out of the Anglo-German naval armaments race before 1914. The threat to Britain's security posed by Germany's fleet expansion, however, left a legacy of distrust of German ambitions. In the 1920s, the view that the arms race inevitably led to war created a powerful momentum for disarmament. The slowness of British and French rearmament after 1936, however, did not stop the outbreak of war in 1939. It may be, therefore, that while an arms race increases international tension, the notion that it inevitably leads to war is not susceptible to proof on the basis of historical evidence.

The role of impersonal forces such as capitalism, imperialism and nationalism in the origins of the war is not easy to establish, partly because of the nature of the evidence but also because of the legacy of politicized views of previous generations of writers. For example, when Lenin dubbed the First World War an 'imperialist war' in

1916, he was writing with a political objective in mind, not as an impartial witness of events. Similarly, when Marx asserted that 'wars are inherent in the nature of capitalism' the fact that a critic of capitalism held such a view is not altogether unexpected. Nor is it all that surprising that generations of the Left should have regarded capitalism and imperialism as the 'hidden causes' of the war.

Some or all of these impersonal forces may constitute long-term underlying causes of the war, even though they cannot explain why the war began in 1914. But Marx's assertion may explain much about the causes of the war, or nothing at all. The notion that industrialists in general and armaments manufacturers in particular provoke wars either to increase their profits or to ruin their competitors has a certain simplistic appeal. It may, however, be quite without foundation. What is demonstrable is that the 'merchants of death', such as Krupp or Vickers-Armstrong, were profiteers of peacetime, rather than prophets of war, who did well out of government contracts and worldwide sales of arms. The latter might well be disrupted by a war in Europe. That they dreaded disarmament is self-evident and hardly requires proof; that they wanted war is not. As regards industrialists, there were many peaceful uses for iron and steel and the process of steel manufacture involved considerable two-way trading, even between Britain and Germany, creating a form of interdependence before 1914. In the decade before the war Britain became Germany's best trade customer, while Germany ranked as Britain's second best market for its products. That international bankers had even less desire for war seems evident from the stock exchange slump in Berlin in 1911 and the crisis in the City of London in 1914.

If capitalism and trade rivalry were the hidden causes of war, then logically Britain should have fought against the United States in 1914. If the origins of the war lay in imperial rivalries, then Britain had more reason to fight Russia than Germany in 1914. Imperialism may have been a contributory factor in the origins of the war in other senses, of course. It is possible to argue, as David Kaiser does, that Germany opted for war in 1914 out of a feeling of 'dissatisfied imperialism', having failed to add significantly to its overseas empire after 1890. There is some plausibility also in Fischer's contention that the failure of *Mittelafrika* led Germany's leaders to revive the *Mitteleuropa* scheme in 1914. The combination of both expansionist plans into the September Programme of 1914, before hopes for a rapid victory were dashed at the battle of the Marne, is highly informative of Germany's appetite for territorial gains as the prize of a successful war. Whether it provides a reliable explanation of German objectives before the outbreak of the war is more debatable. Such reservations notwithstanding, it seems probable that the era of imperialism almost inevitably affected the attitudes and decisions of many, if not all, of the statesmen in July 1914.

Nationalism might be seen as a more obvious underlying cause of war than either capitalism or imperialism. Aggressive nationalism was far from being confined to the Balkan states, as the record of the Pan-German League clearly shows. The crises and tensions of the decade before 1914 aroused nationalist feelings in many of the European states, as in the 'nationalist revival' in France after the Agadir crisis. The tendency of the popular press to excite xenophobia also seems undeniable. What is not so easy to ascertain is how deeply felt or long-lasting such animosities were before the horrors of the First World war intensified them. Political leaders in Europe seemed surprised at the popular rejoicing which greeted the declaration of war and it was they, not the public or the press, who made the decision for war in 1914.

SOURCES AND FURTHER READING

Bridge, F. R., *From Sadowa to Sarajevo. The Foreign Policy of Austria-Hungary 1866–1914*, London, Routledge & Kegan Paul, 1972.

Dedijer, V., *The Road to Sarajevo*, London, Macgibbon & Kee, 1967.

Ekstein – see Hinsley.

Ferguson, N., 'Germany and the origins of the First World War: new perspectives', *Historical Journal*, 1992, vol. 35(3): 725–52.

Fischer, F., *Germany's Aims in the First World War*, London, Chatto & Windus, 1967.

Geiss – see Schöllgen.

Geyer, D., *Russian Imperialism 1860–1914* (transl. B. Little), Leamington Spa, Berg, 1987.

Hinsley, F. H. (ed.), *British Foreign Policy under Sir Edward Grey*, Cambridge, Cambridge University Press, 1977.

Jarausch, K. H., 'The illusion of limited war. Chancellor Bethmann Hollweg's calculated risk', *Central European History*, 1969, vol. 2: 48–76.

Joll, J., *The Origins of the First World War*, Harlow, Longman, 1984.

Koch, H. W. (ed.), *The Origins of the First World War*, London, Macmillan, 1984 (2nd edn).

Langhorne, R., *The Collapse of the Concert of Europe 1890–1914*, London, Macmillan, 1981.

Miller, S. E. (ed.), *Military Strategy and the Origins of the First World War*, Princeton, Princeton University Press, 1985.

Pogge von Strandmann, H. and Evans, R. J. W. (eds), *The Coming of the First World War*, Oxford, Clarendon Press, 1988.

Remak, J., 'The third Balkan war: origins reconsidered' (see Koch).

Schöllgen, G. (ed.), *Escape into War? The Foreign Policy of Imperial Germany*, Oxford, Berg, 1990.

Snyder, J., *The Ideology of the Offensive. Military Decision Making and the Disasters of 1914*, London, Cornell University Press, 1984.

Schmidt – see Schöllgen.

Steiner, Z. S., *Britain and the Origins of the First World War*, London, Macmillan, 1977.

(The titles in this series for the other great powers have been cited previously: in ch. 5, Berghahn on Germany; in ch. 6, Keiger on France, Lieven on Russia and Williamson on Austria-Hungary.)

Stokes, G., 'The Serbian documents from 1914. A preview', *Journal of Modern History*, 1976, vol. 48, September.

Trumpener, V., 'War premeditated? German intelligence operations in July 1914', *Central European History*, 1976, vol. 9: 58–85.

Turner, L. C. F., 'Russian mobilization in 1914', in P. M. Kennedy (ed.), *The War Plans of the Great Powers 1880–1914*, London, Allen & Unwin, 1979.

Van Evera – see Miller.

Wilson, K. M., *The Policy of the Entente*, Cambridge, Cambridge University Press, 1985.

Serbia's role in the July crisis is described in detail in Dedijer. Good brief accounts can be found in Bridge and Williamson while Stokes has some interesting snippets. Remak is useful.

Austro-Hungarian policy is very well discussed by both Bridge and Williamson. For Russian policy see Geyer (especially chapter 13) and Lieven and a useful essay on Russia in Pogge von Strandmann.

The views of some of the critics of German policy can be pursued in Fischer, Pogge von Strandmann and Berghahn. Schöllgen contains a brief restatement by Fischer. The 'apologists' include Jarausch, Gustav Schmidt (in Schöllgen) and Koch *et al.*

Ekstein's views on British policy are in Hinsley (chapter 18) and a collaborative essay with Steiner (chapter 23). Schmidt's views are also relevant and there is an essay on England in Pogge von Strandmann. Keiger is good on France.

Military planning is covered very well in essays by Snyder, van Evera and others under the editorship of Miller.

Sources on the origins of the war extend from here to eternity, but Joll is essential reading.

Epilogue
The German problem, 1919–1925

In the spring of 1918 Germany's alleged decline as a military power was hardly evident on the battlefields of France and Belgium. Victory on the eastern front enabled it to launch an offensive in the west that brought the German armies to within forty miles of Paris before their advance was checked. By the end of the summer, however, the German army was in full retreat and incapable of further serious resistance to the Allied forces. The entente powers had seemingly been saved from defeat or deadlock on the western front by the intervention of the United States, which entered the war in 1917, though the benefits of this were slow to materialize. Hence Adamthwaite's assertion that 'the war showed that Germany, with only modest help from Austria-Hungary, could defy a coalition of four leading European powers.'

In early October the German government requested the American president to negotiate a peace settlement on the basis of his Four-teen Points, which resulted in an armistice being signed in November 1918. The armistice signified the end of the war, but not the ending of the German Problem. It was rather the reverse since, according to Sally Marks, 'the net effect of World War One and the Peace Treaty was the effective enhancement of Germany's relative strength in Europe.'

Some elements of the apparent paradox are readily identifiable. For some years after the revolutions of 1917 and the ensuing civil war, Russia ceased to count as a great power. It remained something of an enigma in international affairs for at least a decade. The collapse of the Austro-Hungarian empire also left a power vacuum in much of central and eastern Europe. The combined effect of the demise of the Romanov and Habsburg empires was to provide Germany with eastern neighbours much weaker than those that had existed in 1914. Although France was able to conclude alliances with Poland and Czechoslovakia, this did not compensate it for the loss of the Franco-Russian alliance. In addition, the creation of an independent (and fiercely anti-Russian) Polish state meant that Russia no longer had a common frontier with Germany. Clearly, some of the changes brought about by the war and the peace treaty in central Europe tilted the power balance decisively against France, making it more dependent than ever on an alliance with Britain for its security in the future.

All the belligerent nations obviously suffered from the effects of such a long and destructive war but France, despite being one of the victors, has been called 'the greatest casualty of all the nations involved'. With a population of only 40 million to face Germany's 60 million, French losses in manpower (which included 1.35 million dead) were proportionately much greater than those of the other great powers. The war period created the phenomenon of the 'hollow years' ('les années creuses') in the mid–1930s, when the size of the annual contingent of conscripts fell dramatically to about half its former figure.

French finances were also weakened by the war, which was largely financed by loans, creating a legacy of debt and a depreciating currency. Alone of the great powers, France had to shoulder the burden of reconstructing devastated regions (covering 8 million acres, including much of the country's industrial base) fought over or occupied by the Germans during the war. Not only had the occupying power ruthlessly exploited the economy of the region for its own war effort, but the Germans had also wantonly destroyed much of the infrastructure, including coal mines, in the course of their retreat in 1918. The damage suffered has been estimated as amounting to something like £2,000 million.

Britain had an equivalent to France's devastated provinces, it has been suggested, in the form of 2 million unemployed. The disruption of world trade during the war affected Britain quite severely, especially through the loss of markets to the advantage of 'non-belligerents' such as the United States and Japan. To pay for the war, overseas investments had been disposed of on a substantial scale, thereby reducing the 'invisible' earnings which had long been vital to Britain's balance-of-payments position. War debts to the United States had also been incurred. The war acted as a catalyst to Britain's pre-existing decline as a leading industrial and commercial nation, concealing the fact that recovery, a 'return to normalcy', after 1918 was an illusion.

The German economy was also affected by the war effort and the

British blockade. Its recovery was complicated by the disruptive effects of the territorial losses imposed by the peace treaty, in which Germany forfeited valuable industrial regions to France and Poland. The government's policy of meeting war expenditure through loans rather than taxation had also put a severe strain on the financial system and weakened the currency. By the end of the war the mark had lost half its pre-war value, standing at eight to the dollar in 1918, plunging to sixty by May 1921. On the other hand German territory had not been occupied or fought over during the war years, so that the economic infrastructure was largely untouched and the country was not encumbered with devastated regions in need of reconstruction. It could be said, therefore, that Germany, in common with Britain, had an interest in restoring pre-war patterns of trade as the surest route to general economic recovery. For France, however, the way forward was not so clear. A 'return to normalcy', without a special recovery package, would inevitably result in German economic superiority and ultimately restore its position as the most powerful nation on the continent.

The peace settlement did not solve the German Problem. In fact it probably exacerbated it in the long run, while providing a temporary respite from the threat of 'Prussian militarism'. The incomplete nature of the Allied victory in 1918 precluded the dismemberment of the defeated nation, as effected in 1945. This was, in any case, far too drastic a concept for the British and Americans, even though the French aimed to separate the Rhineland from the rest of Germany. Germany therefore remained a great power which would regain its strength in due course.

In general, the Allied leaders shared a common starting point in their approach to the peace settlement with Germany. They believed that Germany had provoked the war and waged it in an unacceptable manner. This called for some punishment and justified requiring Germany to make restitution for some of the damage and suffering it had caused. They also agreed that steps should be taken to reduce Germany's ability to make mischief in future. On each of these issues, however, the allied leaders held divergent views, some of which were not easily reconcilable with the high moral tone or idealism of President Wilson's numerous utterances, to which the Germans attached significance. They chose to regard the Fourteen Points (issued in January 1918) in particular as a guarantee of a just and honourable peace. The net result was a peace settlement, based on a series of compromises among the Allied leaders, which was regarded as too severe by the Germans, yet which required both the cooperation of the German government and also persistence and determination on the part of the victors for its enforcement.

France's demands at the peace negotiations in Paris reflected the French high command's obsession with Germany's potential power and the underlying need to bolster France's security, by artificial means if need be. Hence the demand for the 'indefinite occupation' of the left bank of the Rhine, with control of the strategic bridge-heads. Alternatively, Paris wanted the Rhineland, which gave the Germans opportunities for a lightning invasion of France, to be made into an independent or autonomous state. France also sought to regain the frontiers of 1814 in the Saar, including the use of its coal resources.

Clemenceau, the French premier since 1917, stood no chance of persuading Wilson or Lloyd George to accept Marshal Foch's draconian peace plans. The best he could achieve was a compromise which created a 'demilitarized zone' extending 50 kilometres to the east of the Rhine and provided for Allied occupation of the Rhineland, with staged withdrawals over fifteen years. By way of compensation, Britain and America promised a treaty of guarantee against future German aggression, but this proved worthless when the United States Senate failed to ratify the Versailles treaty. There is even doubt whether the Americans were genuine in their offer of a guarantee in the first place. The French had good reason to feel, therefore, that their demands for security against invasion in the future had not been taken seriously by their allies.

That the French would recover Alsace-Lorraine after Germany's defeat in 1918 was a foregone conclusion. It was the extent of Germany's territorial losses in the east which created dissension among the Allies and deep resentment on the part of the Germans. For Wilson, justice for an independent Poland, especially access to the Baltic at Danzig, took precedence over German objections to the 'Polish corridor' which cut off East Prussia from the rest of Germany. Lloyd George's insistence on plebiscites in the most disputed regions significantly reduced the number of (culturally superior) Germans placed under Polish rule, but the ethnic mix was too complex to permit an acceptable solution, except in the case of Danzig, predominantly German, which became a 'free city'.

As a result of the territorial changes in the west and the east, Germany lost about 7 million people (not all of whom were German) and about 13 per cent of its territory and economic potential. Although severe, these terms were nothing like as harsh as those imposed by Germany on Bolshevik Russia in the Treaty of

Brest-Litovsk (March 1918). The forfeiture of German overseas colonies, to the advantage of the states which had occupied them during the fighting, an expedient dressed up by the invention of the 'mandates' system, was an added humiliation for Germany, but hardly a serious economic loss.

The attempt to disarm Germany was, not surprisingly, deeply resented by the military, whose influence remained great under the weak republican Weimar regime, which needed the army's support against extremists of the right and left. By limiting the army to 100,000 men, without aircraft or armoured vehicles, abolishing the general staff and reducing the fleet to a mere token force, the Allies hoped to destroy 'Prussian militarism' and deprive Germany of the means of waging a war of aggression in the future. Ostensibly, the disarmament of Germany was to be the first stage in a general reduction of armaments, but this ideal made little headway while France remained fearful for its security.

As a peace settlement, the way the negotiations were conducted in Paris left much to be desired. The domination of the decision-making process by the Council of Four (usually three, in fact) was probably inevitable. It was the procedural chaos and the resultant amount of time wasted between January and early March that led to serious flaws. Consequently the British delegation was appalled when the totality of the terms affecting Germany was finally put together, but at this late stage of the conference expediency determined that a reassessment should not be attempted. Similarly, the original intention to invite a German delegation to participate in negotiations on a draft of the peace terms had to be abandoned for lack of time. As a result, the Germans had little option but to accept most of the terms as they stood.

Furthermore, the Germans were unwisely saddled with the concept of 'war guilt' (although the phrase itself does not appear in articles 231 and 232 of the Versailles treaty) so as to create a theoretical justification for British claims for reparations. The reference in the pre-armistice agreement in November 1918 to Germany's 'invasion of Allied territory' (a fact they could hardly dispute) had been amended to 'the aggression of Germany' (a moral judgement) at Britain's insistence. The concept of Germany's 'aggression' was consequently carried forward into the peace treaty and 'war guilt' became a highly emotive phrase, unacceptable to German opinion from the outset and subsequently embarrassing to an increasingly appeasement-minded British government.

If the Versailles treaty did contain injustices, the Germans certainly devoted much energy to highlighting them during the next two decades. Nevertheless, the enormity of the problems facing the peacemakers in 1919 has to be borne in mind. The collapse of the Romanov and Habsburg empires, on top of the war itself, led to massive turmoil, confusion and strife in central and eastern Europe. Not surprisingly, showing consideration for the sensitivities of those who were held responsible for causing such upheaval carried less weight at the conference than attending to the demands of those states which had supported the Allies and suffered from the war.

The peace treaty has been criticized both for being too severe and for being too lenient. Lloyd George's conversion to the idea of a more lenient settlement might have lessened German hostility to Versailles but, some historians argue, for it to have been acceptable to the Germans the treaty would have to have been so mild as to make it unacceptable to British public opinion in 1919. In the event, the victors seem to have ended up with the worst situation, imposing 'Napoleonic conditions to be executed by Wilsonian methods' – a treaty severe enough to antagonize the vanquished but one which was not easily enforceable.

The Versailles treaty's lack of 'moral validity', as A. J. P. Taylor has put it, did not arise from its failure to conform to Wilson's Fourteen Points and other pronouncements, or to the terms of the armistice, except perhaps for the gloss the Germans chose to put on them. Indeed, two of the issues they resented most – reparations and the creation of Poland – were explicitly referred to in one or both of them. The lack of dialogue between the peacemakers and the vanquished constituted a more valid grievance, but the 'dictated peace' was largely the unintended outcome of the procedural disorganization of the peace conference.

However, the root cause of the German rejection of the *Diktat* of Versailles, Sally Marks suggests, was self-delusion. Misled by the government about the true outcome of the crucial battle of the Marne in September 1914, the German people were encouraged to believe that the war ended as a draw in 1918, as a war 'without victors or vanquished'. This led to the misconception that Wilson's talk of a 'just peace' implied a return to the *status quo ante bellum* and that any alterations in the 1914 situation would probably be in Germany's favour.

This self-delusion arose from several factors. Perhaps the most important was the simple fact that no fighting took place on German soil. It was after all parts of Belgium and northern France that lay in ruins in 1918, not Germany. The reality of defeat was not brought home to Germans as it might have been by an Allied victory march in Berlin. Occupation of the Rhineland was seemingly too peripheral to make much impact on German opinion as a whole. The victors may have erred also, Sally Marks suggests, in using the term 'armistice' in November 1918 when the German army had in fact surrendered. Worse still was Chancellor Ebert's salute to German troops in December 1918 returning 'unconquered from the field of battle', giving credence to the myth of the 'stab in the back', which the army was sedulously fostering. The reality of defeat was obscured by Weimar republican leaders who demonstrated their patriotism in the face of nationalist hostility by resisting enforcement of the hated Versailles peace terms.

An unforeseen problem arose, therefore, in trying to implement the treaty, several of whose key clauses were predicated on the assumed cooperation of the German government. Enforcement of the treaty required determination on the part of the victors. If this was lacking, as it soon was in the case of Britain and America, the German government was able to exploit the disagreements among the Allies to its own advantage. What has been called the *mésentente cordiale* of the years 1919 to 1923 aided Germany's revival, so that 'post-war became the continuation of war by other means'.

The disagreements between Britain and France were fatal to the success of enforcing the treaty in the face of German non-compliance. On the issues of reparations and security the differences were in some regards quite fundamental. Once the immediate passions and bitterness aroused by the war died down, the British felt that Germany had been taught a salutary lesson and that the conflict was now over. In misreading the long-term power balance in Europe (unlike the French) the British paid little heed to questions of security but seemed more anxious to satisfy German grievances. 'If France feared that Europe could not live with Germany, Britain feared that it could not live without her', as Sharp neatly puts it.

Aided by Keynes's influential polemic, *The Economic Consequences of the Peace*, the Germans succeeded in persuading British leaders that reparations were not only excessive but unjust. Once faith in the justice of reparations was undermined, it was not difficult to convince British opinion of the unfairness of the Versailles treaty as a whole. Such grievances coincided with Britain's desire to restore its substantial pre-war trade links with Germany, so that the British tended to see Germany as a commercial opportunity – not, as the French did, as a military threat. It is not surprising, therefore, that

British governments came to attach greater importance to Germany's economic recovery than to Berlin's adherence to the London Schedule of Payments, devised by the Reparations Commission in 1921.

French governments, by contrast, had no incentive to hasten Germany's recovery, except as a factor in Berlin's ability to meet reparations demands. German defaults in reparations payments were of no great consequence for Britain, whose share was substantially less than that of France, for whom the effects were serious. The French needed reparations to help pay for the cost of reconstructing the devastated provinces. If the Germans did not pay, French taxpayers, already more highly taxed than their German counterparts, would have to foot the bill.

The security issue was even more important for France, whose leaders read the long-term power balance equation correctly. Denied the reassurance of the Anglo-American Treaty of Guarantee, the French feared that Germany's recovery of its continental dominance was only a matter of time. Conscious of how close to breaking point France had been in 1917, its leaders insisted on containing Germany through strict enforcement of the peace treaty, while seeking to exploit their temporary military superiority to alter the power balance in Europe to their advantage.

In so far as French governments had a coherent strategy to achieve this aim, its success depended on regular reparations payments. When Germany defaulted in its payments, France's leaders attempted to employ the coercive powers contained in the treaty and also resorted to more dubious activities, such as the ill-fated attempt to encourage separatist movements in the Rhineland. The British government disapproved of legitimate coercion as well as the other more questionable policies. It also gave no support to more constructive measures to resolve the economic imbalance on the continent.

The recovery of Alsace-Lorraine provided France with ample supplies of iron ore (in which Germany was now deficient), but the country lacked suitable coal, which existed in abundance in the Ruhr. The crux of the problem for France was how to create a Franco-German economic partnership which did not end in German dominance. French attempts to resolve this dilemma, linked to the reparations issue, through the Seydoux Plan and the Wiesbaden Accords (October 1921), were unsuccessful.

Consequently France fell back on the extraction of reparations in cash or kind from a Germany that was either unable or unwilling to pay them. The outcome of this struggle was important. In Schuker's view, 'whether Germany paid reparations and how much it paid would largely determine the European balance of power in the 1920s.' Britain's leaders, however, unduly alarmed by the signs of 'French militarism' in the early 1920s, failed to appreciate France's predicament or understand the deeper issues at stake. Hence the view that British policy was a combination of 'blindness and ruthlessness encased in elevated rhetoric'. But, Sally Marks contends, the reparations question was a political issue; it was 'a struggle for dominance of the European continent and to maintain or reverse the military verdict of 1918'.

Poincaré's comment in 1922 that 'the problem of reparations dominates all others' suggests that it had become the key issue of the post-war years. It provided a focus for German grievances against the whole Versailles treaty, while the defaults exacerbated French fears of Germany's future economic superiority. Reparations also sourced Anglo-French relations to the extent that the Entente Cordiale was all but destroyed. The constant bickering between the two allies made enforcement of the treaty virtually impossible and enabled the Germans to play one off against the other. On several occasions Britain seemed to be siding with Germany against France. That 'the Treaty of Versailles was never fully accepted or enforced' is ascribed by Ruth Henig to the crumbling of the victorious alliance, rather than to the actual provisions of the peace terms.

The peacemakers at Paris eventually decided not to set a figure for the total reparations debt demanded of the central powers, including Germany; instead they assigned the task to a Reparations Commission. By the time it reported in April 1921, the absurd figures bandied about in 1919 of 800 or 500 billion marks had been reduced to the seemingly more realistic figure of 132 billion marks of £6,600 million. Even then, this figure was largely window-dressing to satisfy public opinion in Britain and France, whose expectations had been raised by the irresponsible utterances of their leaders. In reality, the amount the Germans were required to pay was 50 billion marks, at a rate of 2 billion a year plus a variable sum according to the value of Germany's exports.

Since the Germans had previously offered to pay this amount in recognition of their liability for damage to civilian property in Belgium and France, the notion that the Allies' demand for reparations was vindictive is absurd. Yet Keynes, who should have known better, fostered that notion both in Britain and Germany. The Germans were therefore presented with a valuable propaganda weapon against reparations, which they systematically attempted to avoid paying. Yet as Sharp points out, the Allies had a 'legitimate and pressing claim against Germany, particularly for the deliberate damage she had inflicted in the closing stages of the war'. What confused the issue was the attempt by Lloyd George and, to some extent, the French to pass off pensions to war widows as part of the claim for 'civilian damages', despite the dubious legality of this move. This casuistry 'squandered a strong moral position' and reduced the amount that France would receive for reconstruction. Whether Lloyd George was trying to link Allied war debts to the USA with German reparations is not clear, but his devious tactics certainly blurred the clear case for France's entitlement to compensation for the damage done to civilian property.

Some historians, notably David Felix, have disputed Germany's ability to pay the 'real' figure of 50 billion marks. But if a notional debt of about £6,000 million (132 billion marks) implied an annual levy of about 7 per cent of Germany's GNP in the late 1920s, as Trachtenberg's calculations suggest, the 'real' figure of 50 billion seems a not unmanageable sum. This is inevitably a highly complex and technical issue, involving an assessment of Germany's tax system, currency situation and the condition of the country's economy in the aftermath of the war. There is little doubt, however, that France was considerably more impoverished than Germany in 1919. The suspicion also exists that the German Government wilfully embarked on the destruction of the currency in 1922–3 through hyper-inflation as a means of proving its inability to meet the reparations bills. If the damage done to the social fabric by hyper-inflation was enormous, it conveniently enabled the government to pay off its domestic debts – an expedient not open to the victor states. The whole debate on Germany's ability to pay reparations seems to underline the pressing need for American financial involvement, either in the form of loans or by cancellation of war debts, which would have made capital available for reconstruction while the German economy was still recovering from the effects of the war.

By 1923 the French government faced the stark fact that despite several years of conferences since the end of the war, the problem of Germany and the reparations issue remained unsolved. But when the Germans defaulted on the payment of reparations in cash and coal in 1922, the British came up with a proposal for a four-year moratorium without any guarantees of resumption in the future. The French, with reluctant Belgian and Italian support and despite the strong disapproval of the British government, occupied the Ruhr in January 1923 to coerce the German government into accepting its liabilities. Germany's policy of passive resistance, combined with France's diplomatic isolation and financial weakness, eventually forced the French into a settlement on terms injurious to their interests. Nevertheless, Poincaré's resolute action at least resulted in American involvement in the reparations question, which may have been his underlying objective from the outset.

At the London Conference in the summer of 1924 the Dawes Plan was agreed, under which France had to forfeit the right to impose sanctions on Germany in the event of future defaults in reparation payments. Schuker calls this the 'first unmistakeable augury of the demise of the Versailles system'. The Dawes Plan provided a loan to Germany of 800 million gold marks. This was to facilitate the payment of reparations at the reduced rate of 1 billion marks in 1924, rising in stages to 2.5 billion. With the aid of substantial foreign loans, the Germans honoured their commitments under the Dawes Plan until the onset of the depression in 1929 resulted in a further scaling down by the Young Plan. The ultimate irony was that Germany received more in foreign loans (most of which were not repaid in the 1930s) than it paid out in reparations. It therefore made a profit out of reparations and it was, Sally Marks contends, 'the victors who paid the bills'.

In their quest for security, French governments could find little solace in the achievements of the League of Nations. By 1925 the League had failed to fulfil the high hopes which President Wilson, as well as much of European public opinion, had placed in it as a world forum which would inaugurate a new era of peace and stability. Articles 10 and 16 of the League Covenant did not provide the basis for 'collective security' as intended. Two attempts to negotiate a security pact, the Draft Treaty of Mutual Assistance and the Geneva Protocol, failed to secure British approval. It remained to be seen whether the Disarmament Commission could overcome not only the technical problems involved but also the French refusal to agree to equality of armaments with Germany in the absence of guarantees for its own security.

Given the disappointed hopes of the immediate post-war years, the mood of euphoria that greeted the conclusion of the Treaty of Locarno in October 1925 is readily understandable. It seemed as if a new era of reconciliation was about to begin when Germany voluntarily accepted the permanence of its western frontiers and the demilitarization of the Rhineland and agreed to join the League of Nations. Between 1926 and 1929 the regular meetings at

Geneva of the Locarno statesmen, Austen Chamberlain, Briand and Stresemann, was another reassuring sign of international goodwill.

The 'spirit' (*Geist*) of Locarno, however, was also a 'ghost'. The motive behind Stresemann's proposal for a non-aggression pact with France and Belgium was to head off a possible Anglo-French alliance, which Chamberlain was contemplating in order to allay French fears for their security. Stresemann also wanted to advance the date for ending the Allied occupation of the Rhineland, 'the rope of the strangler', as he called it, so as to strengthen his domestic position with the nationalist right. A sense of urgency was also imparted to Stresemann's policy by the danger that the evacuation of the Cologne region, due to take place in January 1925, would be delayed because of the report from the Military Control Commission indicating German non-compliance with the disarmament clauses of the Versailles treaty. In other words, Stresemann's conciliatory stance as a 'good European' concealed the ambitions of a German nationalist, anxious to dismantle as much as possible of Versailles, especially the remaining sanctions contained in it for non-compliance with its terms. In this he was largely successful.

The disbanding of the Control Commission meant that there was no longer an effective check on Germany's disarmament. The last Allied troops left the Rhineland in 1930, five years ahead of schedule. France could not occupy German territory without invoking British aid to Germany nor counter a German attack on its eastern allies by invading the Rhineland. If Germany infringed the demilitarized zone in a way that did not constitute a 'flagrant violation', France had no automatic right of assistance to retaliate. Indeed, the country's entitlement to assistance from Britain, now (with Italy) one of the treaty 'guarantors', was of questionable value since Anglo-French staff talks were not appropriate to the status of a guarantor power, as opposed to an entente partner. In short, France may well have sacrificed substantial rights under the Versailles treaty in return for little in the way of worthwhile guarantees for its security from Locarno.

Why then did France agree to Locarno? The answer seems to be that Briand felt that there were few options left for France. The policy of standing on treaty rights had alienated Britain and left France isolated, and in any case these rights would not last indefinitely. By signing the Locarno agreement France secured a British commitment of sorts to the integrity of France's frontiers. In addition, there was a chance that Germany might become reintegrated into the European states system, instead of being a threat to it. Such was the 'spirit' of Locarno.

From the British point of view, Locarno represented an important stage in the return to normalcy in international relations. The foundations laid by the Dawes Plan ended the tiresome bickering over reparations and ushered in a period of German economic recovery – a desideratum of British policy since the end of the war. Locarno symbolized a more constructive period of reconciliation which, while seeming to satisfy French demands for security, avoided the more binding commitment of a formal alliance with France. Furthermore, Chamberlain genuinely believed that Locarno was the beginning of a new era of peace and stability. He seemed not to be conscious of the irony that 'a largely disarmed Britain became the primary instrument for the enforcement of peace.' Such was the spirit of Locarno.

For Germany, Locarno marked a decisive stage in the undermining of the Versailles system and the beginning of 'revisionism'. Germany had not recognized its eastern frontiers as permanent and had merely agreed to arbitration treaties with Poland and Czechoslovakia. Its non-compliance with the disarmament provisions had been tacitly ignored, while the first stage of the Rhineland evacuation had gone more or less according to schedule, with the promise of complete evacuation in five years' time. Locarno also paid financial dividends. The conclusion of a security pact greatly facilitated securing further loans from the United States and other nations, including Britain. If, as A. J. P. Taylor suggested many years ago, Locarno marked the true end of the First World War, then the war ended, in Sally Marks' view, 'with the defeat of France and the return of Germany to diplomatic equality and potential superiority.'

SOURCES AND FURTHER READING

Adamthwaite, A., *The Lost Peace*, London, Macmillan, 1976. (Mainly documents.)

Felix, D., 'Reparations reconsidered with a vengeance', *Central European History*, 1971, vol. 4, June: 231–55.

Henig, R., *Versailles and after, 1919–1933*, London, Methuen, 1984; repr. Routledge 1989, 1991. (Short but useful.)

Jacobson, J., 'Strategies of French foreign policy after World War I', *Journal of Modern History*, 1983, vol. 55(1): 78–95.

Marks, S., *The Illusion of Peace*, London, Macmillan, 1976.

——, 'The myths of reparations', *Central European History* 1978, vol. XI(3): 231–55.

Martel, G. (ed.), *The Origins of the Second World War Reconsidered*, London, Allen & Unwin, 1986. (Ch. 1 by Marks; ch. 2 by Schuker).

Sharp, A., *The Versailles Settlement: Peacemaking in Paris 1919*, London, Macmillan, 1991. (Good discussion.)

Trachtenberg, M., 'Reparation at the Paris Peace Conference of 1919', *Journal of Modern History*, 1979, vol. 51: 24–55, 81–5.

——, 'Versailles after 60 years', *Journal of Contemporary History*, 1982, vol. 17: 487–506. (Useful points.)

Index